63 Ready-to-Use Maker Projects

63

Ready-to-Use

MAKER
PROJECTS

EDITED BY

Ellyssa Kroski

An imprint of the American Library Association

CHICAGO | 2018

Ellyssa Kroski is the director of information technology at the New York Law Institute as well as an award-winning editor and author of thirty-six books, including *Law Librarianship in the Digital Age*, for which she won the American Association of Law Libraries' Joseph L. Andrews Legal Literature Award in 2014. Her ten-book technology series, *The Tech Set*, won the ALA's Best Book in Library Literature Award in 2011. She is a librarian, an adjunct faculty member at Drexel University and San Jose State University, and an international conference speaker. Her professional portfolio is located at www.ellyssakroski.com.

© 2018 by the American Library Association

Extensive effort has gone into ensuring the reliability of the information in this book; however, the publisher makes no warranty, express or implied, with respect to the material contained herein.

ISBNs
978-0-8389-1591-2 (paper)
978-0-8389-1661-2 (PDF)
978-0-8389-1662-9 (ePub)
978-0-8389-1663-6 (Kindle)

Library of Congress Cataloging-in-Publication Data

Names: Kroski, Ellyssa, editor.
Title: 63 ready-to-use maker projects / edited by Ellyssa Kroski.
Other titles: Sixty-three ready-to-use maker projects
Description: Chicago : ALA Editions, an imprint of the American Library Association, 2018.
Identifiers: LCCN 2017024393| ISBN 978-0-8389-1591-2 (pbk. : alk. paper) | ISBN 978-0-8389-1662-9 (epub) | ISBN 978-0-8389-1661-2 (pdf) | ISBN 978-0-8389-1663-6 (kindle)
Subjects: LCSH: Makerspaces in libraries. | Libraries—Activity programs.
Classification: LCC Z716.37 .A15 2018 | DDC 025.5—dc23
LC record available at https://lccn.loc.gov/2017024393

Book design by Alejandra Diaz in the Adobe Jenson and Filson Soft typefaces.

♾ This paper meets the requirements of ANSI/NISO Z39.48–1992 (Permanence of Paper).
Printed in the United States of America

22 21 20 19 18   5 4 3 2 1

Contents

Circuitry, Wiring, and Wearables Projects   107

Milling, Soldering, and Cutting Projects   145

High-Tech Programming and Robotics Projects   199

Digital Media Projects   241

3D Printing Projects   285

Figures

Acknowledgments

I WOULD LIKE to thank all of the talented, creative authors who generously dedicated their time and expertise to contribute to this unique work.

Preface

LIBRARY MAKERSPACES ARE informal, creative spaces where patrons can learn, invent, build, and make in partnership with the library and fellow makers. They offer fantastic opportunities for libraries to provide valuable tools, machines, resources, and STEM (science, technology, engineering, and math) skills to their community through instruction or simply by providing access to their spaces and equipment. As more and more libraries design makerspaces of their own, the need to plan engaging programming around them increases. This is a one-stop guidebook on how to do just that!

63 Ready-to-Use Maker Projects is an all-in-one recipe book for makerspace programming that is chock-full of practical project ideas for libraries, each authored by librarians and makers. The projects range in cost, topic, and difficulty as well as space and equipment requirements, so there is something for every size and type of library, even those without makerspaces.

Projects run the gamut from sewing and crafts projects such as do-it-yourself chain mail, creating cardboard standups, and hydro-dipping flower pots to high-tech and robotics programs such as building solar robots and creating an ultrasonic speed detector. Also included are digital media projects such as video editing to remix films and light painting, as well as a plethora of milling, soldering, and cutting projects, programs involving 3D printing, and circuitry, wiring, and wearables projects. Each project includes step-by-step instructions, a materials and equipment list, learning outcomes, and recommendations for next projects.

Public, school, and academic librarians, including those in libraries without a dedicated makerspace, who are looking to learn and create programming around makerspace topics will benefit from this resource.

Ellyssa Kroski
Director of Information Technology
The New York Law Institute

Create Your Own Lava Lamps

JESSICA LOGAN / BRANCH MANAGER

Hamilton Mill Branch, Gwinnett County Public Library

Type of Library Best Suited for: School or Public

Cost Estimate: Under $50

Makerspace Necessary? No

PROJECT DESCRIPTION

Create your own lava lamp using basic household items like recycled plastic bottles, vegetable oil, food coloring, and fizzy tablets. Have a blast from the past with these colorful, take-home projects that are sure to result in a hit maker program.

This program is a one-hour stand-alone event that can easily be held at any time during the year. The Gwinnett County Public Library hosts this event with a target audience of teens and tweens in grades 6–12, but this project is also suitable for a younger age group. Even before adding the fizzy tablets, children enjoy watching their creations bubble and swirl inside the plastic bottles.

OVERVIEW

Aimed at teens and tweens in grades 6–12, the participants work to create lava lamps using basic household items, including plastic bottles (20-ounce beverage bottles work especially well), vegetable oil, food coloring, and fizzy tablets. Because many of the participants become excited at the prospect of creating their own lava lamp, be sure to provide step-by-step written instructions for the activity prior to beginning so that they can be used as a reference. Before and throughout the activity, explain not only what steps to take, but also the science behind each one.

We do not limit this program to a specific number of participants, but we do make sure to have enough materials on hand so that everyone can take home a lava lamp. Start collecting bottles early so that you have enough. You can always use smaller bottles if you have a limited budget to purchase the other materials, or end up needing to stretch your vegetable oil a little more than planned.

MATERIALS LIST

- Clear, empty, and clean plastic bottles (20-ounce ones work great)
- Food coloring
- Water
- Vegetable oil
- Alka-Seltzer tablets (or other tablets that fizz)
- Tablecloths

NECESSARY EQUIPMENT

- Funnels
- Water pitcher
- Tables
- Flashlight (optional)
- Camera or other device to take pictures (optional)

STEP-BY-STEP INSTRUCTIONS

Prior to the start of the event, make sure to cover any tables to be used during the project with a tablecloth for easy cleanup. The plastic, disposable variety of tablecloths are an inexpensive option that works well for this purpose.

Throughout the program, be sure to explain both the steps and the science behind the project. For example, oil and water do not mix very well. The water and oil separate from each other and the oil ends up on top of the water because it has a lower density. The piece of an Alka-Seltzer tablet that you drop in the bottles fizzes and releases small bubbles of carbon dioxide gas that rise to the top of the bottle. Some of the colored water is taken with the gas up to the top of the bottle as well. The gas escapes when it reaches the top and the colored water comes back down. The reason Alka-Seltzer fizzes in such a way is because it contains citric acid and baking soda (sodium bicarbonate): the two react with water to form sodium citrate and carbon dioxide gas (those are the bubbles that carry the colored water to the top of the bottle).

Once the participants have had an opportunity to read over the instructions and ask any related questions, you may distribute the needed materials. If we have been

FIGURE 1.1 ··

Fizzing Alka-Seltzer

able to collect bottles of various shapes and sizes, we allow the participants to choose which one they would prefer. Because food coloring is an inexpensive material, we also make sure to have several different colors available for the students to personalize their lava lamps with.

To begin creation of the lava lamps, pour water into the plastic bottle until it is approximately one quarter full. You may wish to use a funnel when pouring to avoid spills. Next pour in vegetable oil until the bottle is nearly full. Wait (patiently, if possible) until the oil and water have separated . . . this step should not take too long. Add about a dozen drops of the chosen food coloring to the contents of the bottle. Have the participants observe as the food coloring falls through the layer of oil and mixes with the water. Finally, break your Alka-Seltzer tablets into pieces (about 4–5 pieces per tablet will do) and drop one piece into the bottle. The contents of the bottle should immediately begin fizzing and bubbling around like a real lava lamp. In our experience the children are always enthralled with this process, so it is a good idea to try having enough Alka-Seltzer pieces so that each participant can make their lava lamp come alive several times. You can also use this as an opportunity to reiterate that the reason the Alka-Seltzer fizzes in such a way is because it contains citric acid and baking soda (sodium bicarbonate): the two react with the water to form sodium citrate and carbon dioxide gas, which are the bubbles that carry the colored water to the top of the bottle. If you opted to provide a flashlight for the event, you can now shine it through the bottom of the bottle to give the contents more of a glowing lava lamp effect as it bubbles . . . this also makes for an excellent photo opportunity!

Groovy lava lamps

When the bubbling stops, you can always add another tablet piece and watch the fun reactions begin again. We allow our participants to take their groovy creations with them to enjoy (with the addition of more Alka-Seltzer tablets) at home.

LEARNING OUTCOMES

- Learn about molecular reactions and liquid density.
- Observe chemical reactions as the ingredients are combined to create a truly uplifting experience.

RECOMMENDED NEXT PROJECTS

This maker project has been a huge success at our branch each time it has been hosted, and several of the other branches within the Gwinnett County Public Library system have adapted it for their own use as well. The students always have a blast and we find that the materials are fairly inexpensive . . . or even free, in the case of our collection of recycled plastic bottles. If you have leftover bottles, you may consider trying a "Tornado in a Bottle" program to use up the remaining materials and to give your library users a new experience with a similar feel.

Feeling brave? If you have a place, such as a suitable outdoor area, you might also think about having your participants learn about chemical reactions on a larger, more explosive scale by trying out a Diet Coke and Mentos eruption. We have not tried this one ourselves, but I can only imagine the lasting impression it would make.

Host an Upcycled Fashion Show

SPRING LAVALLEE / YOUTH SERVICES LIBRARIAN
Salt Lake County Library Services

Type of Library Best Suited for: School or Public

Cost Estimate: $0–$100

Makerspace Necessary? No

PROJECT DESCRIPTION

Upcycling means to take something old and discarded and turn it into something new, useful, or more valuable. Unlike recycling (which breaks materials down into their most basic structures before re-forming them into new materials), upcycling can be done by anyone, anywhere, with little to no resources, equipment, or money. Libraries are full of raw materials just waiting to be upcycled, from cardboard boxes to old newspapers to pages from discarded or damaged books. Wouldn't it be great to put all that (free) material to good use?

The Upcycled Fashion Show is a one-hour program geared toward children, tweens, and/or teens. In one session, participants explore fashion and construction and create a garment or outfit using upcycled materials. The program is virtually free, and the participants get hands-on experiential learning on how to design and create custom fashion pieces and accessories. Additionally, participants have an opportunity to directly participate in the environmental process of reusing old materials in order to reduce consumption and waste.

Children working

OVERVIEW

The Upcycled Fashion Show could be a one-time program or it may be a series of programs, with each project focusing on a separate genre of fashion or type of construction. Each one-hour session includes a short presentation on the focus of this fashion show, a few minutes to design, lots of time to experiment and discover different fabrication techniques, and a fun-filled runway show at the end. Due to time constraints, the program should be limited to 20 participants; alternatively, the time of the program could be extended to 1.5 or 2 hours to accommodate a larger group. Additionally, this is a project that travels well, and it can easily be transported to an outreach event, if desired.

MATERIALS LIST

- Old, unused materials (cardboard, newspaper, magazines, book pages, cloth scraps, plastic bags, felt pieces, etc.)
- Tape (duct tape and/or masking tape) or glue (glue guns or glue dots)
- Colored pencils, crayons, or markers
- Scrap paper (for designs and drawing)

- Optional: construction paper or drinking straws
- Optional: paint and brushes
- Optional: decorative materials (ribbon, aluminum foil, plastic wrap, yarn, sequins, puff balls, feathers, etc.)
- Optional: thread and needle

NECESSARY EQUIPMENT

- Scissors
- Rulers
- Optional: rotary cutter or box cutter
- Optional: cutting mat
- Optional: sewing machine
- Optional: lights, runway music, and cameras

STEP-BY-STEP INSTRUCTIONS

Preparation

To prepare for the program, first consider what genre of fashion or construction techniques you would like to focus on during your program. For example, you might choose a time period (1920s or ancient Egyptian), a cultural fashion (like Japanese street fashion), or something more creative (e.g., superheroes, pirates, or sports uniforms). Or you can focus the program on a construction technique such as pleating, layering materials, hemming, or creating hidden pockets. Once a focus has been chosen, create a short presentation with lots of pictures. Explain what the focus of the program is and, if it uses specific techniques, how to achieve the look.

Next, take an inventory of what kind of materials you have available for this program. Any material (paper, cloth, metal, plastic, etc.) may be useful, if you can get enough of it. Remember that you will need construction materials for twenty or more participants, so if you do not have enough of one item, consider holding a short donation drive at your library to make up the difference. Whenever possible, do not buy materials! It's easy to spend lots of money on this project, buying materials and decorations; however, spending money on this program is unnecessary and undermines the environmental message of reusing old items.

During the Program

In setting up for this program, consider the age group that will be participating. Children may prefer working on the ground, rather than at tables, whereas teens probably want to sit at tables in small groups and pairs. Remember to leave a space for the runway, and consider marking the runway out on the floor with masking tape before the program starts. Materials and equipment can be placed around the edge of the room, to create more workspace in the middle.

The program starts with a brief presentation on the fashion genre or technique that is the focus for the day. Make sure to include lots of pictures, and consider bringing fashion magazines or books from the library in order to demonstrate and inspire new designs. Allow the participants to draw their designs on scrap paper during the presentation and shortly afterward. No more than ten minutes should be spent on both the presentation and design portion of the program.

Next comes the construction portion of the program. This should take up the bulk of your time, 40–45 minutes, depending on the size of the group. During this time, encourage participants to work together, if possible. If one participant discovers a new technique, or makes something really cool, have that person share with the group. Some helpful tips and tricks follow:

- Cardboard is a very hard material to cut, so don't cut all the way through. Instead, score one side of the cardboard and bend it around the "seams" of your garment.
- Newspaper is very delicate material, but it can be made stronger by using multiple layers taped together.
- Small-sized materials like book and magazine pages may need to be taped or glued together to create a piece large enough for use. Layer the pages on top of one another and glue or tape all of them on the same side to hide the seams and make the finished look more polished.
- Cloth materials may need to be prepared by cutting them into strips or small patches before they can be used. When using cloth, focus your participants on creating a single item, rather than an entire outfit; they will not have time to make multiple items when using cloth.
- Encourage participants to construct a piece fully before decorating. Children may get distracted by the decorations and need to be brought back to the task of constructing a garment first.
- Rolled construction paper or drinking straws can be used to create a garment that sticks out (e.g., instead of creating and using petticoats for a full skirt, tape straws on the inside in straight, vertical lines to give it the same effect).
- Plastic is very heavy. Consider using it with sturdier base materials (e.g., cloth, felt, etc.) or in very small pieces as decoration (e.g., as buttons, appliques, etc.).

Finally, in the last few minutes of the program, hold a real fashion show, showing off your creations! Turn off the lights, play upbeat music, and have each participant stroll down the runway. If you do not have floor lights or strobe lights, use a flashlight to "spotlight" each participant during his or her walk. Encourage caregivers to arrive

FIGURE 2.2

Superhero shirt

back at the program in time to see the finale; then clap, whistle, and cheer each other on, as you strut your stuff in front of the crowd!

LEARNING OUTCOMES

- Social and personal development are encouraged by enhancing qualities such as confidence-building, resiliency, problem-solving, and individual expression.
- Participants exercise translation skills and artistic prowess by working in multiple mediums. They also learn about fashion and potentially improve body image and body awareness by dressing themselves.
- Basic artistic and construction skills are learned in this project. Basic sewing skills are fostered when using needle and thread.

RECOMMENDED NEXT PROJECTS

Variations on this project are endless. Different combinations of recycled materials and types of fashion can be tried out, or a special speaker in the fashion industry can attend, in order to provide new perspectives on design and construction. Dolls, paper dolls, action figures, and stuffed animals could also be dressed, for a different take on the same concept. Additionally, creating accessories such as hats, jewelry, or purses may be more appropriate with certain demographics or material types.

Do-It-Yourself Chain Mail

HEATHER BUHLER / YOUTH SERVICES LIBRARIAN

Salt Lake County Library Services

Type of Library Best Suited for: Any

Cost Estimate: $200–$500

Makerspace Necessary? No

PROJECT DESCRIPTION

Making chain mail is a flexible project for many age ranges and groups, and is based around the concept of completing a custom work of chain mail. This project details how to create a European 4-in-1 chain mail weave.

OVERVIEW

Chain mail may seem outdated and irrelevant to a modern makerspace, but it is precisely this uniqueness that gives it its potential. Making chain mail is extremely accommodating and can be modified to any variety of library program ideas. Anime clubs, STEM/STEAM groups, teens, tweens, live-action role-players (LARPers), history enthusiasts, reenactors, medieval/jousting clubs, home businesses, jewelry designers, "lost arts" enthusiasts, and more can find a unique angle to this versatile project material. Making chain mail can also appeal to other niche constituents who may not be normally considered or currently reached by your library. The sky is the limit as new ideas are implemented to fit the needs of individual communities and niches of patrons. Learning to make chain mail can be a single event or it can be designed as a registered series over weeks, months, or a year during which a fully realized project, such as a customized suit of chain mail, is jump-started as a final result. From drop-ins to a fully programmed series, it is as adaptable as your imagination and can be repurposed over and over again.

MATERIALS LIST

- Chain mail rings (these can be purchased on Amazon as well as from custom suppliers such as Etsy, weavegotmaille.com, and others)

NECESSARY EQUIPMENT

- Smooth, bent (curved) needle-nose pliers (two per person)

STEP-BY-STEP INSTRUCTIONS

Preparation

Have pliers and chain mail rings available for participants to choose from at the start of the workshop. You also have the option of having them create their own chain mail rings, which will be cut from a wire wound around a rod and cut to make the links. You can certainly have them do this themselves with something as simple as a drill press and dowel to save extra on costs, but you will need another tutorial for that, and there is a time-cost ratio to consider because this will involve a few extra steps. Instead, it is recommended to start them off with the ready-made rings.

Creating Chain Mail

After participants select the gauge of the links and metal type, such as steel, aluminum, or other variety they want to work with, walk them through how to close several rings before linking them together. To close the rings, use toothless, curved, needle-nosed pliers to pull against the two ends of the open ring, twist and line them up, and then press them together so they form as close to a seamless link as possible. This procedure falls into a nice rhythm very quickly. This is also why toothless, curved, needle-nosed pliers are the most recommended tools here (pliers with teeth can nick the rings, which can then catch on skin and clothing), though you are welcome to adapt other pliers as you need.

Once they get the hang of it, this part will go by very quickly. For a novice, over 120 individual rings can be made in less than an hour, which is more than enough for the start and completion of a simple jewelry project, such as a necklace or chain mail bracelet.

Next, show them how to create a weave by linking the chain mail rings together. Drop four rings inside an opened, fifth ring. Close this fifth ring. Split these four rings in half, lay them down on your surface, and spread them apart. The orientation of the inner and outer rings is absolutely essential here. The first and most important thing you need to know is that the center rings need to be facing the same direction. The outer rings also all need to be facing the same direction. If they do not, the chain mail will not be seamless. Since (from a Western standpoint) we work from left to

FIGURE 3.1

Closing the rings

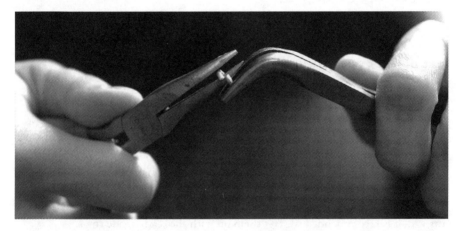

FIGURE 3.2

Creating the pattern

FIGURE 3.3

Continuing the pattern

right, be sure the center rings lean forward while the outer rings all lean back. This will be easier and more intuitive to work with.

Using the two rings to your right, loop another opened ring (with two new closed rings already attached) through these two rings going *down* through the first ring and *up* through the second. Picking up and pinching your chain mail weave together makes the manipulation of linking these easier. Then you will repeat this procedure for as long as necessary to complete the project. This pattern is all it takes. As long as the center rings face one direction while the outer rings face the other, this is how to create a basic, European 4-in-1 chain mail weave.

LEARNING OUTCOMES

- Participants will learn the foundation of the art of chain mail creation.
- Participants will also gain skills in mathematics, pattern-making and recognition, self-directed learning, and independent problem-solving.

RECOMMENDED NEXT PROJECTS

There are hundreds of chain mail patterns and tutorials available on websites such as the following ones:

- www.mailleartisans.org/weaves
- www.artofchainmail.com/patterns

Once participants have the foundation skills mastered, you can follow up with successive workshops on other chain mail weaves, or workshops focused on creating a particular chain mail garment or accessory. Some other chain mail weaves include:

- Japanese *hitoye-gusari* (4-in-2 square weave)
- Japanese *hana-gusari* (6-in-2 hexagonal weave)
- Persian 6-in-1 (note: not place of origin; possibly more modern)
- Etruscan chain mail
- Byzantine (decorative)
- Helm chain mail (decorative)
- Orbital chain mail (decorative)
- Spiral chain mail (decorative)
- Celtic chain mail (decorative)

Note: there are many other weaves available.

How To Make Your Own Cardboard Standup

MELISSA SALNAVE / BRANCH MANAGER
Pearland Westside Branch Library

Type of Library Best Suited for: Any
Cost Estimate: $5–$50 each, depending on what supplies you already have
Makerspace Necessary? No

PROJECT DESCRIPTION

Learn how to easily (and inexpensively!) create your own cardboard standup figures. These can either be used by the library for signage and marketing purposes, or you can teach patrons to create their own.

OVERVIEW

I used to run a small public library with a limited budget, so I had to get creative when it came to decorations. I decided to start making my own standups as a way to advertise various programs at the library. You can make these standups any size you'd like, so they can be used for a variety of different purposes. And since it uses basic supplies and a color printer, you don't need a makerspace to create them. You can run workshops to teach your patrons how to create standups of themselves, their pets, or whatever else they'd like.

MATERIALS LIST

- Paper
- Foam core board or cardboard (available at hobby/craft stores in multiple sizes, starting at $4.99 for a 20 × 30-inch sheet)
- Duct tape
- Spray adhesive (available at groceries, superstores, hobby/craft stores)
- Mod Podge (available at hobby/craft stores)
- Self-adhesive Velcro (available at hobby/craft stores)

NECESSARY EQUIPMENT

- Color printer
- A computer
- Cutting mat (to protect the surface you're cutting on)
- Ruler
- Rotary cutter or X-ACTO knife
- Foam brush

STEP-BY-STEP INSTRUCTIONS

1. Find an image. You can take your own photos or find one online. The higher the resolution of the photo, the better it will look when enlarged. If the image has a background that you don't like, use a photo-editing software program to clean it up. I have computers with Photoshop on them, but you can also use Microsoft Paint; it's just a bit more difficult and time-consuming.
2. Figure out what size you want your final standup figure to be. The site below does a fairly good job of converting pixels to inches and inches to pixels: http://auctionrepair.com/pixels.html.
3. Download Smilla Enlarger, http://sourceforge.net/projects/imageenlarger/.
4. Drag and drop your image into Smilla Enlarger.
5. Then set your output height. There are other options, but height generally gives the best results. The number is in pixels. Use the site from step 2 to figure out how many pixels will give you the height you desire.
6. Pick a name for your enlarged photo and choose where you would like it to be saved.
7. Click Enlarge & Save to save the photo.

Now you are ready to print your enlarged photo. There are several different businesses, both online and brick-and-mortar, which have the ability to print large images on a large sheet of paper. Most libraries don't have that ability, so you will have to print your photos across multiple sheets of paper.

FIGURE 4.1 ···

Smilla enlarger

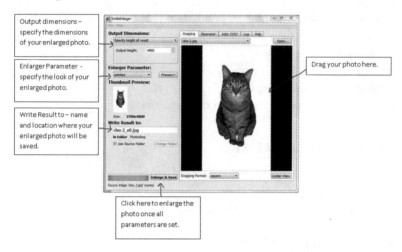

Output dimensions – specify the dimensions of your enlarged photo.

Enlarger Parameter - specify the look of your enlarged photo.

Write Result to – name and location where your enlarged photo will be saved.

Drag your photo here.

Click here to enlarge the photo once all parameters are set.

8. Open up your enlarged image in Microsoft Paint. Then go to File > Print > Page setup.
9. On the Page Setup screen, set your margins all to 0. It will then default to the smallest number possible. Under Scaling, select Adjust to 100% normal size. It will then show you how many pages the picture will print across.
10. Hit OK and then print your picture.
11. Now you will have to trim all the pages to remove the white borders. I used a quilting ruler and a rotary cutter, but any straightedge and blade should work.

Now it's time to mount the papers onto a board. I used foam core board. It's easy to find and inexpensive. You can use cardboard, but it's not as stiff and doesn't work as well for larger standup figures.

12. I recommend laying out all the pieces of paper on the foam core first. That way you can plan how many pieces of foam core you need and see what type of layout will work the best.
13. If you need more than one piece of foam core board, attach the pieces together with duct tape before you start gluing the paper to them.
14. Now you're ready to start putting the papers onto the board. Start by spraying the foam core with a spray-on adhesive. I've found that 3M Multipurpose Spray Adhesive works the best.
15. Once you've sprayed the adhesive, start laying down the papers one row at a time. Most spray adhesives are tacky, so you have the ability to adjust the papers for a short amount of time.

16. Once all the papers are glued down, you need to seal the seams. Using a foam brush, cover all the seams with Mod Podge. I used the one that was just for paper and it has a matte finish.

17. Once the seams have dried, trim the edges of your project.

The final part of this process is putting a stand on the character. If you just want a standup figure to attach to a wall or the end of a bookcase, you can ignore these last steps.

18. Cut a piece of cardboard or foam core board that is about three-fourths of the height of your standup character and about 4 inches wide.

19. On the bottom cut about a 5-degree angle. This will cause the standup to lean very slightly backwards. If you want it to lean more, cut a steeper angle.

20. Take self-adhesive Velcro and attach one strip to the middle of the cardboard standup and the other strip to the edge of the stand piece. You want the Velcro to be even with the bottom of the standup.

21. Attach the stand piece to the back of your standup.

Congratulations! You have made your very own standup figure!

LEARNING OUTCOMES

- Participants will be able to use a photo-enlarging program to enlarge a photograph.
- Participants will be able to use Microsoft Paint to print objects across multiple pages.
- Participants will be able to create a standup.

RECOMMENDED NEXT PROJECTS

- 3D wall art
- Paper circuits
- Decoupage

FIGURE 4.2

Final result

Hydro-Dipping
Flower Pots

SILVIA GUTIERREZ / TEACHER LIBRARIAN

Palos Verdes Peninsula High School Library Media Commons

Type of Library Best Suited for: Any

Cost Estimate: $3 per participant

Makerspace Necessary? No, but must be held outdoors because of the strong nail polish odor

PROJECT DESCRIPTION

Nail polish is not just for fingers and toes anymore. This long-lasting pigment comes in an ever-growing palette of colors, and the painted results are eye-catching. A bit of paint and a few drops of nail polish will make plain terra-cotta pots pop with designs in vibrant colors.

In this project, you begin with a plain terra-cotta pot (used to hold plants and flowers) and you end up with a piece of art. The results are dazzling and yet simple to achieve. No special artistic talent or skill is needed. Just ordinary nail polish! The technique involves swirling the terra-cotta pot in a container of water and polish. The polish forms a design on the pot that looks difficult to paint but isn't. The swirling action creates the design. Use colors to match your flowers, your home décor, or just go wild!

OVERVIEW

I hold twice-monthly "Crafternoon" sessions at my high school library, and many of the projects revolve around holidays or special occasions. This is a "Mothers and Others Day" craft project held in the month of May. Luckily, May brings warm weather, and this craft needs to be held outdoors due to the strong odor of nail polish, and because it can be quite messy with spilt water and polish. Our "Crafternoon" projects usually attract our teenaged young ladies, but young men are enticed into this one when we advertise, "If you don't have a Mother's Day gift ready for your mom, aunt, grandma, come make one free at the library!"

The teens will decorate a plain clay terra-cotta plant pot with paint and nail polish. The easy technique requires no art skill, yet results in a beautiful, one-of-a-kind piece that is ready to give. It is safe for a live plant.

This session is an hour in length. The clay pots are prepared in advance and the materials and equipment are displayed and ready as the session begins. We have two adults supervising and twelve crafty teens. We limit the program to twelve teens because it is a fast-paced craft and the adults need to be constantly circulating among the teens. More adults = more teens.

MATERIALS LIST

- 6-inch terra-cotta pots—one or two for each participant
- Nail polish with no glitter, sequins, or sparkly fillers. Minimum of three colors per participant, but bottles may be shared
- White acrylic paint and paintbrush or white enamel spray paint
- Several Popsicle sticks
- Bucket of clean, lukewarm water
- Container large enough to fit the length and width of the plant pot
    - The container doesn't need to be deep. The pot will not be submerged but will only skim the surface. The container does have to be large enough for the length and width of the pot to fit into easily. Larger is better so the pot can be rotated without scraping the sides

- One 10-ounce or larger tin can for each pot to dry upon
- Pair of disposable gloves for each participant
- Polish remover
- Cotton balls
- Roll of paper towels
- Clear varnish spray

Many of these items are available in your library's supply cabinet or from your staff, and do not need to be purchased. Put the call out to your staff and patrons, and donations of nail polish will be plentiful! Who doesn't have a few bottles of unwanted nail polish?

Someone may have recently finished a house painting job and have leftover white paint. Or you may purchase paint samples that are available in small jars for just a few dollars. A little goes a long way, and one sample jar or spray bottle will paint several pots. Terra-cotta pots can be purchased from craft or home improvement stores for less than one dollar apiece. If your budget allows, provide more than one pot per teen.

STEP-BY-STEP INSTRUCTIONS

Preparation

The pots need to be painted white in advance of your event. Terra-cotta clay is a dull brown and doesn't create a contrasting background. White paint is a wonderful backdrop, and the polish will pop and look vibrant on this painted background. Use acrylic paint with a medium paintbrush or enamel paint spray. The spray paint is easier and quicker to apply. The paint will dry within an hour, but it is best to paint a day ahead and have the white pots ready for your group when they arrive, rather than having them paint the pots themselves and then wait for the paint to dry.

Advisory

You must do this craft outside due to the strong odor of nail polish. We began inside with all the doors open and the odor was still so strong we had to move outside. It was a big disruption to cart everything outside.

You are ready to begin. Assemble the supplies and have each participant collect

- terra-cotta pot
- a few Popsicle sticks
- container for water
- one tin can for each finished pot
- pair of disposable gloves
- paper towels

Have a wide selection of nail polish colors. The polish must have no glitter, sequins, or sparkly fillers. This is because if the polish is too heavy, it will sink; instead, it must float. Group the polishes by color and display them on the table. Participants choose three bottles. They can select various shades of one color, or they can mix it up with different colors for a wild look. Bottles may be shared.

Fill each plastic container halfway with lukewarm water. Not cold, not hot. Wear gloves. You are now ready to add the polish.

The teens work in pairs; one teen will drizzle the polish into the water, the other teen will "paint" the pot.

Starting with the lightest color, one partner slowly and gently drizzles the polish into the water close to the surface to prevent the polish from sinking to the bottom. The polish should stay floating at the top and not sink to the container's bottom. If it sinks, slowly drizzle more polish on the surface. If it sinks a second time, discard that polish; it is too heavy. Make a spiral pattern with the polish as it is slowly poured. Use a Popsicle stick to swirl the polish if it has not spread.

Have the pot ready to be "painted." It must be "painted" quickly before the polish dries. Yes, the polish dries in the water. Don't believe it? Try it! If the polish is left in the water for a few minutes it will congeal into clumps.

One teen holds the pot as the polish is poured. Hold the pot horizontally. Clasp firmly around the pot's top ridge with the fingertips of one hand; the other hand holds the bottom. Holding the pot, lightly roll the pot's surface through the polish until the entire pot has been rotated. The polish will adhere to the pot. Remove the pot from the mixture but continue to hold it. Do not set it down.

The partner repeats the above with the second shade of polish. Drizzle the second color. Quickly rotate the pot through the polish.

Repeat one more time with the darkest color. Drizzle and "paint." After the final coating, take the pot out of the water and gently place it upside down over the tin can

FIGURE 5.1

Polish drizzled in pot

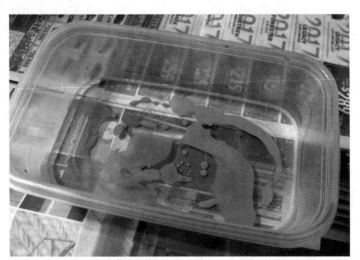

to dry. If spots have been missed, you may fill them in by lightly dabbing polish on them with the nail brush.

FIGURE 5.2 ·······························

Finished pot with flowers

Ready for another pot? It's easy to change colors. Remove the polish from the container using the Popsicle sticks to catch the nail polish. The polish will bond to the stick. Or mop up the nail polish with paper towels.

Begin again. Drizzle the polish and "paint" the pot with multiple colors.

Wait about fifteen minutes after painting and do a "touch" test. It the polish is dry to the touch, it is ready for the varnish. Spray clear varnish on the inside and outside of the pot. The varnish will set the color and also make it more water-resistant.

The teens may take the pots home immediately or return the next day to pick them up. Wait overnight for the varnish to dry before planting live flowers in the painted pots, or arranging a bouquet of silk flowers in them.

This little artistic piece will bring smiles and oohs and ahhs from the recipient!

LEARNING OUTCOMES

- Teens learn that nail polish is a decorative paint for more than toes and fingernails.
- There is more than one use for an item. Teens are encouraged to look for alternative uses for common items.

RECOMMENDED NEXT PROJECTS

Teens may try other nail polish projects. Mugs, glass jars, ceramic bowls, and tiles can all be painted with nail polish. Use the polish-in-water method or paint with the nail brush directly on to the surface.

- Bookmarks can be created with this same method by using cardstock of special watercolor paper from an art supply store.
- Bling a cell phone case with nail polish polka dots.
- Fabric can be painted with nail polish. Highlight a sweatshirt or jeans. The polish won't come off in the wash!

6

Create Magnetic Slime

JESSICA LOGAN / BRANCH MANAGER
Hamilton Mill Branch, Gwinnett County Public Library

Type of Library Best Suited for: School or Public

Cost Estimate: Under $50

Makerspace Necessary? No

PROJECT DESCRIPTION

The Hamilton Mill Branch of the Gwinnett County Public Library hosts an event that challenges teens to explore magnetism and chemical reactions by creating their very own magnetic slime. Building upon the ever-popular DIY slime programs, we incorporate an additional learning component by having participants create slime that is also attracted to magnets.

This program is a stand-alone event that can easily be held at any time during the year and is designed for middle school and high school students. Students enjoy comparing the reactions of the slime before and after the addition of iron oxide and are always thrilled to learn they can take some home to show off to friends and family . . . and to continue experimenting with on their own time.

OVERVIEW

Magnetic Slime is a program that works well with teens and tweens, ages 12–18. It is best to start things off with an explanation of what will be accomplished during the hour-long program. Plan to explore the mechanics of magnetism with the participants and explain how the magnet will attract the iron oxide powder in the slime. Give participants instructions on how to create slime and demonstrate that the mixture does not interact with the neodymium magnet prior to the addition of the iron oxide. Once the final ingredient has been added, allow the participants time to test it and explore the magnetic reaction of the slime through play. We do not limit this program to a specific number of participants, but we do make sure to have enough materials on hand so that everyone is able to mix and take home a small batch of magnetic slime. Were you to have a larger than expected crowd, it would still be possible to accommodate everyone by having participants work in groups and then evenly dividing the mixture among those who wished to take some home.

MATERIALS LIST

- 3 ounces of white school glue/ per person
- ⅛ cup warm water/ per person
- ⅛ cup liquid starch/ per person
- 2–3 teaspoons black iron oxide powder/ per person
- Neodymium magnet—at least one for sharing; it is not necessary to have one per person
- Tablecloths to cover the tables during the program
- Disposable gloves (nitrile preferred in case any participants are allergic to latex)
- Plastic "Ziploc" baggies (or collect and recycle small jars or other containers with lids)
- Printed instructions for reference

NECESSARY EQUIPMENT

- Measuring cups
- Bowls and utensils for mixing
- Tables
- Camera or other device to take pictures (optional)

STEP-BY-STEP INSTRUCTIONS

Prior to the start of the event, make sure to cover any tables to be used during the project with a tablecloth for easy cleanup. The plastic, disposable variety are an inexpensive option that works well for this purpose.

Begin the program with a brief explanation of what will be accomplished. Discuss the mechanics of magnetism with the participants and explain how the magnet will attract the iron oxide powder in the slime. Distribute printed instructions on how to create slime and, using a batch of already mixed slime, demonstrate that the mixture does not interact with the neodymium magnet prior to addition of the iron oxide.

Once the participants have had an opportunity to read over the instructions and ask any related questions, distribute the mixing bowls, stirring utensils, and measuring cups. We have the participants measure out their own ingredients for creating the slime, but it would be possible to have everything measured out in advance and then just have the students mix it together; this may work well if you anticipate a large crowd or have limited time in which to host the project.

Add the three ounces of school glue to a bowl and stir in the ⅛ cup of water. Once it is fully incorporated, add the ⅛ cup of liquid starch until it comes together. If your mixture is not coming together easily or does not have the desired "sliminess," you may need to use warmer water or make sure your measurements are correct.

FIGURE 6.1

Making slime

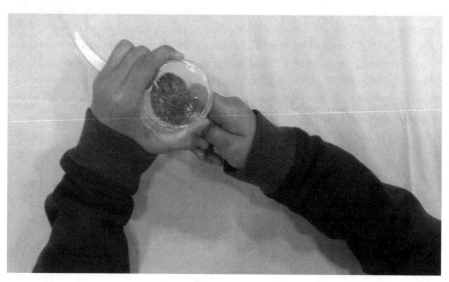

Remove the slime from the bowl and knead it, stretching it to make it more pliable. At this point you should have a glob of white slime. Have the participants use the neodymium magnet to see if it will attract the white slime. Spoiler: It will not.

Now it is time to add the iron oxide powder. Have your students put on their disposable gloves and then make a small indentation in the slime and add a teaspoon of iron oxide powder. Fold the slime over the powder and knead it to incorporate the powder throughout. The slime will begin to turn black. Repeat the process until you have added enough iron oxide that the slime reacts to the neodymium magnet.

Allow the participants some time to play with their slimy creations and watch them react with the magnets. Take pictures of the fun and then distribute plastic baggies or small jars so that the students can take their magnetic slime home.

LEARNING OUTCOMES

- Learn the mechanics of magnetism and magnetic attraction.
- Explore the use of magnetic fields through hands-on play and experimentation.
- Observe chemical reactions as ingredients are added together and new characteristics arise to form a new, and decidedly slimy, substance.

RECOMMENDED NEXT PROJECTS

If the children at your library enjoy hands-on, messy fun (and who doesn't, really?), you may consider a variation on this project that uses glow-in-the-dark paint as an ingredient rather than iron oxide. You will need to have a very dark room available for the participants to take their slime into so that they can see the effects of adding the glow paint, but this version is always a hit. You could even get really crazy by making slime that is simultaneously magnetic *and* glow-in-the-dark! You can also create variety by using transparent gel glue to create slime that is not opaque. Experiment with fun additions such as colored paint or glitter to make galaxy slime or slime that reflects the personality of the creator! DIY Play-Doh is another fun variation that is a bit easier to mix successfully than the slime and may be more suitable for younger participants.

Duct Tape Crafts: Wallet and Rose

CATHERINE BLAIR / MIDDLE SCHOOL SERVICES LIBRARIAN
Gail Borden Public Library

Type of Library Best Suited for: Public or School

Cost Estimate: $1–$2 per participant in consumable materials;
$6–$30 per participant in reusable equipment

Makerspace Necessary? No

PROJECT DESCRIPTION

Duct tape. It's available in a kaleidoscope of colors and patterns; it can be used to create dozens of useful items; and it absolutely fascinates kids and teens. Thus, it is a popular material to use in makerspace programming.

Duct tape crafting programs inspire mathematical questions: "How long is this strip of tape? How many more strips will I need to complete my project?" They present engineering problems: "How can I turn these flat lengths of tape into a three-dimensional object? How can I modify that object to make it stronger, more useful, more secure?" And they inspire artistic reflection: "Which tape patterns look best next to each other? Have I succeeded in making my creation beautiful?"

For this project, students will learn how to manipulate duct tape to produce two objects—a wallet and a rose.

OVERVIEW

Gail Borden Public Library offers duct tape programs for students in grades 6–8 monthly during the school year and weekly during the summer reading program. The programs are run on a drop-in basis and are supervised by one staff member. Attendance ranges from three to fifteen teens, with most sessions on the higher end of that range. While instruction is available for beginners, teens can also choose to work on self-directed projects.

If you are working with older teens, you can include some or all of the optional extras mentioned in the instructions below. To adapt the program for a younger audience whose fine motor skills and arm strength are less developed, focus the session on either wallet or rose construction, but not both. Limit enrollment to ten students or recruit helpers (staff members, parents, experienced teen volunteers) to provide one-on-one assistance.

MATERIALS LIST

- Duct tape
- Plastic drinking straws

Duck, Scotch, Platypus, and other brands offer unique tape colors and patterns. Rolls of tape from different brands can differ in terms of surface texture, rigidity, and adhesive strength. For this reason, when starting off, you may want to buy tape from only a single brand, like Duck, for consistency's sake. On the other hand, using tape from multiple brands offers teens a chance to analyze and evaluate the differences between them.

Brick-and-mortar hardware stores offer large rolls of basic colors of duct tape, often at a lower price per yard, whereas craft supply stores will offer more trendy patterns. Online, Tape Planet (www.tapeplanet.com) has good prices and a wide selection of patterns. If you are planning to make duct tape programs a regular part of your programming, keep an eye out for sales at Staples (www.staples.com), Jo-Ann Fabric and Crafts (www.joann.com), and Michaels (www.michaels.com).

NECESSARY EQUIPMENT

- Fiskars Duck Edition eight-inch scissors
- Self-healing cutting mats (preferably with grid lines for measuring) (optional)
- Craft knives (optional)
- Rulers (optional)

Fiskars Duck Edition scissors cut through duct tape without getting gummed up from adhesive. They cut as smoothly after many uses as they did the day you bought them. What's more, they do not present the safety issues that craft knives do, so they are great for younger, clumsier, or more boisterous groups of participants. If your budget is tight, you can have participants tear the duct tape by hand, or use regular scissors that you clean after each program. But these specialized scissors are well worth their price.

STEP-BY-STEP INSTRUCTIONS

Preparation

Make at least one sample of each project. Take photos of each step in the process. Use these photos to create an illustrated instruction sheet for participants.

Gail Borden Public Library's teen population prefers receiving verbal instructions over using written directions. Even if your program participants feel the same way, it can be helpful to have a piece of paper to share with them, especially if they are working at different speeds or arrive late.

At the Beginning of the Program

Participants examine project samples, then make their tape selections (if you offer a choice). At Gail Borden's programs, teens grab their scissors, cutting mats, and tape from a supply table or cart as they arrive. You might place supplies at each seat ahead of time to expedite distribution.

If your participants will be using craft knives, review the safety rules. (Consult the project "Create Papercraft Toys" in this section for information about Gail Borden's use of craft knives at teen programs.)

Constructing the Wallet

Cut four strips of tape, each about seven inches long, and lay them on the cutting mat with their sticky side down. Overlap them lengthwise by about half an inch each to make a single "sheet" of duct tape.

Cut four more seven-inch strips of tape. Then turn the first sheet of tape over so that its sticky side is facing up. One at a time, place the second set of tape strips on top of the first with their sticky sides facing down, overlapping them as you did for the first set. This should create a double-sided sheet of tape that has no adhesive showing except around the edges.

Use scissors to trim off the remaining adhesive. Then fold the sheet in half, creating a wallet shape that is close to four inches tall and seven inches wide. Seal the two shorter sides of the wallet with tape.

Participants who finish their wallets quickly may wish to add credit-card pockets, make a closure, or decorate their wallets with cut-out shapes.

Constructing the Rose

Cut off a strip of tape the length of the plastic straw and place it sticky side up. Roll the straw over the tape to make a stem.

Cut a two-inch square of duct tape and place it sticky side up. Fold the top right corner down, into the middle of the square, to make a shape that looks like a letter L with a colored triangle. Then fold the top left corner in the same way, overlapping your first fold. The two folds should overlap so that no adhesive is showing in the middle of the shape, and a line of adhesive should still be visible at the bottom. This shape is your first petal. Wrap it around the stem to create a rosebud.

Cut more two-inch squares and repeat the petal-making process. When wrapping the petals around the stem, make sure each petal is slightly offset from the one before it. As the rose gets bigger, move new petals higher up to create a fuller look.

No set number of petals is required. Some participants will be satisfied with a smaller rose, while others will wish to continue adding petals until the rose is almost too heavy for its stem.

FIGURE 7.1

Rose

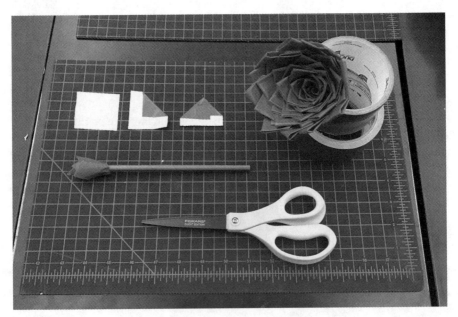

FIGURE 7.2

Teen-designed wrist cuff with attached kunai

Participants with time to spare can try adding a calyx below the petals, creating leaves, or arranging different-colored petals to make a pattern. They might also try changing the petal size to see how it affects the look of the finished product.

At the End of the Program

As participants are finishing their projects and cleaning up their workspaces, ask them to talk about the parts of the process that they struggled with, the parts they found most rewarding, and what advice they would give to future participants. Encourage them to share any special techniques they discovered and explain design decisions they made.

Use a camera to document the final products. You might want to share the photographs on social media, use them to market the program, or add them to an inspiration board that you bring to future sessions.

LEARNING OUTCOMES

At the end of this program, participants will be able to:

- Estimate and measure lengths of material.
- Construct duct tape "sheets," simple duct tape wallets, and duct tape roses without assistance.

- Describe to peers the steps necessary to construct a wallet and a rose.
- Assess how their construction process affected their finished project. What aspects of their project are they satisfied with? What, if anything, would they change when doing the project again?
- Recognize ways in which other duct tape projects (bags, bracelets, pencil cases, etc.) use the same techniques they used for the wallet and rose.
- Use a craft knife safely (if craft knives were used at your program).

RECOMMENDED NEXT PROJECTS

Once teens have grasped the fundamentals of duct tape crafting, the sky's the limit. They can use the same techniques to create bookmarks, bags, bracelets, collages, earbud holders, pillows, masks, mustaches . . . the list goes on and on. Let your teens browse through any duct tape project books you have available. Encourage them to come up with their own ideas. Ideally, *they* will tell *you* what they want their next project to be.

To facilitate self-directed projects, stock your program cart with items like toilet paper tubes, paper towel tubes, empty cardboard tape rolls, cardstock, used Tyvek envelopes or bubble mailers, flattened boxes, hook-and-loop fasteners (Velcro), and bobby pins. Then stand back and watch the magic happen.

Create Papercraft Toys

CATHERINE BLAIR / MIDDLE SCHOOL SERVICES LIBRARIAN
Gail Borden Public Library

Type of Library Best Suited for: School or Public

Cost Estimate: 90 cents per participant in consumable materials

Makerspace Necessary? No

PROJECT DESCRIPTION

Paper toys, often referred to as papercrafts, are flat templates that can be cut, folded, and assembled to make three-dimensional figures. They are a valuable addition to library makerspace programming for a number of reasons:

- They are inexpensive, easy to acquire, and easy to store.
- They are portable. All the materials required to make them can easily be moved between classrooms, branches, or outreach sites.
- Many teens, and even some elementary-schoolers, can figure out how to assemble simple paper models with minimal assistance. Thus, papercrafts are ideal for passive programs and for times when you are not able to offer lots of one-on-one help.
- The wide variety of papercraft models available allows you to customize your offerings to meet the specific interests of your library's kids and teens. Whether they are interested in sports, video games, anime, or cute animals, there's a papercraft out there for them.

- The variety of papercraft models available also facilitates differentiated instruction. Some library users are already adept at cutting shapes cleanly and folding with precision. Others struggle with scissors. By offering models at different difficulty levels, you give both groups the opportunity to improve their skills.

Gail Borden Public Library currently offers papercrafting both as a stand-alone event and as an add-on or individual station at large events. The toys have proved popular with library users of all ages. While the program described in this chapter is geared toward students in grades 6 and up, it can be adapted for use with students as young as kindergarten or first grade.

OVERVIEW

Gail Borden's teen papercrafting programs are drop-in, with a single library staff member supervising. They run for an hour and attract anywhere from a handful of teens to more than two dozen. Each participant selects templates from a "papercraft library" that is stored in file boxes and refilled after each program. Teens are encouraged to go at their own pace. Beginners are usually able to complete two to three simple papercrafts during their first session. Returning participants might choose a more complex template and spend the whole time working on it.

For your first program, limit the number and complexity of the templates you offer. If you are worried about running out of supplies or are concerned that your user population will need more one-on-one assistance, you may want to require registration and cap enrollment at fifteen students. For participants in grades 3–5, you should offer only two papercrafts, and use tape instead of glue. For grades K–2, spend the hour making one simple papercraft.

MATERIALS LIST

- Cardstock
- Glue
- Tape
- Small plastic bags (to keep pieces together if unfinished projects are carried home) (optional)

Gail Borden Public Library uses 65 lb. cardstock. If your library has budget constraints, you can print on copy paper instead. Glue sticks will work better on copy paper, whereas liquid craft glue adheres better to cardstock. If possible, offer both glue and tape. That way participants can choose their favorite adhesive or they can experiment to see which works better in different situations.

NECESSARY EQUIPMENT

- Computer or tablet with Internet and printer access
- Color printer
- Scissors
- Craft knife or knives
- Self-healing cutting mat(s)

Gail Borden offers teens the option of using a craft knife if they agree to follow the necessary safety rules. If your teens will be using knives, consider paying extra for Fiskars Softgrip, X-ACTO X2000, or other knives with a molded ergonomic grip. They cost more than the cheapest X-ACTO knives but they are easier to grasp, they do not roll when placed on a surface, and their blades seem less likely to come loose when in use. Even if your participants will not be using craft knives, cutting mats can be useful for corralling paper scraps.

STEP-BY-STEP INSTRUCTIONS

Before the Program

Identify three papercraft templates that match the interests and skill level of your teens. It's safest to start with simple, boxlike templates and let your teens work their way up to more complicated models. Boxcats by Goopymart (available at https://www.flickr .com/photos/goopymart/8456144433/in/photostream/) and I Heart Mammals by Salazad (http://salazad.com/papertoy/heart-mammals/) are excellent for beginners. Both are Creative Commons (CC) licensed for noncommercial use.

For your third papercraft, you might consider a Cubeecraft-style model like those available at www.cubeecraft.com. Cubees can be assembled without the use of glue or tape. Be aware that Cubee arms are a challenge for most beginners.

To find models of a specific animal, character, vehicle, and so on, do an image search online for *[name of character] papercraft*, *[name of character] paper toy*, and/or *[name of character] cubee*. In general, the more closely the model resembles a cube, and the fewer pieces it has, the easier it will be to assemble. Multi-page templates are not necessarily more difficult, but they do cost more to print.

Locating templates online is easy. Ensuring that they comply with copyright law can be a challenge. Many papercrafts featuring popular characters are fan-made and thus have the same murky legal status as other fan art and fan fiction—see https:// www.plagiarismtoday.com/2010/05/13/the-messy-world-of-fan-art-and-copyright/ for a more in-depth discussion of this issue. Meanwhile, officially sanctioned templates are usually made available "for personal use only," a term that some creators of original papercrafts also set on their websites.

When faced with this issue, some libraries (including Gail Borden) have decided that character-inspired papercrafts are an officially tolerated and therefore acceptable part of fan culture. You may wish to consult your library's legal expert for guidance on using fan-created papercrafts, particularly if you are using them at a large-scale event. Ways to be absolutely sure that you are following copyright law include:

- Using original, nonderivative templates that are CC licensed for noncommercial use
- Obtaining permission to distribute copies from an original template's creator
- Creating your own templates or adding CC-licensed art to existing, CC-licensed templates

Gail Borden Public Library has used all three of these methods with success.

Print out enough copies of each model for your anticipated group size. If you are printing out JPG and PNG files from Windows Photo Viewer, uncheck "fit to page" and choose the 8x10 option to ensure that the model prints out fully.

Some templates include cut lines that require the use of a craft knife. If you do not wish to provide participants with craft knives, you will need to make sure those lines are precut.

Make a sample of each paper toy for participants to examine.

During the Program

If your participants will be using craft knives, review how to use them safely. Gail Borden's rules boil down to: "Don't cut your fingers off. Don't cut other people's fingers off. And don't cut the table." While these rules may sound funny, it is made clear that knife safety is no joke. Teens are reminded to cut only when their template is flat against a self-healing mat that is fully supported by the table; to avoid jostling each other or the table; and to keep the safety cap on their knife whenever they are not actively cutting (the hardest rule for most to remember). Teens who have not used a craft knife before may also need to be shown the correct way to grip it.

Use scissors or a knife to cut out the first template. (Many papercrafters score their models before doing any cutting. Turning the model over to its unprinted side and using a ruler to guide them, they press down along any fold lines with a bone folder, dull butter knife, or dried-out ballpoint pen. Performing this step helps to ensure that each fold will be straight and crisp. However, Gail Borden's papercraft programs have not yet incorporated scoring instruction, mostly because it would take extra time and delay the gratification of having a finished model.)

Fold the appropriate lines and tabs as indicated on the model. Participants who are having trouble folding straight lines can try holding a library card or other piece of thin, straight plastic against the fold line while creasing it.

Use glue or tape to secure the model into its final shape.
Repeat these steps for the second and third models.

Teen-embellished Cubee model atop Minecraft block

Circulate throughout the room during the program. Ask how things are going with each teen, and offer suggestions or assistance where needed. Some students may need encouragement to continue working on a model they believe they have "messed up."

If you will be offering the program again, ask participants what characters or animals they would like to try making at future sessions. You could even bring a laptop or tablet into the programming area and work together with students to search for appropriate templates online.

LEARNING OUTCOMES

After participating in this program, students will be able to:

- Explain the papercraft assembly process to their parents and peers.
- Evaluate the assembly process, explaining which parts were hardest or easiest for them, and what (if anything) they would do differently in the future.
- Assemble similar models without assistance.
- Recognize cube shapes when they see them in unfamiliar papercraft templates.
- Use a craft knife safely (if craft knives were used at your program).

RECOMMENDED NEXT PROJECTS

Papercraft programs offer excellent replay value. Some returning participants will be happy to construct the same basic shape over and over, as long as the art on each iteration of that shape depicts a different animal or character. That's great—the repetition will help them to improve their fine motor skills. Other participants will want to move on to more complex papercrafts. That's great, too—they can challenge themselves by tackling any of the following:

- Chibi papercrafts
- Hexagons, dodecahedrons, and other non-cuboid geometric figures
- Templates that utilize pinching rather than folding techniques to create more rounded figures
- Templates with ten or more pieces
- Automata (papercraft with moving parts)

Trying each of these model types can help you become more comfortable assisting students, but you do not need to create a sample of every single papercraft you make available during programs. Look for images of completed models online for students to consult when a template does not come with assembly instructions.

Teens who prefer art to engineering can be encouraged to draw their own designs onto existing blank templates using markers, a drawing app, or a papercraft-specific app like Foldify. Budding paper engineers can learn how to use 3D modeling software and the Windows application Pepakura Designer to create their own unique templates.

FIGURE 8.2 ....

A variety of papercraft figures

9

Card-Making
with Conductive Paint

LYSSA TROEMEL / MAKER LAB GUIDE

Allen County Public Library–Georgetown

Type of Library Best Suited for: Any

Cost Estimate: $20–$40

Makerspace Necessary? No

PROJECT DESCRIPTION

In this project you will make a card using conductive paint. Participants will learn how to make a card, how to draw a simple circuit, and get a chance to be creative without restrictions. At Georgetown, conductive paint pens from Bare Conductive were used. Conductive paint is paint that's electrically conductive, which means that you can paint wires onto any surface such as walls, furniture, and so on.

OVERVIEW

This is done as a one-day, two-hour program that is usually open to six people of all ages. This is a program that has proven popular with all age groups and is great to do with families. It is also offered multiple times during the month. Usually this program is offered in December to go with the holidays, but it can be done at any time during the year.

MATERIALS LIST

- Paper for folding
- LEDs (light-emitting diodes)
- Batteries (coin cell, CR2032 works well)
- Battery holders
- Conductive paint pens or conductive paint pot with paintbrushes
- Colored paper for cut-outs
- Any other craft supplies like glue, stickers, crayons, markers, and so on
- Scissors

NECESSARY EQUIPMENT

No specialized equipment is needed for this project.

FIGURE 9.1 ·

Two examples of cards

STEP-BY-STEP INSTRUCTIONS

Step 1

Make the base of your card by folding paper in half or in quarters. Depending on the thickness of the paper, quarters may be more stable. The paper can be either cardstock or regular copier paper.

Step 2

Decorate the card and decide where you want to have your LEDs. Decorate as much as possible before adding the LED because you will need time to let the conductive paint dry, and it is very easy to brush and smear the paint while decorating. People can use whatever craft supplies they would like to decorate the front, insides, and back of the card. Have markers and other kinds of paper out so participants can draw or cut out designs. If stencils are available, those would be good to bring out too.

Step 3

Insert the LED into your design. There are two ways to do this:

If you don't want to see the conductive paint, poke the LED legs through the paper and bend outwards. Insert the battery holder an inch or two away. Draw the circuit with the conductive paint. Make sure the paint for the negative does not cross the paint of the positive. Place a glob of paint under the legs of the battery holder.

If you don't want the LED to stay on all the time, leave a gap for a switch on either the positive side or the negative side. Add a piece of paper with a blob of conductive paint on one end and glue on the other.

Step 4

If you want to see the paint, follow step 3 except for poking the LEDs through the paper. You can just separate the legs of the LED and place them flat on the paper. If you want to incorporate the paint into the design, trace the outline of the shape. Remember to keep the positive and negative separate. If they are not separate, the circuit will not work. Try not to get any paint on your hands; it is very hard to wash off, but will wash off eventually.

Step 5

The LED will not light up right away. The paint will need to dry before you start to see any results. If the participant has decided not to add in a switch, they will probably start to see the LED light up as the paint dries.

FIGURE 9.2

Circuit example with switch

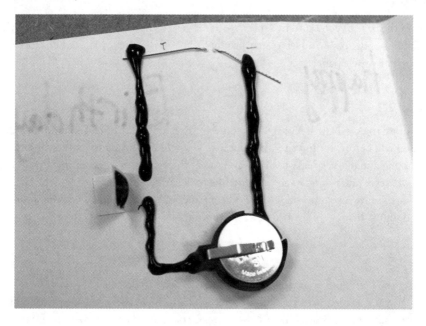

FIGURE 9.3

Circuit example without switch on front

Step 6

If the LED does not light up, check to make sure the participant didn't connect or accidentally smear the paint so the positive and negative are connected. If this has happened, they may need to start over. If the participant hasn't connected them, check the paint for breaks or weak spots. If this is the case, draw another line of paint, keeping the flow as consistent as possible.

LEARNING OUTCOMES

Participants should learn how to:

- Make a circuit with a switch.
- Make a circuit.
- Simple folding techniques.

RECOMMENDED NEXT PROJECTS

More complex circuits with more LEDs can be tried with the conductive paint. A good non-messy next step may be to use copper tape instead of conductive paint. There are also sticker circuits that have positive and negative marked on the sticker. You could also add in other card-making techniques like pop-ups, and other folding and engineering projects. Bare Conductive also has a store that has card kits with preprinted designs and other projects. They also have a touch board that allows for other components and is programmable like an Arduino. This would also be a good project to supplement with a paper-cutting machine like a Silhouette Cameo or similar device.

Build and Launch Foam Rockets

NICK MADSEN / YOUTH SERVICES SPECIALIST AND MAINTENANCE MANAGER
Community Library Network: Kootenai and Shoshone Counties
Project originally developed by Randy Zepeda

Type of Library Best Suited for: Any

Cost Estimate: $45–$75

Makerspace Necessary? No

PROJECT DESCRIPTION

This project details how participants can build a foam rocket and assemble a rocket launcher to launch their own rockets more than 100 feet.

OVERVIEW

The rocket launcher for this project is designed with PVC pipe and a sprinkler valve. Air is loaded into the launcher with a bike pump or air compressor, and when the air is released, a small rocket can be launched over 100 feet through the air. Insulation tubing, cardstock, and duct tape are used to create the rocket. The sprinkler valve can be manually released to launch the rocket. Alternately, a push-button switch can be wired to the sprinkler valve to launch the rocket.

Please note: This launcher does not include any inherently dangerous components, but the rocket is launched by releasing pressurized air. Be aware of the pressure ratings of each of your components, and practice safety and common sense while using the rocket launcher. For additional safety, wrap the exterior of your rocket launcher in duct tape.

MATERIALS LIST

Rocket Materials

- 1-inch or ¾-inch insulation tubing (1 foot long of this size per participant)
- Cardstock
- Duct tape

Rocket Launcher Materials

- ¾-inch PVC pipe (6 feet long approximately)
- 2-inch PVC pipe (2 feet long approximately)
- PTFE thread seal tape
- PVC pipe cement and primer
- Duct tape
- Large zip ties
- 1-inch inline sprinkler valve
- ¾-inch blowout plug
- ¼-inch NPT bottom mount gauge
- ½-inch MIP × ¼-inch FIP brass pipe bushing
- 2 × ¾-inch PVC pipe brush with female thread

FIGURE 10.1 . . . .

Materials

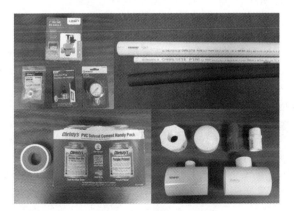

- 2 × 2-inch × ½-inch PVC pipe female threaded tee
- 2 × 2 × 1-inch PVC pipe female threaded tee
- 1 × 3-inch PVC pipe male threaded joint
- 1" × ¾-inch PVC pipe male threaded adaptor
- 2-inch cap PVC pipe

NECESSARY EQUIPMENT

Bike air pump or air compressor

STEP-BY-STEP INSTRUCTIONS

1. Build the Rocket Launcher

Decide whether your participants will assemble the launcher at the event or if it will be assembled by a staff member beforehand. Allow 30–45 minutes for assembly. The bulk of your launcher will be 2-inch PVC pipe, and will measure about two feet across when completed. There will be a measurement assembly on one end, a launcher assembly in the middle, and a cap on the other end. Zip ties and pieces of PVC pipe will be used to stabilize the launcher. Keeping safety in mind, use thread seal tape and PVC pipe cement to join your pieces together.

Measurement/Fill Assembly
Put the ¾-inch blowout plug into the 2 × ¾-inch brush with female thread and insert that into one side of the 2 × 2 × ½-inch female threaded tee. Put the ½-inch MIP × ¼-inch FIP brass pipe bushing onto the ¼-inch NPT bottom mount gauge and attach that to the top of the 2 × 2 × ½-inch female threaded tee. This assembly will let you fill the launcher with air and will also let you measure the pounds per square inch inside of the launcher. Attach a one-foot length of 2-inch PVC pipe to the opposite side of the female threaded tee.

Sprinkler Launcher Assembly
Put the 1 × 3-inch male threaded joint onto the top of the 2 × 2 × 1-inch female threaded tee. Put the 1-inch inline sprinkler valve onto the male threaded joint, and place the 1 × ¾-inch male threaded adaptor on the other side of the inline sprinkler valve. Take a one-foot length of ¾-inch PVC pipe, and attach that to the top of the ¾-inch male threaded adaptor. Place one side of this completed assembly onto the other side of the one-foot length of 2-inch PVC pipe from the measurement/fill assembly. Finally, place a second one-foot length of 2-inch PVC pipe onto the opposite side of the 2 × 2 × 1-inch female threaded tee. Close the other side of this second piece of PVC pipe with the 2-inch cap.

Stabilizers

Cut two 2-foot lengths of ¾-inch PVC pipe. When completed, these lengths will be stabilizers for your rocket launcher. Each stabilizer should be perpendicular to the finished rocket launcher, one positioned near the measurement/fill assembly, and the other close to the 2-inch cap. For each of the two stabilizers, create two holes in the PVC pipe. The holes should be positioned near the center of the PVC pipe around three inches apart from one another. Thread a zip tie down through one hole and back up the other. Join the zip tie together over the top of one of the ends of the finished rocket launcher. The following picture shows the completed "H" shape that is created.

FIGURE 10.2 ....

Rocket launcher stabilizers

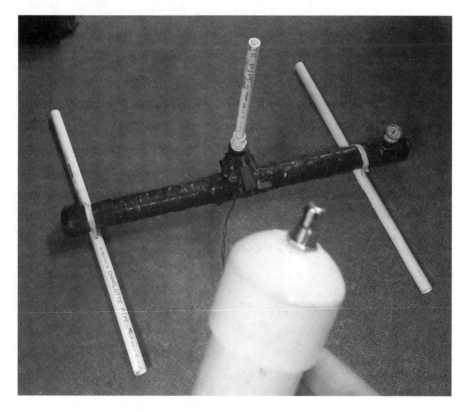

2. Build the Rockets

The majority of the participants' time will be spent building, testing, and redesigning their rockets. The simplest form of rocket is built with a one-foot length of ¾-inch or 1-inch insulation tubing, a rocket nose cap made from cardstock or thin cardboard, and fins made from cardstock or thin cardboard. Individual rockets can be wrapped in duct tape to ensure they are airtight. After launching their rockets, participants should brainstorm how they could improve their design (i.e., changing fin shape, trimming weight, rebuilding the nose shape), and then spend time rebuilding their rockets for another round of launches. Each round of building, redesign, and launching can take between 30 and 45 minutes.

3. Launch the Rockets

The sprinkler valve assembly will have an open and closed setting. Make sure the valve is in the closed setting while filling the launcher with air, and then release the air by switching the valve to the open setting. As mentioned previously, use common sense and safety while launching these rockets. Determine the piece of your assembly that can handle the lowest amount of pressure and do not exceed that amount of pressure.

LEARNING OUTCOMES

- Participants learn that their ideas can improve with time and persistence.
- Participants adapt plumbing parts into a rocket launcher.
- Participants learn about aerodynamics and flight in a hands-on way.
- Participants troubleshoot and improve rocket designs.

RECOMMENDED NEXT PROJECTS

- PVC pipe stomp rocket launcher
- Model rocket kits and launcher
- Pumpkin launcher or trebuchet

Create Pet Rocks and Rock Pets

HEIDI COLOM / YOUTH SERVICES LIBRARIAN
Tampa-Hillsborough County Public Library

Type of Library Best Suited for: Public or School

Cost Estimate: $50

Makerspace Necessary? No

PROJECT DESCRIPTION

This project details how to make pet rocks and rock pets using simple materials. Pet rocks can be made using just one rock, wiggly eyes, and other decorations. They can also be painted with markers or paint, while rock pets involve several rocks, construction paper, wiggly eyes, and other decorations. They can also be painted with markers or paint. Both of these crafts require scissors and glue which can be liquid or a glue stick.

Pet rocks and rock pets can be made as part of a staff-led program, or at a table in an outreach—not just in the library's makerspace. This type of program is recommended for ages five and up due to the small pieces involved.

OVERVIEW

Back in the 1970s, pet rocks were very popular. But why just have a blank rock sitting there? You can make your own pet rock with wiggly eyes that gaze back at you—as well as a face, a hat, and maybe even hands and feet.

If you like pet rocks, you can take your imagination up a notch by creating a rock pet! Arrange your rocks in shapes to form your favorite animal—and give it a home with a background.

All materials and supplies will be provided by the library's makerspace—and you get to take it home. They can be created individually, or as part of a class led by an instructor.

MATERIALS LIST

- River rocks
- Wiggly eyes
- Feathers
- Pom-poms
- Foamies
- Felt
- Craft gems
- Markers
- Craft paint
- Glue—stick or liquid
- Construction paper of various colors

All materials can be easily obtained at craft supply stores, such as Michael's and Jo-Ann Fabrics.

NECESSARY EQUIPMENT

- Makerspace, table, or any other flat surface
- Scissors

STEP-BY-STEP INSTRUCTIONS

Creating Pet Rocks

1. Glue wiggly eyes onto a flat and smooth surface of the rock.
2. Use a marker to draw a mouth and nose on the rock.
3. Add feathers, pom-poms, felt, and craft gems to the rock as a hat.
4. If the rock is large enough, you can also give it an outfit made out of felt.
5. If you would like to make the rock stand up, add two Foamies under the rounded surface below the face.
6. You can also add Foamies to the rounded surfaces on both sides of the face in order to portray hands.
7. Don't forget to give the rock a name!

FIGURE 11.1

Pet rocks

Creating Rock Pets

1. Begin with a piece of blue construction paper . . . if you would like a diurnal outside pet. You can use black if your pet is nocturnal. Or you can use any other color for an indoor pet.

2. Cut out green construction paper in the shape of grass. Glue at the bottom of the blue construction paper. You can also create a rug. But you need something for your pet to stand up on.

3. Glue the largest rock onto the center of the paper in order to make the pet's body. Next add the second largest rock to make the head. Add at least two others to make the paws.

4. Glue Foamie ovals to the head to make ears. Glue a larger oval to the body to make a tail.

5. Glue wiggly eyes to the head.

6. Use markers to give your pet a nose, mouth, hair, and claws. You can also use paint.

7. If you wish, you can add gems, feathers, and other decorations to give your pet a collar or hat.

8. Rock pets do not have to be just mammals. You can make any kind of animal. You can even make fantasy creatures—such as dragons or unicorns. Use your imagination!

9. Draw or glue any other plants or toys your pet would enjoy. You can also add the sun, moon, or stars.

10. Don't forget to give your rock pet a name!

FIGURE 11.2

Rock pet

LEARNING OUTCOMES

- Makers will use their creativity and fine motor skills while creating the pet rocks and rock pets.
- Makers will learn about the history of 1970s popular culture thanks to the pet rocks background info. If part of a class or makerspace, a display of books about the 1970s can be created.
- Makers will also learn about zoology and ecology thanks to the rock pets. If part of a class or makerspace, include books about animals and biomes.

RECOMMENDED NEXT PROJECTS

Other fun crafts from other decades include:

- Tie-dyed handkerchiefs from the 1960s
- Shrinky-Dinks from the 1980s
- Recycled crafts from the 1990s

Sewing
and
Textiles Projects

Fidget Flannels

AMANDA KRAMER

DIRECTOR OF ACCESS SERVICES/LIBRARIAN/ASSISTANT PROFESSOR
Library and Academic Technology at Washington College

Type of Library Best Suited for: Any

Cost estimate: $2 per participant

Makerspace Necessary? No

PROJECT DESCRIPTION

In this simple project, designed to get everyone "making," students use a sewing machine and two pieces of cotton flannel material to stitch together a rectangular case with a small opening, essentially creating a pocket. This pocket is turned inside out and lines are stitched on the right side of the fabric to create a maze. Students insert a standard-sized marble and sew or hand seam the opening.

OVERVIEW

Whether it's a student in third grade or a student in her third year of college, there's nothing quite like prepping for a test or listening to a long talk in a classroom or a packed lecture hall. For some young people, situations like these are a piece of cake. For others, they're the stuff of nightmares.

As part of the Washington College first-year research and writing course "Cultivating a Maker Mindset," professors Amanda Kramer and Brian Palmer worked with students on this simple project called a Fidget Flannel—a small trinket that might be just what some need to make it peacefully through an anxiety-ridden situation.

Teaching students how to construct these flannels will sharpen their knowledge of sewing machine basics, but could also make a larger impact on your organization or campus. Creating a set of these simple trinkets—which allow the user to move or "fidget" a marble between seamed lines—and then donating them to a public library or a college's disability services office teaches students the importance of sharing their gifts with others—one of the keys to cultivating a true "maker" mindset.

MATERIALS LIST

- One spool of 100 percent white cotton sewing thread. *Note:* 100 percent cotton thread should be used because it is sturdy; nylon thread has a tendency to break. Because these small flannels are meant to be handled frequently, cotton is important.
- 1 to 2 yards of soft, cotton flannel fabric with varying patterns. Some stores will advertise this flannel as "cozy" or "snuggle" fabric. One hundred percent cotton plaid flannel shirts from a thrift store would also fit the bill.
- Piece of paper and a pencil
- Chalk
- Assortment of round glass marbles

NECESSARY EQUIPMENT

- Any basic sewing machine in good working condition. *Note:* At Washington College, we purchased a Janome HD1000 heavy-duty sewing machine with a cast aluminum body. This type of machine is hard to break and easy to fix, which is critical when you have a high volume of student use on a machine.
- Basic sewing accessories like bobbins and assorted feet that come as part of the machine.
- A standard or quilting ruler, or a measuring tape
- Scissors
- Sewing pins
- Hand sewing needle

STEP-BY-STEP INSTRUCTIONS

Note: Prior to beginning the project (which will move quickly if you have several sewing machines that enable students to spread out), spend a class period showing students how to use a sewing machine—make sure it's a hands-on session. Help them fill a bobbin, thread the machine, and sew a few rows of stitches on scrap fabric. This will build their confidence before starting this project.

1. Lay out your fabric, folded so that when you cut, you'll be cutting out two pieces at a time.
2. Using your ruler or measuring tape, and your piece of paper and pencil, craft a simple "pattern" by measuring a rectangle that's approximately 6 inches wide by 4 inches deep. Cut out the pattern.
3. Lay the pattern on the flannel and pin it to the fabric in two spots so it's stable.
4. Use your scissors to cut around the pattern. Unpin the pattern from the fabric and you will have two pieces of rectangular fabric.

FIGURE 12.1

Cutting the pattern

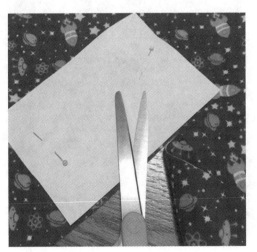

---

5. Put the fabric right sides (the side or pattern image you want to appear on the finished product) together and pin in two or three spots so they are secured.
6. Move to the sewing machine (which should be threaded and set to a simple straight stitch). Sew a ¼-inch seam around three of the sides, leaving some room before hitting the end of each side to rotate the fabric. (Show students that the distance from the end of the fabric to the sewing line is ¼ inch.)

7. Rotate one last time and sew the final side, leaving a 1½-inch opening (this will be the place to slip in your marble).

8. Remove the pins from your fabric and snip away excess thread. Then, by gently placing your thumb into the opening you've left, carefully pull the inside out so that the pattern side of the fabric is now visible.

9. Lay your project down on your table—it should look like a rectangle. Lay the ruler or measuring tape across the center of the rectangle and make three chalk marks in the middle of the fabric—at approximately 1½-inch intervals.

FIGURE 12.2 ....

Chalk-marking the flannel

10. You will now sew three lines of straight stitching that stop about an inch from the top of the fabric to create the maze. You will alternate your starting point for the lines. Your first line will start at the bottom of the rectangle (in line with your chalk mark) and move up to the middle chalk mark. Remove the fabric from the machine and turn it, stitching from the bottom of the opposite side (in line with your chalk mark) up to the second middle chalk mark. Remove the fabric again and turn it one last time, stitching again from the bottom of the opposite side up to the third middle chalk mark.

11. Place your marble inside the fabric pocket and move it around the maze, making sure that it can pass through easily.

12. At this point, you may choose to neatly sew the opening closed with the machine, or have students thread a hand-sewing needle, fold the ends of the opening in slightly, and use a few simple slip stitches to seam it shut, tying off the end into a knot.

13. Trim off all excess threads—and test it out!

LEARNING OUTCOMES

- Students learn sewing machine and hand-stitching basics.
- If paired with a brief discussion on forms of anxiety or characteristics of autism spectrum disorder, students will learn a little more about why "fidgeting" or touch can help regulate heightened sensory systems.

RECOMMENDED NEXT PROJECTS

Fidget flannels are a fantastic, simple "stepping-stone" project. In the course at our college, this project was used to get students comfortable with sewing machines and fabrics. Suggested next projects are:

- Sew a simple throw pillow and fill it with Poly-Fil stuffing
- Use a basic store-bought pattern to create pajama pants
- Teach beginner quilting by having students sew a potholder

Sew a Glowing Ghost Marionette

LYSSA TROEMEL / MAKER LAB GUIDE
Allen County Public Library–Georgetown

Type of Library Best Suited for: School or Public

Cost Estimate: $30–$40

Makerspace Necessary? No

PROJECT DESCRIPTION

This is a simple marionette that is made on a single control bar to look like a ghost. Participants use a sewing machine to make the understructure, and use conductive thread and LEDS (light-emitting diodes) to make the eyes glow. The understructure can also be done only by hand sewing.

OVERVIEW

The ghost marionette is typically made around Halloween and is made in one two-hour program. If there is no sewing machine available, this can be done by hand, but doing so will more than likely take longer. Participants are generally children, even though this is a class offered to all ages. During this two-hour program they learn how to use the sewing machine, how to hand sew, and how to make a simple circuit.

MATERIALS LIST

- White cotton fabric cut in a rectangle
- Two pieces of white tulle
- Long skewers or dowel rods
- Conductive thread
- Wearable LEDs
- Double battery holder or two LilyPad switched battery holders
- Two 2032 batteries
- Fiberfill
- Fishing line or thread
- Hot glue

NECESSARY EQUIPMENT

- Sewing machine
- Hand sewing needle

FIGURE 13.1

The finished ghosts

STEP-BY-STEP INSTRUCTIONS

Step 1

The first step is to make the marionette's head. The fabric needs to be cut into a rectangle. The bigger it is, the bigger the head can be. On the white cotton fabric, sew a zigzag stitch on the two longest sides. It should be on the widest and longest stitch. Back stitch at only one end and leave a long tail at the end of the stitch. If you don't have a sewing machine, make big single stitches. Then pull the top string gently and make a ruffle with the fabric on one side.

FIGURE 13.2 ....

Example of making the ruffle

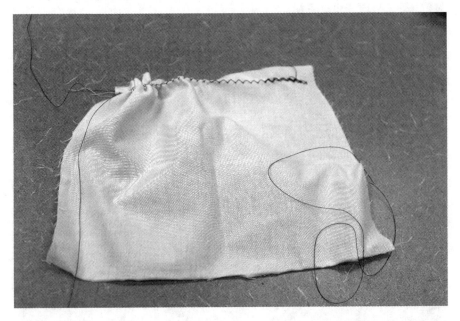

Step 2

Put the right sides together and sew along the edges, leaving one side open. You should leave the non-ruffled side open and you don't have to stitch along the folded edge. Fill the head with fiberfill and pull the top thread to make a ruffle. Close up by hand stitching. If you don't have a sewing machine for this, hand stitch two straight lines. Pull on the end of the thread to ruffle it. Sew up the side and follow the rest of these instructions.

Step 3

Hand sew on the LEDs with conductive thread with the battery in the back. The LEDs should be positioned so that the holes of either the positive or the negative LEDs are facing each other. If you are using two LilyPad battery holders, they can be sewn on directly. If you are using a double battery holder, you will need to snip the ends of the wire and strip them. The thread can be tied around the ends and the wire bent over the knots. Secure the connection with electrical tape. If you find people are having problems keeping any of the components in place, a little bit of hot glue will hold them down. Be sure to emphasize the importance of sewing in a straight line.

Step 4

A pocket made of scrap cotton fabric can be sewn onto the back to hold the double battery holder in place. To do this, simply fold in the edges and hand stitch the pocket to the back of the head.

Step 5

Now we make the rest of the marionette. You should have two pieces of tulle; suggested sizes are one piece that is 18 inches by 22 inches and one piece that is 18 inches by 24 inches. Place the larger tulle over the head that you now have and tack on the bottom ruffle and the top of the head. Don't go all the way through to the other side of the tulle. Leave this open so the batteries can be changed. Place a second piece and also tack it on the top of the head.

Step 6

This is the last part. There should be at least three strings total: one from the head, and one from each side for arms. To attach the head, take a hand needle and stitch through to the head. If you have a thick needle, use it because the fishing line is thick and can be difficult to get through with a small needle. Take the other end of the string and tie it to the bar. For the arms, tie it to the edge of the bottom, larger tulle. Put a little bit of hot glue on the end tied to the bar.

Troubleshooting

If the eyes don't light up, check to make sure the positives and negatives aren't touching. If you are using the double battery holder, it is very easy for the wires and thread to cross if electrical tape has not been applied. If it still doesn't work after this step, take out the stitches and re-sew. Chances are that the threads crossed somewhere inside where it can't be seen.

LEARNING OUTCOMES

People making this marionette should learn how to:

- Use a sewing machine (if available).
- How to hand sew.
- Circuitry basics.

RECOMMENDED NEXT PROJECTS

After making this, people should work on a few more simple sewing projects to get familiar with the machine or hand stitching. Some projects that have been done at the Georgetown Branch are handwarmers, coasters, tomato and strawberry pincushions, and small tote bags. If they liked working with the conductive thread, Sparkfun has some tutorials and different projects that would also work; a superhero mask is another popular program we have done. They can also add any Arduino wearable into a conductive sewing project and use it to program the LEDs for a more advanced project. Once people are familiar with the sewing machine, they can start to work on closures like zippers and buttons.

Hand Sew a
Mini Stuffed Animal

LEANNE POSEY / YOUTH SELECTION AND TEEN PROGRAMMING LIBRARIAN
Grand Prairie Public Library

Type of Library Best Suited for: Public or School

Cost Estimate: $50–$100 (20 participants)

Makerspace Necessary? No

PROJECT DESCRIPTION

This project aims to provide teens and tweens with the knowledge of how to do several basic hand stitches, including the running stitch, backstitch, and blanket stitch. This is a two-part project: "Learning Basic Hand Stitches" and "Creating a Mini Stuffed Animal." These projects can be done during one program time, but they work best when split into a multipart program with two separate projects.

This program is geared toward novice sewers who have minimal experience with hand sewing. Participants learn a new skill in this hands-on program, and are given the opportunity to apply this new skill in a practical project.

OVERVIEW

This craft project consists of two 45–60 minute programs: "Learning Basic Hand Stitches" and "Creating a Mini Stuffed Animal." Program participants will first learn how to do the stitches necessary to create their mini stuffed animal, and take time to practice these stitches. During the second part of the program, attendees will apply their new skills and create a mini stuffed animal. This program used a template for a penguin mini stuffed animal, but other templates can be used. Templates can be purchased, created from a line drawing, or copied from a craft book as long as all copyright laws are followed.

MATERIALS LIST

Learning Basic Hand Stitches

- Scrap felt or fabric
- Embroidery thread (preferably a contrasting color to the fabric)
- Handout with explanation of stitches

Penguin mini stuffed animal

Creating a Mini Stuffed Animal

- All supplies from first list
- Black felt
- White felt
- Orange felt
- Any color felt
- Black embroidery thread

- Colored embroidery thread
- Penguin stuffed animal template
- Sharpies (black and silver)
- Stuffing (i.e., Poly-Fil Premium Polyester Fiber Fill)

NECESSARY EQUIPMENT

- Scissors
- Needles

- Optional: laptop with Wi-Fi and access to YouTube

STEP-BY-STEP INSTRUCTIONS

Part 1: Learning Basic Hand Stitches

Begin by viewing some videos on each of the stitches; this will help participants see the stitches being done and will help when they read the instructions on the handout. The YouTube videos by Red Ted Art offer simple and clear instructions for the stitches, but there are many videos to choose from. Then hand out the supplies needed for the first project: "Learning Basic Hand Stitches."

After watching the videos, have participants read the handout and start practicing the stitches; have them spend approximately ten minutes on each stitch. During this time, walk around and offer assistance as needed. After participants have done each stitch, let them spend the remaining time asking questions and practicing the stitches they had the most trouble with. Participants may take their needle, thread, and fabric home with them; encourage them to practice before the second part of the project.

Hand Stitch Instructions

Running Stitch

Start by threading your needle and knotting the end of the thread. Place your needle on the back or "wrong" side of the fabric. Bring your needle through the fabric until the knot hits the fabric. Move your needle over to the left or right of where the thread comes through the fabric. How far over you move it will determine how large your stitch is. Push your needle through the fabric and pull until all excess thread is on the back side of the fabric. Your needle is now on the back side of the fabric. Move your needle over (how far over will determine how big of a space you will have between stitches), and bring the needle back through to the front of the fabric. Repeat.

Backstitch

Start by threading your needle and knotting the end of the thread. Place your needle on the back or "wrong" side of the fabric. Bring your needle through the fabric until the knot hits the fabric. Move your needle, however large you want your stitch to be, in the opposite direction you want to go in. If you are sewing a line to the right, move your needle to the left. Push your needle through the fabric and pull until all excess thread is on the back side of the fabric. Your needle is now on the back side of the fabric. Move your needle in the direction you are sewing in. You want to move your needle over one stitch length from your starting point. Bring your needle and thread through to the right side of the fabric. There should be a stitch-sized blank space between where your thread is now and the first stitch you made. Push your needle and thread back to the other side of the fabric at your starting point. Move the needle over again so there is a stitch-sized blank space; pull the needle and thread through to the front side of the fabric. Go to where your previous stitch starts, and push the needle and thread through the back side of the fabric. Repeat.

Blanket Stitch

This stitch is done on the edge of fabric. Line up two edges of fabric. Start by threading your needle and knotting the end of the thread. Place your needle on the back or "wrong" side of one of the pieces of fabric so that the knot is between the two pieces of fabric. Bring your needle through the fabric until the knot hits the fabric. Bring your thread around the edge of the fabric and push it back through the same spot you started the stitch in. *Don't* pull the thread completely taut; leave a small loop. Bring your needle through this loop and finish pulling it through. Move a short distance to the right or left. Repeat.

Part 2: Creating a Mini Stuffed Animal

The second part begins by reviewing the stitches; this can be done verbally or by rewatching the videos. Next, make sure everyone has the supplies that are needed. Participants will begin by cutting out the template pieces and tracing them onto the various colored pieces of felt with black and/or silver Sharpies.

Template and Instructions
1. Cut out all template pieces.
2. Trace shape A onto black felt twice. (Body)
3. Trace shape B onto white felt. (Belly)
4. Trace shape C onto black felt twice. (Eyes)
5. Trace shape D onto orange felt. (Beak)
6. Trace shape E onto any colored felt. (Bow tie)

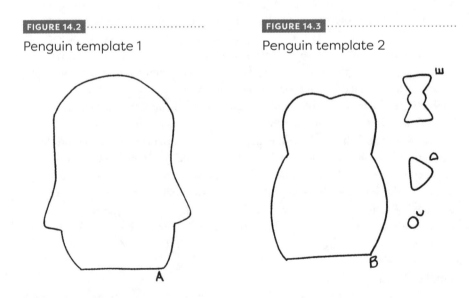

FIGURE 14.2 ···································

Penguin template 1

FIGURE 14.3 ···································

Penguin template 2

You can resize this template on your copier to your desired size. Be sure to resize and adjust Template 2 to the same size.

You can resize this template on your copier to your desired size. Be sure to resize and adjust Template 1 to the same size.

7. Cut all felt shapes out.
8. Using black thread, use the backstitch to sew the eyes and beak onto the white belly piece.
9. Using black thread, use the running stitch to sew the bow tie onto the white belly piece.
10. Using black thread, use the backstitch to sew the white belly onto one of the body pieces.
11. Using colored thread, use the blanket stitch to sew the two body pieces together. When they are three-quarters of the way sewn together stop, but do not knot off your thread.
12. Stuff the penguin with the desired amount of Poly-Fil.
13. Finish sewing the body pieces together with the blanket stitch.
14. Knot your thread as close to the fabric as possible and tuck the knot in.

LEARNING OUTCOMES

- Attendees understand and are able to do the various types of simple hand stitches.
- Attendees know when to use certain types of stitches on a project.
- Attendees complete a practical project using their new skills.
- Attendees should feel confident enough to attempt other hand sewing projects on their own, and undertake learning other types of stitches.

RECOMMENDED NEXT PROJECTS

There are several ways to expand on this project. This project could also be used as a stepping-stone that leads to teaching more complicated sewing classes using sewing machines. This route will require access to multiple sewing machines (depending on how many participants you have). This is a great opportunity to foster relationships with community business partners because many libraries, especially those without dedicated makerspaces, do not have the space to store or the funds to purchase multiple sewing machines.

Potential community partners may include craft stores that teach classes like Jo-Ann Fabrics, local businesses, or local nonprofits that emphasize creativity and similar skills. Reaching out and cultivating relationships with businesses and nonprofits benefits both parties. The library gains access to supplies and equipment it may not have the funds or storage space for, while the business or nonprofit gets advertising and exposure to program participants.

Another way to expand upon this project would be to continue with hand stitching. Future sessions could focus on teaching new stitches, such as the split stitch, stem stitch, threaded backstitch, satin stitch, and French knots. Additional programs could also offer more complex projects such as embroidering pillowcases or hand towels.

15

Transform a T-shirt to Tote Bag in Ten Steps

SILVIA GUTIERREZ / MEDIA COMMONS TEACHER LIBRARIAN
Palos Verdes Peninsula High School Library

Type of Library Best Suited for: Any

Cost Estimate: $3 per participant. Will be less if teens provide their own T-shirts

Makerspace Necessary? No

PROJECT DESCRIPTION

We've all heard the three "R's." Reduce. Reuse. Recycle. Let's add "Upcycle" to the "R's." Or, stick with the "R's" and call it "Repurposing." Recycling takes a used item and extracts useful material from it. Upcycling takes a used, no longer wanted item and creates a completely different "new and improved" item. Recycling is tearing an old T-shirt to make rags; upcycling is transforming an old T-shirt into a tote bag.

Our ancestors upcycled out of necessity. Old clothes were stitched into quilts. An old door was crafted into a table. Now we upcycle to save the earth, save money, and express our own creativity.

Participants will create a tote bag from a T-shirt in just ten steps. This project is quick, fun, and environmentally friendly because a gently used T-shirt is upcycled into a tote. Makers can show their school spirit, advocate for a cause, or be artsy when that too-tight tee is no longer wearable. The end project is a lightweight, versatile tote bag that shows the individual's personality. This practical item will earn the user many compliments and admiration when it is revealed to be upcycled from an old T-shirt. Upcycling is the fun factor of environmentalism.

OVERVIEW

This T-shirt to tote project can be easily completed in one 45–60 minute session. Have a few T-shirts for those teens who don't supply their own, but it is more rewarding if they bring one that is special to them. Most of the work involves cutting the T-shirt and tying knots. Just a bit of sewing—straight stitching on a printed line by hand or machine—is needed, and shouldn't discourage those with no previous sewing experience. One or two sewing machines are all that are needed. One adult per 8–10 teens can supervise. Teens can sit around a table, and each should have enough room to lay the T-shirt flat on the table. Adults should position themselves at the head of the table to be easily seen by all as they demonstrate each step for the teens to follow.

MATERIALS LIST

- T-shirt—gently used
- Pen or pencil
- Pot lid or large bowl
- Thread

NECESSARY EQUIPMENT

- Fabric scissors, not paper scissors
- Straight pins
- Sewing needles
- Ruler
- Tape measure
- Sewing machine in good working condition and threaded (optional)

STEP-BY-STEP INSTRUCTIONS

A word on T-shirts. Choosing an appropriate T-shirt is crucial. The wrong type of tee will not create a long-lasting, useful bag. Instead, it will stretch out of shape when filled or be too small or flimsy to be useful. Sturdy, heavyweight T-shirts like Hanes Beefy T or Gilden Heavy Blend are best. The neckline may be round or v-neck. But don't choose a shirt with holes. You don't want your loose change slipping out!

Size matters. An Adult Small or Child Large are good choices. Estimate the size of the finished tote by measuring the T-shirt circumference around the chest area, then measuring the shoulder to bottom hem, and subtracting four inches. This will give the approximate length and width of the finished bag.

T-shirts can be purchased at bargain prices at thrift stores. But remember, we are upcycling, so no new tees!

Step 1

Lay the T-shirt on the table surface. Have the arms straight out from the body of the shirt. In other words, lay it in a T. Cut off the sleeves by cutting on the outside of the seam, leaving the seam attached. This section will be part of the shoulder strap, and the seam prevents stretching and fraying.

Step 2

Place the sleeveless T-shirt on the table with the design or graphic face up. Smooth the shirt out to minimize wrinkles or folds. Using a round bowl or pot lid, place it between the shoulders. The lid should be half on the shirt and half off, creating a half circle for the cutting line. Check that the shoulder strap will be about 1½ to 2 inches wide when cut and that your graphic design is complete and not chopped off. You may need to use another size bowl, or make adjustments. If you feel confident, you may do without the bowl and draw freehand in the next step.

Step 3

Trace around the pot lid with a pen or pencil on the front side only. You will cut on the line in the next step, so don't worry if the mark is unsightly.

Step 4

Cut on the traced line through both thicknesses—the front and back.

Step 5

If the shoulder straps look too short, place the lid down lower on the T-shirt and trace again. Then, cut.

Step 6

Look over the design and decide how long you want the bottom fringe. The fringe should be at least four inches

FIGURE 15.1 ·

Sleeves and neckline cut

long in order to tie easily. The bottom of the tote bag will be right above the fringe. Draw a horizontal line on the front of the T-shirt at least four inches above the bottom edge. Pin the front and back together by pinning through both thicknesses, horizontal to the traced line and an inch above the traced line. The pins hold the T-shirt firmly together for the next step.

Step 7

The front of the T-shirt will be sewn to the back by sewing on the traced line. There are two options—hand sewn or machine sewn.

If hand sewn, cut a long piece of thread about two feet long. Thread the needle and knot one end of the thread. Sew through both back and front, making about six stitches per inch. When one end of the T-shirt is reached, knot the thread and repeat by sewing again. This will strengthen and reinforce the tote's bottom. The stitches do not have to be perfectly straight because the thread will not show when the tote is completed.

If machine sewn, set the stitch length to six per inch and choose the straight stitch. Sew on the marked line to the end, and knot. Cut the thread, and begin again at the first end. You are sewing the back and front together twice to reinforce the bottom.

When finished sewing, remove the pins.

Step 8

Lay the shirt flat on the table and make marks one inch apart along the bottom edge and just under the stitched line.

Step 9

Cut through both thicknesses up to the sewn line. Caution: do not snip through the thread. The first and last slits, which are the side seams of the T-shirt, will need to be cut on the seam to make into two slits.

Step 10

Keep the T-shirt carefully laid flat so the slits line up front and back. Tie the front fringe to the coordinating back fringe twice, in a double knot.

Congratulations! Your T-shirt is now transformed into a tote bag and is ready to use. It's lightweight and compact and can be taken anywhere. Bag your lunch, bag your groceries, bag your gym clothes.

FIGURE 15.2

Fringe cut and tied

FIGURE 15.3

Finished tote bag

LEARNING OUTCOMES

- Teens learn the benefits of upcycling.
- Instead of recycling or discarding, teens are encouraged to look for alternative uses for various items they already own and learn that there is more than one use for an item.
- Teens have an introduction to machine sewing.

RECOMMENDED NEXT PROJECTS

- Teens may try other fabric projects that require little or no sewing. Flannel or fleece blankets and pillows are projects that use strip tying.
- Stuffed animals created from old socks can be cleverly crafted without sewing a single stitch.
- Many other ideas may be found on Pinterest.

Yarn Painting

JESSICA LOGAN / BRANCH MANAGER, HAMILTON MILL BRANCH
Gwinnett County Public Library

Type of Library Best Suited for: Any

Cost Estimate: Under $50

Makerspace Necessary? No

PROJECT DESCRIPTION

The Hamilton Mill Branch of the Gwinnett County Public Library hosts a regularly scheduled event for young children to explore their artistic ability. Held once per month, our Little Leonardos program offers a new craft or project that introduces a specific art skill or style at each meeting.

The project presented and explored here is yarn painting, a popular program that is recommended for children ages 4–8 and which can take place at any time of the school year. Each event lasts approximately one hour, and we make sure to schedule the program during times when the students are not scheduled to be at school. Because this program is known to get a bit messy, we always encourage participants to dress in clothing they do not mind getting paint or glue on . . . and we also make sure to provide a supply of freshly washed, oversized T-shirts for anyone who forgot or would like an extra layer of protection.

OVERVIEW

Yarn Painting is a project that works well for young children (ages 4–8) with parental participation. To begin the event, you may want to explore the history of the Huichol—an indigenous people of Mexico who originated this art form. Be sure to present images of traditional yarn painting and discuss the purpose of this art form within the Huichol community and culture. Next, it is helpful to present images of modern yarn paintings and then review the materials needed and demonstrate the technique to your participants.

FIGURE 16.1

Little artists

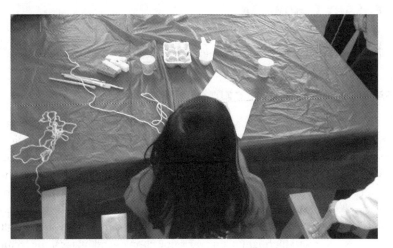

FIGURE 16.2

Traditional yarn painting

MATERIALS LIST

- Samples of traditional yarn painting
- Samples of how yarn painting is used today
- Picture templates
- Cardstock
- Construction paper (assorted colors)
- Glue (both glue sticks and liquid variety)
- Skeins of yarn (assorted colors)
- Pencils
- Crayons

NECESSARY EQUIPMENT

- Scissors
- Camera or other device to take pictures (optional)

STEP-BY-STEP INSTRUCTIONS

Once you are ready to introduce your yarn painting project, begin by sharing facts and information about the Huichol (pronounced Wettchol) people of Mexico. For example, the Huichol did not have a written language and used stories and symbols heavily within their society. Next, explore some information and images of Nierika (pronounced Near-eeka), or the traditional style of yarn painting. Nierika was created using natural glue from tree resin or beeswax, and wooden boards. The yarn was then pressed onto the board in a pattern or to create a particular image, using the glue to secure it. It is helpful to highlight (using various examples and images) the technique of using both long and short strands of yarn to create different effects.

Using one of the templates that will be provided to the children, give a quick technique demonstration to the group and then answer any questions they—or the parents—may have. Once everyone is prepared to begin you may distribute the materials, including pictures or templates of various objects and animals that they can use for guidance, glue/glue sticks, crayons, pencils, and yarn.

Yarn painting is a simple technique that can produce vibrant and fanciful works of art. Begin by selecting a background material for your painting. Some options include colored construction paper or cardstock. Strong paper or some other material is recommended to support the weight of the yarn and glue. You may also work from a guiding template printed or drawn on the material. Next cut your first strand of yarn. When first familiarizing yourself with the technique, it may be useful to start with shorter strands because they can be easier to manage. Once your first strand is ready, begin by laying down glue on your background material precisely where you wish to attach the yarn. Press the yarn firmly into the glue until it is secure. Try not to lay down too much glue at a time so that it does not begin to dry, or get in your way and become a sticky mess. Repeat this process of laying down glue and yarn until you have completed your very own yarn painting. A helpful tip is to use a pencil or toothpick to press the yarn into the glue so that it does not get on your fingertips; this can make the yarn increasingly difficult to work with. You may wish to adjust the lengths, colors, and/or textures of yarn throughout the piece to create various effects.

Allow your participants ample time to create their works of art and be sure to remain available to answer questions or to provide assistance. In our experience, many of the parents also wish to create a yarn painting alongside their child, and this is an activity that we certainly encourage. Yarn painting is truly fun for all ages and makes for excellent quality time spent working together. With an age group of young children, be sure to offer plenty of encouragement and praise throughout. Nothing makes the children light up quite like knowing they've impressed the adults with their skill and imagination.

FIGURE 16.3 ....

Yarn paintings

Once your participants have completed their yarn paintings, you may wish to ask permission to create an art display of the pieces until your next art program. While some participants are eager to take their work home (and that is totally okay), many are excited at the prospect of having their art on display at the library. We regularly display works of art in our branch, and the children's displays are always highly appreciated. They add a special energy and pop of color to the space . . . and serve as excellent advertising for your maker/art projects. The displays also give the children a reason to come back; many return not just to pick up their art but to show off their work to friends and family.

LEARNING OUTCOMES

- Learn and practice a new art technique.
- Explore different cultures both around the world and throughout history.
- Adapt and repurpose art techniques of the past.

RECOMMENDED NEXT PROJECTS

As mentioned, this project is one that has been appreciated at our library by individuals of all ages. Consider using yarn painting as a multi-generational project with both seniors and children collaborating on a yarn painting.

Other Little Leonardos projects with a similar feel have included dot painting from the aboriginal people of Australia and shaving cream painting. Shaving cream painting is an easy-to-produce mixture of shaving cream, liquid glue, and food coloring (optional) to create a thick, puffy paint that dries with volume intact and with a "foamy" feel. We have used this style of painting successfully in both Little Leonardos and as a component of one of our recent Sensory Storytimes.

Create a Woven Communi-Tree

SPRING LAVALLEE / YOUTH SERVICES LIBRARIAN
Salt Lake County Library Services

Type of Library Best Suited for: School or Public

Cost Estimate: $200–$500

Makerspace Necessary? No

PROJECT DESCRIPTION

Football games, farmers' markets, and county fairs. What do all of these events have in common? They are community gathering places, experiences where we can unite with a greater goal in mind and come together to celebrate our collective and individual achievements. Community art is another opportunity to work toward a common goal and embrace a moment of collaborative achievement, but art differs from experience in one major way: art creates. When the football field lights turn off and the local farmers go home, all we are left with are the memories of the fun and camaraderie we shared during those events. When we are finished making art, though, we have a physical representation of our efforts and experiences, a constant reminder of our bonds to our neighbors and community.

The Communi-Tree weaving project is an easy, beginner option for creating a beautiful piece of community art without needing much in the way of resources or space. Individuals or community groups create woven leaves and a tree trunk out of plastic mesh canvas and recycled textile materials. Once the leaves and trunk have been created, the pieces are sewn onto a blank canvas or painted backdrop. The finished product is a stunning, one-of-a-kind representation of your community.

Child weaving

OVERVIEW

The Communi-Tree weaving project is completed in three stages: preparation, weaving, and final construction. In the preparation stage, the librarian(s) or library should plan and collect and prepare materials according to the size of the finished item they wish to create. The finished tree in this project is 9 × 12 feet; the tree can be scaled up or down, depending on your needs, time constraints, and funds. In the weaving stage, participants throughout the community can create a leaf in a one-hour session hosted by the library; this project travels well and is great for outreach activities at schools, senior centers, homeless shelters, housing units, and so on. For this size tree, 300 leaves are recommended, and these can be completed in a series of one-hour sessions. Since the tree trunk is very large, several sessions will be needed to complete it; around 5–10 hours total will be needed, depending on the size of the group working on it. The final construction involves sewing the trunk and leaves onto the canvas, which takes about 25 hours total. However, a small group of 5–8 can work on sewing together, so the final construction could be completed in one long session, if multiple one-hour sessions are undesirable. The entire project can take several months to one year to complete.

MATERIALS LIST

- #5 plastic mesh canvas (clear, 10.5 × 13.5 inches)
- 3.75 Mesh Graph N' Latch rug canvas (36 × 60 inches)
- 9 × 12-foot fabric canvas, painter's tarp, or painted cloth backdrop
- Variety of recycled or new textile materials such as old T-shirts, scrap fabric, shoelaces, sheets, pillowcases, fabric ribbon, paracord, yarn, and so on
- Black thread
- Masking tape
- Black and clear spray paint
- Black Sharpie markers

NECESSARY EQUIPMENT

- Scissors
- Sewing needles
- Cutting mat or cardboard

STEP-BY-STEP INSTRUCTIONS

Preparation

The finished project is 9 × 12 feet in size. It can be scaled up or down, depending on your needs. Each sheet of plastic mesh will produce about 8 (6 × 4-inch) leaves; for 300 leaves, you will need about 40 sheets total. Once a master has been created, trace the leaves onto the plastic mesh, using a black Sharpie, and cut them out. Then spray paint the leaves black; after two coats of black spray paint, use one coat of clear spray paint to seal the leaves.

The trunk is made out of six Graph n' Latch mesh canvases stitched together. Place the canvases three across and two wide; using black Sharpie markers, trace the outline of a tree trunk onto the canvas and cut it out. Sew the pieces of the trunk together, and use thicker black material (paracord, shoelaces, yarn, etc.) to reinforce the seams. Spray paint the trunk with two coats of black spray paint and one coat of clear spray paint to seal it.

Textile materials should all be from the same color palette (e.g., brights/neons, jewel-tones, natural colors, etc.). Mixing color palettes will make the entire tree seem less cohesive. Each leaf requires 2–3 feet of recycled materials, cut into thin strips about ½ inch wide; the trunk will need about 200 feet of material. The final pieces are sewn onto a white painter's tarp that measures 9 × 12 feet.

Once the materials are prepared, consider how you will complete the project, and schedule the sessions. Because weaving takes some fine motor skills, participants should be ages five years or older. One adult should be available for each 10–15 children during a session, to help start the project, switch colors/materials, and troubleshoot. Adults will complete the leaves more quickly, in about thirty minutes.

Weaving

Once the sessions have been planned and the materials prepared, it's time to start weaving! Participants simply weave the cut textile materials in and out of the holes of the plastic mesh to create their leaf. For children, it is best to tie off one end of their material to the plastic mesh and wrap the other end with a small piece of masking tape; that makes it easier to push the material through the holes without pulling the end through as well.

Participants may want to change colors or materials during their weaving. Simply tie off the loose end, for young children, or, for older children and adults, cut off the excess old material before starting the new one. It's okay to skip holes or leave blank places on the leaf; encourage participants to experiment with patterns and different ways of weaving so that each leaf is truly unique. Some of the paint may rub off while weaving; that's okay too. Most of the paint will stay on the leaves, so a little bit flaking off is not a problem.

When weaving the trunk, a small group of 5–10 participants is best. Too big of a group will end up crowding the trunk and making it hard to complete the project. For the trunk, only black materials should be used in the weaving, although different textures of black will make the trunk more interesting to look at. Again, have participants experiment with patterns and weaving techniques on the trunk. The more texture that can be added to the trunk and leaves, the more intriguing the final piece will be.

FIGURE 17.2

Finished leaf

Final Preparation

Before sewing the leaves and trunk onto the canvas, first prepare the leaves by cutting off excess material and taping any stray pieces to the back with masking tape. It is okay to have some loose pieces in the front, as long as the back is taped in place. Additionally, clean up the trunk by cutting off excess materials and taping the back, where needed.

Once the leaves and trunk have been prepared, sew the trunk onto the canvas. Lay out the canvas on a large table or clean floor. Arrange the tree trunk on the canvas and pin pieces in place. Using a whipstitch, sew the outline of the tree trunk onto the canvas with black thread. During this process, watch carefully to ensure the canvas and trunk are straight and not bunching. One to two inches between stitches is fine; the trunk should be pretty light, and it doesn't need to be sewn too tightly or it will bunch the canvas.

Finally, prepare to sew the leaves onto the canvas. First, sew most of the leaves into bunches of 2–5 leaves; layer the leaves so they overlap a little, and sew the touching parts together to create small clusters. Some of the leaves can be left individual to fill in blank spots where needed. Next arrange the leaves on your canvas. Trying putting bunches of leaves in different directions, aligned with the branches of the tree trunk. Some leaves may layer over the top of part of the trunk or branches; this adds depth and texture to the piece. If you have extra leaves once the branches have been filled in, consider piling some leaves at the trunk of the tree to make it look as though leaves are falling to the ground. Once the leaves have been laid out, sew them onto the canvas using black thread and a whipstitch. Like the trunk, the stitches can be spread out an inch or so, so long as the leaf is well-attached.

Once the entire project is complete, display your beautiful, one-of-a-kind piece of community art! The weaving can be displayed by hanging it on a curtain rod with drapery clips, or by cutting small slits in the top of the canvas and sliding the curtain rod through the openings. Consider placing a plaque or small sign near the piece to explain its construction and significance to the community. An unveiling party is also a nice way to celebrate the completion of this large project; invite all the participants who created pieces of this weaving, and thank them for their contributions to the final art piece.

LEARNING OUTCOMES

- Participants will hone fine motor skills that come from cutting/preparing materials, weaving, and sewing.
- Patterning and artistic arrangement are also used to create the leaves and complete the final sewing of the art piece.

FIGURE 17.3 ....

Finished Communi-Tree

- Community art allows the community to participate in a project that expresses their individuality and helps bond members together with a common purpose. Social skills such as communication, teamwork, problem-solving, and cooperation with others are major learning outcomes in this project.

RECOMMENDED NEXT PROJECTS

Once a community art piece has been completed for the library, consider partnering with another organization (such as a school, Boys and Girls Club, YMCA, recreation center, etc.) to create their own community art. A living sculpture made out of individually folded origami pieces is an easy and affordable option, or a more serious undertaking may be to partner with a local artist to create a tile mosaic. Historical societies and senior centers could be potential partners for a community scrapbook art piece, as well.

Sew a Zippered Pencil Pouch

LYSSA TROEMEL / MAKER LAB GUIDE
Allen County Public Library–Georgetown

Type of Library Best Suited for: Any

Cost Estimate: $20–$25

Makerspace Necessary? No

PROJECT DESCRIPTION

This is a simple pouch designed for pencils with a zipper and two buttoned pockets on the outside. It takes less than a yard of fabric to make and is an easy way to learn how to add a zipper to a project.

OVERVIEW

This is a class that is offered to all ages, but has mostly been taken by adults. It is a two-hour class that meets once but is offered multiple times during a period of a month. In the course of the class, participants learn how to change feet on the sewing machine, how to put in a zipper, how to sew a buttonhole and button, and how to follow pattern instructions.

MATERIALS LIST

- Fabric for outside
- Fabric for lining
- Thread
- Zipper
- Two buttons
- Fray Check

NECESSARY EQUIPMENT

- Sewing machine with zipper and buttonhole feet
- Hand sewing needle
- Awl or X-ACTO knife
- Iron and ironing board
- Pencil for marking; water-soluble works best
- Straight pins
- Toothpick or thick hand needle

FIGURE 18.1 ....

Example of the finished pouch

STEP-BY-STEP INSTRUCTIONS

Step 1

First, cut out fabric according to pattern instructions found on the pattern pieces. If you want to make the process go faster, fold the fabric so the right sides are together and cut both layers at the same time. Place the pattern on the fabric, pin in place, and cut out. If you plan on reusing the pattern, I would advise removing the pattern before cutting.

Step 2

Put the right sides of the outer main pouches together. Add the lining fabric to each side. Sew at half an inch seam allowance. Press the seam open. Pin the zipper to the seam flaps and sew using the zipper foot. Keep the fabric flat like an open book so you don't accidentally sew the pouch shut. I usually go all the way around instead of doing two seams. Either works, but the continuous seam allows for the zipper to be cut if needed. Seam rip the opening over the zipper.

Step 3

Take the fabric for the outer pockets. Fold the top down about half an inch and press. Fold in the sides about an eighth of an inch and press again. Keep the side with the half-inch fold at the top. This is where we will put the buttonhole.

FIGURE 18.2

Pouch template

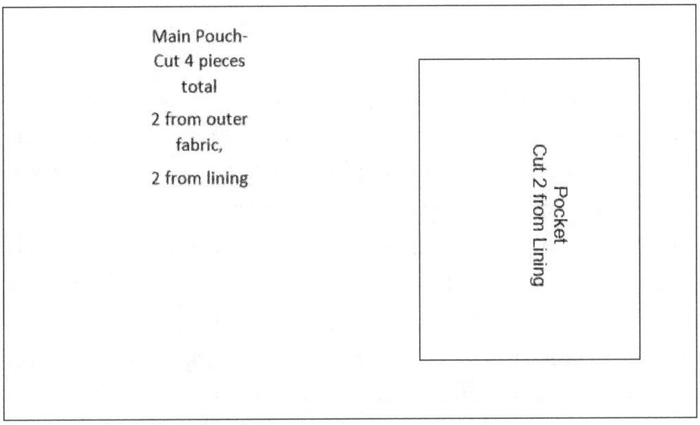

Main Pouch-
Cut 4 pieces
total

2 from outer
fabric,

2 from lining

Pocket
Cut 2 from Lining

You can resize this template on your copier to your desired size.

Step 4

Sew a buttonhole on the two pockets. You can use an automatic buttonhole maker or you can use the following with the buttonhole foot:

- Set your machine to a zigzag stitch. Set your stitch length and width to 1.
- Mark how long and wide your button is on your fabric.
- Stitch/backstitch along the top edge of where your button is going to be a few times.
- Turn the corner and adjust the stitch length and width to 2.
- Stitch/backstitch down the side.
- Repeat steps 1 and 3 for the bottom edge.
- Repeat steps 4 and 5. Make sure to get in fairly close.
- Place Fray Check on the fabric inside the buttonhole.
- Once the Fray Check is dry, use the awl or X-ACTO knife to cut open the buttonhole.

Step 5

After step 4, you can switch to the regular foot or keep the buttonhole foot on a little longer. Place the pockets on the outside and sew down the sides of the pockets to attach to the outer material.

Step 6

Either the normal foot or the zipper foot can be used for this last step on the sewing machine. Put the right sides of the pouch together and open the zipper a little bit so you'll be able to turn out the project. Sew down the sides at 3/8 inch.

Step 7

Attach the button behind the pocket. To do this, use the hand sewing needle to start the stitch on the inside. Then thread the needle through the button. Unless the button has a shank (single hole on the back of a button), place the toothpick between the button and the fabric. If you only have two holes, go from one to the other 3–4 times. If you have four holes in the button, go diagonal, making sure to go through each 3–4 times. Once you are done, take the toothpick out and take the thread around the threads under the button to gather them together. This is now a thread shank. Tie it off by pushing the needle through the thread shank and passing the needle through the loop. Repeat to double knot it and make it secure. The reason for doing it this way is that it puts the pressure and strain on the shank, making the button stay attached longer. If participants are having trouble handling the toothpick, a thick needle can be used and stuck into the fabric. Be careful not to stitch through the eye of the needle.

FIGURE 18.3

Example of the toothpick-under-button method on a scrap piece of fabric

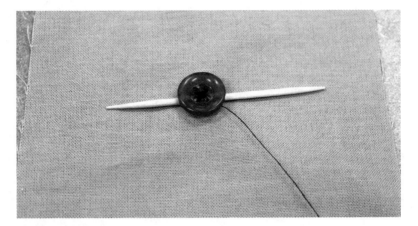

FIGURE 18.4

Knotting off the button

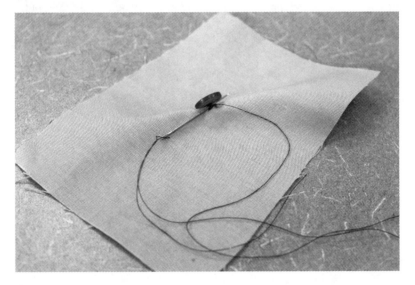

Step 8

Press open the seams if desired and turn right side out. Pressing open the seams will allow it to lay flatter.

LEARNING OUTCOMES

At the end of this project, patrons should know

- How to put in a zipper.
- How to attach a button and make a buttonhole.
- They should also learn about using measurements for seam allowance.
- How to follow pattern instructions.
- How to change feet on the sewing machine.

RECOMMENDED NEXT PROJECTS

After this project, libraries and participants should try to work toward more complex sewing projects. Some suggestions include making a wallet with a zipper section, adding snaps to a project, or adding a zipper into a piece of clothing. It may also be a good idea to have a program about mending clothing that can go through how to fix buttons and replace zippers. Another good project would be to move onto more complex patterns or how to draft patterns based off of measurements.

Sew Your Own Flag

KATHERINE LAWRENCE / LIBRARIAN
Cleveland Heights High School

Type of Library Best Suited for: School or Public

Cost Estimate: $50–$75

Makerspace Necessary? No

PROJECT DESCRIPTION

This was a sewing and textiles makerspace project at Cleveland Heights High School which celebrated diversity and encouraged positive self-expression. Students are tasked with designing a simple flag that represents them: their values, interests, hopes, or dreams. Although the project was originally conducted with high school students, it is appropriate for students of almost any age. There is no formal learning or learning standards involved. This is simply an act of creative, fun, visual self-expression.

OVERVIEW

The Sew Your Own Flag for Self-Expression project can be conducted out of a makerspace cart. It can be an after-school event or, as we did it, a diversionary activity during the lunch periods. A single fifty-minute period is adequate time to have a bite to eat *and* make a flag.

Students view and pattern their flags off of sample flags that are provided and displayed near the makerspace area, and then are provided with the material necessary to craft a flag of their own with any or all of the materials available. The resulting flags may include messages like the following: Peace, Love, Be Happy, Kindness, Infinite Possibilities, and more. When students complete their flags they are encouraged to keep them to decorate their locker or their bedroom, or they are also told that the library would gladly accept and display them. Most selected the latter option and the flags adorn our space to this day.

As students completed them, their flags were taped to the wall behind the "making area." This display helped to recruit others to the activity during subsequent lunch periods. It also allowed our special education participants to copy spelling and themes that appealed to them.

MATERIALS LIST

- Burlap or felt
- Buttons (200 assorted)
- Foam rubber adhesive "emojis" (2 canisters of 50 each)
- "Themed" duct tape (Super Mario, Checkerboard)—8 to 10 rolls

FIGURE 19.1 ⋯⋯⋯⋯⋯⋯⋯⋯⋯⋯⋯⋯⋯⋯⋯⋯⋯⋯⋯⋯⋯⋯⋯⋯⋯⋯⋯⋯

Flags taped to wall behind maker area

- Twine (1 ball)
- Yarn (2 or 3 skeins)
- Ribbon or rick rack (5–7 rolls)
- Colorful papers
- Markers (include Fabric Markers, Sharpies, variety of colors and thicknesses)
- Glue (Elmer's, hot glue gun, rubber cement, glue sticks)
- Prototype flag for display during activity

NECESSARY EQUIPMENT

- Maker cart or storeroom
- Scissors
- Large head needle

STEP-BY-STEP INSTRUCTIONS

Recruit Student Leaders / Design a Model

Recruit a cadre of student assistants or ambassadors about a month in advance of your maker date. We worked through our ELL (English language learners) teacher and AFS Advisor (exchange students), but enlisting any willing teacher or advisor to pitch the idea to a captive audience of students will work. You might also consider approaching student council members, key club students, or even just the usual suspects, your everyday "library rats," to serve as ambassadors for the project.

These project leaders are provided with fabric, ribbon, twine, buttons, and markers and are tasked with making a prototype flag that promotes any message that the maker feels passionate about or compelled by, that expresses a sentiment or design that represents them, or is just aesthetically pleasing to them. These students are also asked to research the origin, meaning, and symbolism of various types of flags and to create a short informational flyer for the future student "makers" When the prototype and research were finished, we had a good idea of what materials and supplies were popular, which led directly to . . .

Sourcing Your Supplies

It's a good idea to start provisioning your makerspace with supplies early in the year, mainly items that glue, staple, cut, and color. After viewing the completed prototypes and noting which materials were most popular, you can shop for more of the same at a local craft store. A visit to the craft store is also helpful for finding other items which would have appeal to the students or add interest to their projects.

It's also helpful and highly economical to think "outside the box" for sourcing items. For example, you might want to keep a box at the entrance of the school and advertise for your cause in a parent newsletter. We were "gifted" some materials by our math teachers who overheard us talking about our upcoming project and voluntarily shopped at a donated supply warehouse for items such as fabric, markers, and decorative ribbons. The more you talk about your project informally to colleagues, the more likely you are to receive donations from others who are grateful to unburden themselves of supplies that are no longer used.

Checklist for a Few Days before Your Event

- Have you arranged for at least two tables and seating for about ten students?
- Have you advertised your project a few days ahead of time using such things as school announcements and posters on bulletin boards and near the prototype flags?
- Have you packed your prototype flag on the cart for display behind the tables to attract interest?
- Have you prearranged with your student ambassadors to be available to assist and "make" during their lunch periods?
- Have you packed your phone or a camera on the cart to be used to document the products and participants?

It's Game Day

Deck your tables out with your trendiest supplies and materials. Invite your student ambassadors to make flags and to enlist their friends and tablemates to do the same. Post the prototype flag somewhere nearby, and even start making a flag yourself. If students are not curious about your activity at first, and business seems to be rolling in too slowly, you might pick up participants by circulating among the masses with the prototype flag and appealing to individuals, reminding them that their creation could adorn their locker, their bedroom, or even the library for posterity. Those first few participants creating at the table are the critical mass that draw attention from others who might want to participate, but don't want to be the first or only participants.

The flags are constructed by cutting, pasting, drawing, and applying the various materials (duct tape, foam appliques, buttons, etc.) to the precut burlap 4 × 6-inch rectangles. The needlework involves threading a large-headed needle with twine and sewing a running stitch through the top edge of the flag, leaving a four-inch tail on each end. Facilitators or student ambassadors may want to do this needlework for special needs students. We used precut burlap rectangles for our flags, but purchasing a yard or so of any sturdy fabric and cutting custom shapes would be a good alternative and would also add variety or interest. Students used fabric markers and fabric paint, and applied materials of their choice, including themed duct tape, Styrofoam stickers, yarn, buttons, fabric swatches, beads, and plastic jewels using glue or needle and thread. Many chose simply to write a message with marker. A few students chose to alter the outline of the flag by cutting it, and others used yarn to create tassels for the bottom of the flag. The flags were left to dry either on an adjoining table or hung on the wall behind our maker area using painter's tape. Encourage participants to consider embellishing their flag by adding tassels, or changing the outline of the form. As students complete projects, painters tape them to dry on the wall behind your maker tables. This helps to draw additional attention to your area, and also serves to "model" some ideas for future "makers" to riff off of.

Snap lots of pictures from lots of angles. Share these with your communications department or principal to get the word out to the community about your maker projects.

FIGURE 19.2 ....

Snap lots of pictures from lots of angles

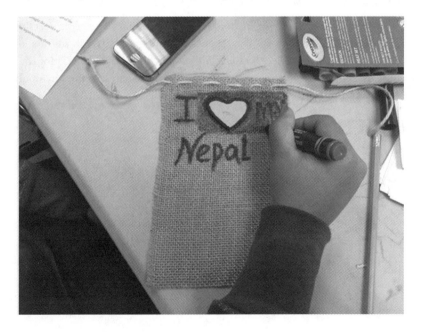

For special needs students you might complete the needlework for them: thread the large-headed needle with twine and sew a running stitch through the top edge of the flag, leaving a three- to four-inch tail on each end. Restock materials between lunch periods and post the finished projects for display around the tables to attract later students.

Be creative in your picture-taking while students are working. Snap a variety of angles, from zooming in on the actual "making" to busy group wide-angle shots. Take lots of pictures and send a few along with a story about the activity to your school communications department or public relations person. Finally, you should post projects that students did not want to keep in the library.

LEARNING OUTCOMES

- Students learn basic sewing skills.
- Students complete a project with their new skills.
- Students learn to craft a message and illustrate it in a creative format.

RECOMMENDED NEXT PROJECTS

We like the idea of extending our makerspace activities into service projects. For example, students could design flags that could be sent to pediatric wards at a local hospital, nursing homes, homeless shelters, and so on with messages like "Hope," "Be Well," and "Strength." Also, this project could be just as easily executed in a public library setting and could include adults as well as young people.

Sew a Pillowcase Photo Frame

SILVIA GUTIERREZ / TEACHER LIBRARIAN
Palos Verdes Peninsula High School Library Media Commons
Rolling Hills Estates, CA

Type of Library Best Suited for: Any

Cost Estimate: $3 per participant. The cost will be less if fabric is donated.
Contact your local American Sewing Guild or Modern Quilt Guild chapter.
These members are passionate about sewing and passionate about fabric.
You will likely find members eager to donate their fabric and share their expertise.
They will be happy to hear that you are teaching sewing skills to another generation.

Makerspace Necessary? A dedicated makerspace is not required, but a space for
sewing machines and accompanying noise will be needed. A community room,
or even the staff lounge may be used. The sewing machines will need electrical outlets.

PROJECT DESCRIPTION

Young adults love photos. How many do they have in their phones? How many do
they post to Instagram, Snapchat, and other photo services? But . . . how many are
printed and displayed in the physical, not virtual, world? This project takes those
fave photos and creates a pillowcase that can be used to display photos in a fun,
eye-catching showcase.

Sewing is no longer for "old ladies" only. Fabric crafts have evolved into a cool activity for old and young, girls and boys. With many high schools eliminating home economics classes, the library may be the only place to introduce sewing to another generation. By the way: those who sew are not called seamstresses; combine *sew* and *artist* and voila—the new trendy term is *sewists*!

OVERVIEW

Participants will sew a pillowcase and add clear vinyl pockets to hold photos. The photos can be easily slipped in and out of the vinyl pockets. Glide a pillow into the pillowcase and this craft is ready to display in a teen's room, or give as a gift.

This project can be completed in one ninety-minute session. One sewing machine per two participants, and ample table space for cutting and pinning fabric will be needed. This project will be most successful if at least one of the adult coordinators is an experienced sewist. One adult supervisor per six teens is adequate. It is assumed that the participants have a standard bed pillow and these will not be provided.

MATERIALS LIST

- Fabric: ¾ yard of a solid cotton (45 inches wide)
- ¼ yard of a coordinating cotton print (45 inches wide)
- Cardstock 4½ × 6 ½-inch template
- Clear vinyl ¼ yard (54 inches wide)
- Standard bed pillow (20 × 26 inches)
- Washable pen for fabric
- White thread, or a color to match fabric

NECESSARY EQUIPMENT

- Sewing machine in good working condition (one machine per two participants)
- Iron
- Ironing board
- Tables with at least a 3 × 3-foot space for each participant for cutting and pinning
- Other tables needed to set up sewing machines
- Chair for each sewing machine
- Electrical outlet for each sewing machine
- Extension cords if sewing machines don't reach outlets
- Scissors for fabric, not paper
- Straight pins
- Sewing needles
- Yardstick

STEP-BY-STEP INSTRUCTIONS

Sewing Terms

Pillowcase cuff: this is the part of the pillowcase that is attached on one end to the body of the pillowcase, and the other end is left open. For this project it is made from a print fabric.

Pillowcase body: the larger, main piece of the pillowcase. One end is closed; the other end is sewn to the cuff. A solid fabric is used in this project.

Blind stitch or slip stitch: method of sewing two pieces of fabric together so that the thread is invisible on one side.

Right side of fabric: the side that is brighter in color.

Wrong side of fabric: the back side of the fabric. The colors are duller.

Stitch length: the number of stitches per inch. The more stitches per inch creates a stronger seam, and vice versa. Ten stitches per inch is the default setting for most sewing machines.

Washable fabric pen: the markings made with this pen are easily removed with a damp sponge or rag.

Cut All Pieces First

Using the 4½ × 6 ½-inch cardstock as a template, draw six shapes on the paper backing of the vinyl and pin. Cut the six pieces but do not remove the pins. The vinyl is slippery and difficult to see and will be easier to manage with the paper backing attached. Note: *Iron the fabric before cutting.*

The print fabric—measure a 9 × 40-inch piece and cut. If uncertain of your cutting skills, you may draw the cutting line with the washable pen.

The solid color fabric—measure a 27 × 40-inch piece and cut. Again, if uncertain of your cutting skills, you may draw the cutting line with the washable pen.

Fold the 9-inch print fabric in half with the wrong sides together so each side measures 4½ × 40 inches when folded. Press the fold with the iron, making a crease. With the wrong sides still together, fold one end ½ inch under and toward the wrong side. One half of the print fabric will measure 4½ inches from the crease and the other will measure 4 inches from the crease to the fold.

Lay the solid fabric right side up. Open the print fabric and place the right side of the unfolded 40-inch edge onto the solid fabric with the raw edges matching. The two fabrics are right sides together, and the wrong side of the print fabric is facing up. Pin the fabrics together about 1½ inches from the raw edge, pinning through both fabrics. The pins can't be too close to the edge or the sewing machine will run over them.

Thread the sewing machine with white thread or a color matching the solid fabric. Set the stitch length to ten stitches per inch.

Sew the two fabrics together with a ½-inch seam, using the guide on the machine. If uncertain, a stitch line may be drawn on the fabric with the washable pen. After the line is sewn, remove the pins and clip the extra threads.

Iron the seam toward the print and it will tuck inside the cuff after the next step. Be careful not to iron out the crease on the print fabric.

The pillowcase is now one piece of fabric, but the cuff is not yet sewn in place. Match the creased ½-inch fold on the print fabric to the stitch line at the bottom edge of the cuff where it meets the solid fabric. Pin the fold to the wrong side of the cuff with the seam hidden in the cuff.

The next step is hand sewn. Double thread the needle for extra strength and knot the end. Blind stitch the cuff in place using about six stitches per inch. Remove the pins as you stitch.

The clear vinyl photo pockets will be pinned and sewn to the fabric in the next steps.

Fold the pillowcase in half, wrong sides together, and press the fold with the iron. Lay it on the table with the longer unsewn edge closest to you. This edge will be the bottom of the finished pillowcase; the fold is the top of the pillowcase. Unfold the fabric. Arrange the pockets on the solid fabric on the front of the pillow, keeping in mind whether the photos will be displayed horizontally or vertically. Rather than arranging all pockets perfectly straight and lined up like yearbook photos, be creative. Place them at angles, in a circle, or in another random arrangement.

Pin the paper and vinyl to the front side of the fabric. Place pins in the corners and halfway between each corner. Write "OPENING" on the side that will be left open because it is easy to forget and sew it closed. With the pockets securely pinned, take it to the sewing machine.

The pockets will be sewn ¼ inch from the edge. Look for the guide on the sewing machine. Begin sewing at one end and then pivot at each corner to create one continuous stitch line. If the pins are close to the stitch line, remove them as you sew. Do not sew over them. Sew three sides of the vinyl, leaving the opening free.

After the six pockets are sewn to the pillowcase, remove all pins and clip the extra threads. Tear away the paper. The vinyl pockets will stay intact.

Take the fabric and fold in half with the right sides together. Carefully match the long edges, the cuff, and the short edges. Pin around the raw edges about 1½ inches from the edge. The stitch line will be ½ inch from the raw edge and may be drawn with the washable pen. Stich around the pillowcase, pivoting at the corner.

Turn the pillowcase right side out. Stuff the pillow form inside. You're almost finished!

Selecting six photos from the hundreds you have saved may be difficult. Select photos that are meaningful to the pillowcase owner. Is that you? Or is it a gift? Look for photos that when displayed together tell a story in six pictures. The story could

FIGURE 20.1

Sewing the pockets

FIGURE 20.2

The completed photo pillowcase

be a timeline of your life, a milestone occasion such as a graduation, or a celebration of a friendship. What story do you want to tell?

Print more photos than needed and create various combos with six at a time. When you're satisfied, or almost satisfied, slip them in the pockets. Remember, they can be easily changed, so don't stress. With the photos inserted—your pillowcase is ready to display!

LEARNING OUTCOMES

Pillowcases are an easy-sew project and are often used in beginner's sewing classes. Participants will learn to follow simple sewing directions; measure, cut, and pin fabric; and sew straight seams on fabric and vinyl.

RECOMMENDED NEXT PROJECTS

Other sewing projects that use straight seams such as skirts or tote bags are appropriate choices for a second sewing lesson. Home décor or accessories such as coasters, napkins, table runners, curtains, and quilts are other easy-to-sew projects with straight seams.

Circuitry, Wiring,
and
Wearables Projects

Create e-Textiles with LilyPad Arduino

HANNAH POPE / EMERGING TECHNOLOGIES LIBRARIAN
Appalachian State University

Type of Library Best Suited for: Any

Cost Estimate: $150 for 10 people

Makerspace Necessary? No

PROJECT DESCRIPTION

Circuitry and sewing are not usually associated with each other, but the projects that can be produced from a combination of these skills are sure to appeal to all audiences. Participants for this project will learn how to add twinkling LED (light-emitting diode) lights to felt bookmarks or bracelets using the basics of circuitry and a small microcontroller.

OVERVIEW

It is never too late to learn STEM (science, technology, engineering, and math) concepts, and working with e-textiles is a great way to introduce patrons to the basics of circuitry. By creating something functional such as a bookmark or a bracelet, participants will be excited to learn, and librarians and staff have the opportunity to build their knowledge base. Participants will learn basic circuitry and how to use conductive thread to sew electronic components together in order to add LED lights to their creations. This project will give patrons the skills that they need in order to work with e-textiles and will encourage an interest in electronics.

MATERIALS LIST

- Standard thread
- LEDs, either for e-textiles, or pronged
- LilyTiny microcontroller
- Coin cell battery pack
- Coin cell battery

- Conductive thread
- Felt fabric in assorted colors
- Fabric glue or puffy paint (optional)
- Alligator clips (optional)

NECESSARY EQUIPMENT

- Standard needles

- Scissors

STEP-BY-STEP INSTRUCTIONS

Step 1: Design Your Circuit

Circuitry and creativity will dictate the creation of participant designs. E-textiles circuitry is relatively simple, so explaining the basic concepts will be the stepping-stone for the design process. All circuitry must have a power source. The source in this case is a small, coin cell battery pack. On the pack, there are two positive and two negative nodes. Connect one of the positive (+) nodes to the positive node on the LilyTiny microcontroller. Make sure to ground the LilyTiny by connecting one of the negative (–) nodes with the negative node on the LilyTiny. This connects the microcontroller to power and also grounds it.

Next, determine how many LEDs you and your patrons will be working with. If there is a large knowledge gap, or the program has severe time constraints, consider starting with only one LED. This program usually works best within a two-hour slot, in which case a maximum of three LEDs is recommended. If some patrons have more advanced skills, additional LEDs are always an option. These LEDs will be sewn to connect with the LilyTiny microcontroller, which will power and control the LEDs. The LilyTiny is already preprogrammed with different blinking patterns on the 0–3 nodes. Each is different, and check out www.sparkfun.com to see what pattern corresponds to each node.

FIGURE 21.1
A parallel circuit

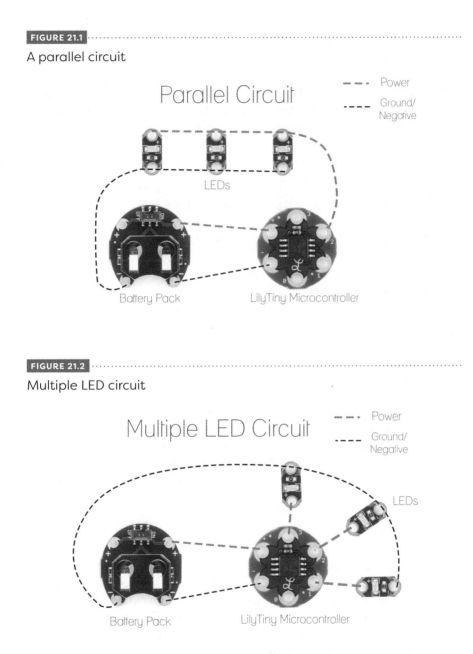

Parallel Circuit

--- Power
--- Ground/
Negative

LEDs

Battery Pack   LilyTiny Microcontroller

FIGURE 21.2
Multiple LED circuit

Multiple LED Circuit

--- Power
--- Ground/
Negative

LEDs

Battery Pack   LilyTiny Microcontroller

Participants have the option of connecting their LEDs to one pattern, or each LED can connect to a separate pattern. See the charts below for each option.

Connect the LEDs by using the conductive thread to go through the positive ends of the LEDs (if using SparkFun e-textiles LEDs, this is marked. If using regular LEDs with prongs, take pliers to twist the legs, then connect the long leg) and sewing onto the pattern node (0–3) of your choice.

Finally, ground the LEDs by sewing through the negative ends (marked on Spark-Fun products, and the short leg of an LED with prongs) and then connecting to the negative in the battery charger. A few things to remember:

- Don't cross any negative and positive threads anywhere in your design. This will cause a short circuit and your LEDs will not work.
- Don't connect a negative directly to a positive.

Have the participants create their designs by drawing out their circuits first. This is very important because it can prevent mistakes later.

Step 2: Prototype

Once participants have drawn their designs, use alligator clips to prototype and test the circuit. Each alligator clip is used to represent a piece of conductive thread. This step allows participants to see the LEDs come to life, and get a handle on how the circuit will look in action. It is also a great tool for debugging.

Alligator clips can be reused and are relatively inexpensive. While they are not a required part of the project, participants will make fewer mistakes if they are able to see their designs work before using the conductive thread.

Step 3: Create

Start sewing the circuit using conductive thread. There should be a different piece of thread for each part of the circuit. The only exception to this is when the positives or negatives are being connected to the same nodes. For example, if all of the LEDs will be using the pattern in node 2 of the LilyTiny, it is okay to use one piece of thread to connect all the LEDs and then the second node. It is also okay to use a separate piece of thread to connect all of the negatives on the LEDs to the negative on the battery pack. Do not use the same piece of thread for negatives and positives! This will cause a short circuit. Some additional things to remember:

- Loop the conductive thread around each component (LEDs, nodes) at least three times. This strengthens the electrical bond and allows the current to flow more smoothly.

FIGURE 21.3

LED bookmark

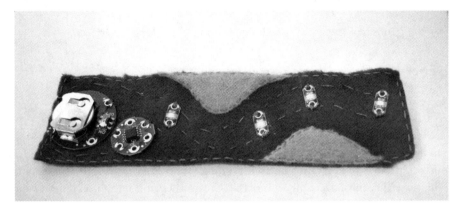

- Clip the ends of each knot of conductive thread as closely as possible. If they are not cut, it can lead to short-circuiting through unintentional overlap.
- Make sure that the circuit has been fully planned before sewing!

Once the conductive thread is used and all of the elements are sewn together, participants can use standard needle and thread to add embroidery, felt pieces, or any other decorative element.

Step 4: Finalize

Once all of the participants have finished their creations, there are a couple of options for sealing the conductive thread. Because some patrons will work at different paces than others, it is expected that there will be some who have not finished by the end of the session. This is fine, but let them know the options for completing their designs.

One option is the use of fabric glue. Take the fabric glue and trace a thin trail over each conductive thread. This seals the thread and keeps it from moving around later. Let the entire project dry overnight. A similar option is using colored puffy paint instead of the fabric glue. The same directions apply. The last option is using embroidery thread to seal the conductive thread. Using a whipstitch, participants can take standard thread and completely cover their conductive thread. This method has been very effective and can be incorporated into the overall design of the project. These methods will keep the conductive thread from tearing and moving within the project.

And with that, you have an LED bracelet or bookmark!

LEARNING OUTCOMES

- Participants will gain a basic knowledge of circuitry, e-textiles, and wearable electronics.
- Patrons will learn sewing techniques, and create a tangible project.

RECOMMENDED NEXT PROJECTS

The circuitry that is used in this project can be applied to many other e-textiles projects. Participants can use what they've learned to add to clothing, pillows, quilts, or whatever other cloth items they find. Once the patrons have mastered the basics, they can build on those skills by using the LilyPad Arduino or Adafruit Flora/Gemma microcontrollers to program LEDs with coding. Another interesting project is combining the 3D printing technique from the "Create 3D Prints on Fabric" project later in this book into your design.

Create a Soft Circuit Bracelet

SUSAN BARNUM / PUBLIC SERVICES LIBRARIAN @ TEEN TOWN
El Paso Public Library System

Type of Library Best Suited for: Any

Cost Estimate: Under $25

Makerspace Necessary? No

PROJECT DESCRIPTION

This project will teach participants how to use fabric-friendly circuitry to create a simple circuit with a custom switch to make a soft bracelet that lights up.

OVERVIEW

Sewing isn't always thought of as a "technology," but it's actually one of the oldest and most influential technologies human beings have ever invented. Recent developments have created conductive thread, which can be used in pairing sewing with electrical projects. Conductive thread conducts electricity. It's often made from stainless steel or regular fibers coated with a conductive substance. It can be bought online from various retailers, or it can be made by stripping old wires to repurpose the thin metal inside to sew with. As you sew with the conductive thread, you will want to use a straight stitch because it won't cross over itself and therefore prevents possible short circuits. For the normal thread, stitch it any way you wish!

Creating the soft circuit is easy, but you want to plan ahead. It's a good idea to roughly sketch out or visually plan where you want to place the electronic elements being used. The circuit can become part of the design of the bracelet itself, or participants can choose to hide the circuitry. The conductive thread is used to create the circuit. A circuit is a closed system that provides electricity from a power source to a device. The circuit described here is very simple and the switch, which is made out of a safety pin, is easy to implement. Participants will learn that when the circuit is open, or when the safety pin is not attached, the device is "off" and it won't light up. You can discuss how batteries provide the power to move electrons through the circuit. This is voltage and is measured (naturally) in volts (V). The current of the flow of electrons is measured in amperes (A). Multiplying the voltage and the amps of the circuit lets you figure out how many watts (W) of power you have. $V \times A = W$. Too easy!

MATERIALS LIST

- Loose LED (light-emitting diode) lights
- Cell-type batteries, at least 3 volts
- Battery holders that fit your type of battery
- Resistors
- Conductive thread
- Plain or normal thread
- Felt (though any fabric will do. Felt is a good choice because the ends will not fray)
- Safety pins

NECESSARY EQUIPMENT

- A clean work surface
- Scissors
- Needles (make sure the eye of the needle can accommodate the conductive thread, which is thicker than normal thread)

STEP-BY-STEP INSTRUCTIONS

Step 1

To begin, cut out a strip of fabric from the felt that will fit easily around your wrist. Make sure it's wide enough to accommodate your electronic parts and any design you want to add to the project.

FIGURE 22.1

Close-up of components, materials, and beginning of the soft circuit

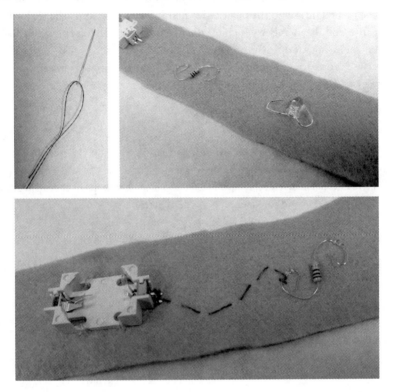

Step 2

Place the battery holder at one end of the strip of fabric. Make sure the negative end is pointing toward the closest end of the fabric. Securely sew it down using the normal or plain thread.

Step 3

Take your resistor and bend it into an interesting shape. It's easier to sew it down to the fabric if you curl the ends into a pretty loop. Just make sure the metal doesn't touch itself. There is no polarity on a resistor, so it doesn't matter which end is pointing towards the battery. Place the resistor somewhere off center on the bracelet. Don't put it right next to the battery holder! Sew it to the fabric using the normal thread.

Step 4

Take your LED light and find the positive, or anode end. This is usually the longest leg on the LED light. Bend the positive leg first into an interesting shape. Next bend the negative end. Remember which is which! Place the LED on the fabric with the anode end pointing towards the positive end of the battery holder. The resistor should be in between the battery holder and the LED. Leave some space between the resistor and the LED. Sew your LED to the fabric with a normal thread.

Step 5

Next, we're using the conductive thread. Thread it through the needle, but don't "double" the thread up. Start sewing, using a straight stitch, from the metal part of the positive end of the battery. Make sure you make a few loops of thread around the metal on the positive end to ensure a good connection.

Step 6

Start sewing your circuit out from the battery holder. You are going to connect to the resistor next. The circuit doesn't have to be a straight line, but it is important not to cross over the circuit with the thread. That will create a short circuit and the bracelet won't light up. Wrap a few loops of thread around the closest resistor wire end. Then cut the thread and knot it on the back.

FIGURE 22.2 ··

Close-up of the "switch," battery, and closed circuit

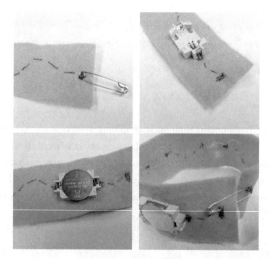

Step 7

Start again with the other end of the resistor. Sew from the resistor to the anode end of the LED. Wrap a few loops around the resistor when you start sewing and around the anode end of the LED. Then cut the thread and knot it.

Step 8

Start again with the negative end of the LED. Sew to the end of the fabric. Take the safety pin. Secure the safety pin to the fabric by sewing with the conductive thread through the small "circle" at the end of the safety pin. Loop through a few times. Cut the thread and knot on the back of the fabric.

Step 9

Using the conductive thread, go back to the battery holder. This time, from the negative metal end of the battery holder, sew until you nearly reach the end of the fabric. Sew a few "lines" of thread next to each other before you cut the thread again and knot it.

Step 10

Now is the moment of truth! Slot the battery into the battery holder. Close the bracelet by pinning the safety pin to the "lines" of thread you sewed on the other side. The circuit should close and the LED should light up!

Troubleshooting

If the LED doesn't light up, check the polarity first. You can often wiggle the LED out of the thread and flip it and replace without resewing everything. If that doesn't fix it, make sure there aren't any short circuits where thread or wires are crossing.

This project describes how to make a very simple, unembellished version. If you have creative kids, encourage them to make their bracelet into something more interesting!

LEARNING OUTCOMES

At the end of this project, participants will. . .

- Recognize and properly use several different electrical components.
- Know how to construct a simple circuit and switch using nontraditional materials.
- Be able to use some simple sewing stitches.
- Gain a basic understanding of different electrical concepts such as conductivity, wattage, and other related topics.

FIGURE 22.3 ....

Rock your finished bracelet

RECOMMENDED NEXT PROJECTS

See my project "Create LED Origami Tea Lights" in the next chapter.

Create LED Origami Tea Lights

SUSAN BARNUM / PUBLIC SERVICES LIBRARIAN @ TEEN TOWN
El Paso Public Library System

Type of Library Best Suited for: Any

Cost Estimate: Under $25

Makerspace Necessary? No

PROJECT DESCRIPTION

This project will teach participants how to create a tea light using origami and simple circuitry.

OVERVIEW

This project teaches participants how to make one of the simplest circuits you can build. It takes less than five minutes to wire your light and turn it on! Because it's so simple, it begs kids to create "variations on a theme." The basic idea of the origami tea light involves wiring and lighting up an LED and then adding it to an origami shape which becomes a pretty tea light. Using origami is a great way to talk about geometry and tessellation, if you choose to do so. However, the shape you choose to light up doesn't have to be a container: you can choose to cut out a spaceship from cardboard and light it up, or maybe create an underwater scene with bioluminescent creatures using LEDs.

The circuitry itself can be modified to teach more complex concepts, such as Ohm's law, which deals with electrical current, voltage, and resistance. For example, you can have participants calculate exactly how much resistance they might need with different battery sizes and amounts of LEDs. You might want to challenge them to serially connect LED lights, or to create a parallel circuit for the project. What happens if you introduce other electronic parts, such as switches or buzzers, to the circuit? Because LEDs and resistors are cheap, it's a good project to allow trial-and-error experimentation with the materials. Overall, kids tend to be excited when they create light, and the light indicates instant success and gratification. You know your kids, so plan accordingly to make this project simple or very complex.

MATERIALS LIST

- Loose LED lights
- Cell-type batteries, at least 3 volts
- 9-volt batteries (optional)
- Resistors (optional)
- Origami paper
- Tape

NECESSARY EQUIPMENT

- A clean work surface

STEP-BY-STEP INSTRUCTIONS

Decide what kind of origami container you will help your kids create. Younger kids benefit from a less-complicated design, while older kids tend to enjoy more advanced origami. The 8-pointed vase depicted in this project comes from Origami-Instructions .com (www.origami-instructions.com/origami-8-pointed-vase.html). Once you have the container folded or created, set it aside.

Because the voltage is low, there is no need to worry about getting shocked by touching the bare wires you are going to construct. This is a good time, though, to talk about the dangers of electricity in most circumstances.

All LEDs (or light-emitting diodes) have polarity, just like a battery. Most often, it is the longer "leg" of the LED that is the positive end, also known as the "anode." Bend the anode leg up at a 90-degree angle so you'll remember which one it is.

Because resistance is an important topic in electronics and in discussing Ohm's law, I usually like to create a circuit starting with the resistors. However, the light will be brighter without the resistor, and if you have too much resistance, it won't light up at all. (You'll need to decide if you want to use resistors or not.)

If you choose to skip using resistors, merely tape the anode leg to the positive end of the battery and the negative, or "cathode" end of the LED to the negative side of the battery: it will light up if you've done it correctly.

FIGURE 23.1

Step by step in pictures

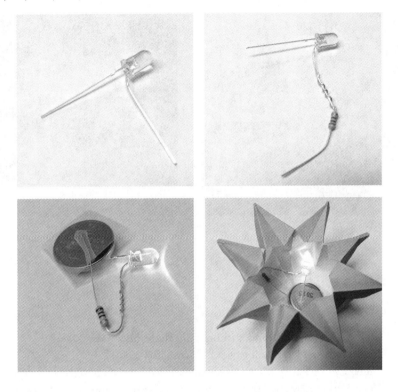

If you are using resistors, wrap any end of the resistor around the anode leg of the LED. Resistors do not have polarity, so it doesn't matter which end you choose. Now connect the other end of the resistor to the positive side of the battery and the cathode end of the LED to the negative end. Now it should light up! If it doesn't, try removing the resistor or check that the anode and cathode are properly aligned with the positive and negative poles of the battery. You can provide different types of resistors for your participants and let them see what happens when there is more or less resistance applied to a circuit. LEDs also have different energy needs. You can discuss this at the same time.

Drop your LED into your origami light. Enjoy!

This project is incredibly simple, so you may want to challenge your kids to do a few different things. Can they power more than one LED with the same battery? Can they make a series of LEDs light up? Can they create a simple "switch" for their circuit in order to save the battery? What happens with higher-voltage batteries? Give them the materials to experiment and find out!

FIGURE 23.2
Variations on a theme

FIGURE 23.3
The tea light at night

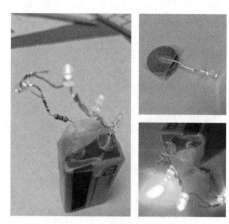

LEARNING OUTCOMES

Participants will . . .

- Learn how to fold origami, turning a 2D shape into a 3D shape.
- Gain a basic understanding of simple circuitry.
- Understand polarity when it is applied to electronic components.
- Understand and recognize several different electronic components: LED, resistor, wiring, and power source.
- Learn electronics safety.

RECOMMENDED NEXT PROJECTS

See my project "Create a Soft Circuit Bracelet" earlier in this section.

Make LED Bookmarks

JESSICA LOGAN / BRANCH MANAGER
Hamilton Mill Branch, Gwinnett County Public Library

Type of Library Best Suited for: Any

Cost Estimate: $50–$100

Makerspace Necessary? No

PROJECT DESCRIPTION

The Hamilton Mill Branch of the Gwinnett County Public Library wanted to help teens and tweens gain an understanding of electrical currents and learn how to create simple circuits in a way that was both fun and encouraged creativity. From this desire arose our do-it-yourself LED Bookmarks program wherein participants could design their own light-up bookmarks with simple circuits using LED lights, colored felt, and conductive thread.

This program is a stand-alone event that can easily be held at any time of the year and is designed for middle school and high school students. This project could also work well for younger participants, provided they have assistance or supervision in using scissors and a sewing needle. Students can let their creativity flow by designing and constructing their own bookmarks that incorporate LED lights in unique and unexpected ways.

FIGURE 24.1 ···

Constructing bookmarks

OVERVIEW

LED Bookmarks is a program that works well with teens and tweens, in grades 6–12. An hour is generally plenty of time for the participants to design and construct their bookmarks. Prior to beginning the project, discuss the use of circuits and demonstrate the construction of the simple circuit needed to create an LED bookmark.

We do not limit the attendance for this maker project, and we have found that the most expensive material needed, conductive thread, went a long way in terms of how many bookmarks could be created.

MATERIALS LIST

- Coin batteries
- LED lights
- Felt
- Needles
- Thread

- Coin battery holders
- Conductive thread
- Paper (optional)
- Pencils (optional)

NECESSARY EQUIPMENT

- Tables
- Tweezers
- Scissors
- Thimbles (optional)
- First aid kit (optional)
- Camera or other device to take pictures (optional)

STEP-BY-STEP INSTRUCTIONS

Discussing the use of circuits and demonstrating the construction of a simple circuit is a great place to start for this project. It is important that the participants understand the use of circuits, and the demonstration of a circuit is always an attention grabber. The basic idea is that the LED light will glow when electricity flows from the positive side of the battery through the conductive thread, through the LED light and back to the negative side of the battery creating a loop, or circuit. You can also use this as an opportunity to demonstrate other forms of simple circuits or encourage the participants to try their hand at creating one. Once all the participants have an understanding of how to create the circuit, encourage them to start thinking of a bookmark design that they would like to create. Some students may need inspiration and it helps to have some samples of bookmarks available, or even images of LED bookmarks if you have not had time to construct your own. Next, display the materials available for use and allow them to select their desired colors of felt. If you have colored LED lights available, you could also let them select those. Simple white LED lights work just fine if you prefer to avoid too many choices.

Prior to letting the participants begin creating their bookmarks, it is important for them to consider their circuit design and the conductive thread connections. Each circuit will have a positive connection, or trace, that connects the positive side of the battery holder to the positive side of the LED, and a negative trace that connects the negative side of the battery holder to the negative side of the LED. Having some paper and pencils on hand is helpful because some students may wish to sketch their design ideas first. Positive traces are traditionally drawn in red while negative traces are drawn in black. All bookmarks should be at least two inches wide so that the battery holder fits on it.

Prior to letting the participants begin creating their bookmarks, it is important to discuss safety with the group since they will be handling sewing needles. Once this has been covered, you can begin to distribute the rest of the materials. We also recommend having a first aid kit on hand that includes antiseptic wipes and Band-Aids should someone accidentally prick themselves with a needle. This has never happened during one of our do-it-yourself LED bookmark programs, but it never hurts to be prepared.

Remain available to assist the participants with any issues they may encounter or to answer any questions they may have. We have found it helpful to have some needles threaded ahead of time because this is a step that the students sometimes struggle with. Some students may also need assistance in sewing secure starting and finishing knots so that their stitching does not come undone. Make sure that participants are pulling their thread tightly when attaching the battery holder in order to create a snug connection.

Once the participants have created their bookmark and sewn in their simple circuit using the conductive thread, LED light(s), and coin batteries, let them have fun showing off their creation to friends and family. If a student is having trouble getting their circuit to work, check the traces to ensure that they are matching on both ends; if the LEDs are connected backwards they will not light up. You will also want to make sure that the positive and negative traces are not touching because this will cause a short circuit.

Finished bookmarks

LEARNING OUTCOMES

- Develop an understanding of electrical currents.
- Explore circuits and learn to create a simple circuit using conductive thread, LED lights, and coin batteries.
- Practice design and sewing skills through hands-on creation.

RECOMMENDED NEXT PROJECTS

You may consider a variation on this project that allows participants to create LED bracelets. This makes for a logical progression in skill because it is a bit trickier to create, and you must ensure that the end product is smooth so that that you don't have any threads poking or irritating your skin. Once this task has been mastered, you can broaden your projects to incorporate wearable tech . . . this is a broad category that can include circuits sewn into shirts, jackets, shoes, and so on. Let the participants use their imaginations to create all kinds of light-up fashions. If you do branch out into the wearable tech realm, just make sure your makers know that all electronic pieces used in this project are washable *except* for the coin cell battery. Should they need to wash their project, they will need to remove the battery prior to washing with a mild detergent.

Create an LED Brooch

CASEY MCCOY / STEAM LIBRARIAN
San Jose Public Library

Type of Library Best Suited for: Any

Cost Estimate: About $0.75 per brooch if buying supplies in bulk

Makerspace Necessary? No

PROJECT DESCRIPTION

Hop on the newest fashion trend by creating your own wearable tech accessory! Learn how a simple electric circuit works while using multiple tools and materials to create a brooch that lights up.

OVERVIEW

Whether you're looking for a unique craft project or a hands-on circuit learning lesson, creating an LED brooch with kids ages eight years and up has it all. This project is suited for all types of libraries.

Wearable technology has grown in the maker world over the years with designs ranging from a simple LED binder clip ring to designing a "sparkle skirt" that lights up when you move (both projects can be found at http://makezine.com), expanding our understanding of both technology and fashion. This LED brooch project fuses technology and fashion together, and you will learn how a simple electric circuit works while using multiple tools and materials to design a fun new accessory.

MATERIALS LIST

- One large (5mm) or two or more small (2mm) LEDs1
- 3-volt button cell lithium battery (CR2032)
- Pinback
- Felt material in multiple colors
- Glue sticks
- Scotch tape

NECESSARY EQUIPMENT

- Scissors
- Embroidery needle
- Hot glue gun

No more equipment is necessary to complete this project, but the following are recommended to expand on the basics:

- Computer and printer: Search online for pattern ideas and print them out to trace on the felt
- Snap circuits: Extend the learning opportunity by adding on more hands-on projects like creating and testing circuits on a Snap Circuits board

STEP-BY-STEP INSTRUCTIONS

1. Trace a pattern or draw your own design onto a piece of felt. If you're layering pieces, trace these on the desired colored felt as well. Cut these out and use the hot glue gun to piece them together. Here are the beginning stages of a spooky glowing eyed skeleton:

FIGURE 25.1

Beginning the skull brooch

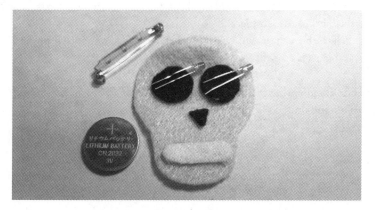

2. Once the glue is dry and cooled off, flip your design over to the back and hot glue a pinback about ½ inch from the top of the main felt piece. This is how you'll attach the brooch to your clothing.

3. To attach the LED(s), first take a pen or fine point marker to mark where the holes should be made to allow the leads (the LED legs) through the felt. Place the LED (leads still straight) over where you want it placed and make two dots where the leads meet the felt. If your design uses two or more LEDs, the pair of holes for the leads of the second LED must be close enough to the first LED so the leads can attach to the same 3-volt button cell battery you will attach in step 10. Smaller LEDs (2mm) are best for adding multiple LEDs to the design because they draw less power from the battery.

Teachable moment: Notice how one LED lead is shorter than the other? Typically, the shorter lead is called the cathode and represents a negative charge, while the longer lead is an anode and represents a positive charge.

4. Now it's time to make two holes in the location where you want to place each lead using an embroidery needle or other fine point tool. Put the two leads through the two holes from the front side. Repeat for each LED you want on the brooch.

5. Bend the two LED leads so they are flat against the back of the felt piece. Now place the 3-volt cell battery flat against the back of the felt piece near the leads. Bend the leads so the negative lead (cathode) is against the negative side of the battery (look for the "−" sign) and the positive lead (anode) is against the positive side of the battery (with the "+" sign). It should look similar to the back of the skull brooch in the photo.

6. When both leads are touching the battery the LED should light up. If it does not light up, play with the placement of the battery and LEDs, make sure the leads aren't touching each other or overlapping, flip over the battery, and so on.

7. With the battery and leads still touching, place a piece of tape across your battery to the back of the felt piece.

8. Attach the brooch to your favorite jacket, backpack, or hat to show off your new wearable tech brooch!

Extra credit: Explore what types of things you can do or add to make the circuit (LED light) turn off and on.

FIGURE 25.2 ....

Battery held on back of the skull brooch

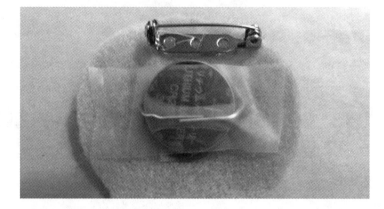

LEARNING OUTCOMES

- Participants gain a basic understanding of how a simple electric circuit works and the negative/positive polarity of batteries.
- Participants use tools and/or materials to design and/or build a device that solves a specific problem or a solution to a specific problem.
- This project also fits within Next Generation Science Standards: Science and Engineering Practices—Constructing Explanations and Designing Solutions.[2]

RECOMMENDED NEXT PROJECTS

The Instructables website has step-by-step instructions for a more involved LED flower brooch online.[3] More wearable tech projects can be found in "Make: Wearable Electronics" by Kate Hartman[4] or on Make's website[5] by searching "wearables" in projects.

Notes

1. EBay has a large variety of small electronics like LEDs and 3-volt batteries, especially if you want to buy in bulk. These items can also typically be found at your local hardware or electronics store.
2. Next Generation Science Standards, Web, www.nextgenscience.org.
3. "Wearable LED Flower Brooch," Instructables, Web, www.instructables .com/id/Wearable-LED-Flower-Brooch.
4. Kate Hartman, *Make: Wearable Electronics* (Maker Media, 2014). "Make," Web, http:// makezine.com.

R'Orchestra: Musical Instruments with Makey-Makey

CORY GREENWOOD / LEARNING COORDINATOR

WITH THANKS TO KATE HANSEN, ARTS AND CULTURE COORDINATOR

Yarra Plenty Regional Library, Australia

Type of Library Best Suited for: School or Public

Cost Estimate: $500–$1,000

Makerspace Necessary? No

PROJECT DESCRIPTION

In response to a simple design brief, participants work in small groups to design and produce a musical instrument with ICT (information and communication technologies) tools and a mix of unconventional materials. There are no restrictions or guidelines to the instrument's form or intended sound. The project is designed to encourage creative thinking and to challenge participants' problem-solving skills through experimentation and the process of design.

OVERVIEW

R'Orchestra is a multidisciplinary science, music, and craft program aimed at acquainting children and young adults with the principles of conductivity and electronic circuits. The program provides an opportunity to explore design thinking and problem-solving, deepens an understanding of computer programming concepts, and provides an introduction to the basics of digital sound production.

A minimum of four hours is needed to run this program effectively, but it can be shortened by removing the sound production module and using a ready-made Scratch project instead of asking participants to create their own.

R'Orchestra (a portmanteau of "raucous" and "orchestra") is noisy. Therefore, it is most suitable for libraries with a soundproof room where noise and mess are permitted. Space to work around computers or laptops that have speakers and Internet access is essential.

MATERIALS LIST

- A variety of random objects—plastic, wooden, and metallic, including soft toys, trinkets and jewelry, paper clips, utensils, disassembled electronics, floristry wire, marbles, and so on. Anything can be used, including fruit, clothing, and people, but make sure plenty of conductive materials are selected.
- Craft supplies—scissors, tape, colored paper, cardboard, pipe cleaners, and so on
- Aluminum foil and/or copper tape
- Butcher's paper (for brainstorming and sketching design ideas)
- Graphite pencils (instruments can be drawn on paper because the graphite is conductive)

NECESSARY EQUIPMENT

- Makey-Makey invention kits—one per group (http://shop.makeymakey.com/products/makey-makey-kit)
- PC or laptop with speakers—one per group
- Audacity, free sound-editing software (www.audacityteam.org/download/)
- Scratch (https://scratch.mit.edu/)

STEP-BY-STEP INSTRUCTIONS

Preparation

1. Set up a station with all the available materials on display.
2. Print or display the design brief—a sample brief is obtainable here: http://bit.ly/rorchestrabrief—and place one Makey-Makey kit at each designated workspace along with some pencils and paper.
3. If this is the first time participants will have seen or used Makey-Makeys, it is advisable to show a short video (there are several on YouTube) demonstrating how the product is used; otherwise, just perform a quick demonstration at the start of the program.

FIGURE 26.1 ···

An example of the materials station

4. Provide participants with the project brief and outline the expected outcomes for the program. Encourage out-of-the-box thinking with an incentive for the most creative design and sounds.

5. It might be necessary to explain that the instruments are to be connected to the computer, and participants can either source digital sound files online or record their own. The instruments can be mobile but will be restricted to the length of the USB cable.

Module 1: Designing the Instrument

1. Participants will first need to brainstorm together and design a blueprint for their instrument on butcher's paper. Allow up to twenty minutes for this module.

2. During this time, encourage participants to peruse the materials and draw or write down their ideas. Part of the challenge is to allow the participants to discover through experimentation, so avoid giving too much guidance at this stage and allow participants to make small mistakes.

3. Regroup and invite some participants to share their design ideas with the group.

Module 2: Coding the Instrument with Scratch

If you are running this program in less than four hours, consider preloading a ready-made Scratch project and have participants swap or modify the sounds instead of coding everything themselves. Search for "makey-makey piano" on the Scratch website;

FIGURE 26.2

Participants presenting their design blueprint

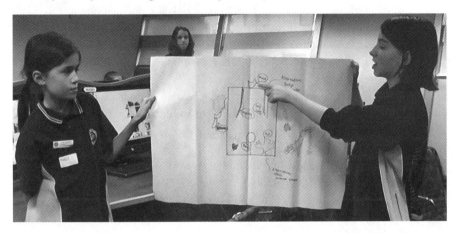

there are hundreds of projects available for use. Note: this program is not intended as an introduction to Scratch; participants should be comfortable using it.

Scratch comes with its own sound library which has a decent range of musical notes and sound effects available, but if time permits, participants can record their own sounds and edit them with Audacity. Consider this for a smaller group size to better manage noise.

- The goal of this module is for participants to program a number of sounds when particular computer keys are pressed. These will later be mapped to their instrument with the Makey-Makey.
- For this module, allow up to an hour for participants to source or record a number of sounds. Advanced participants could be challenged to invent a "switch" that changes their instrument to a whole new set of sounds; a musical harp could easily become a chime of dogs barking, and so on. Some advanced knowledge of Scratch is required to achieve this task.

Module 3: Putting the Band (Back) Together

1. Once participants have chosen their sounds, the raucous (and messy!) part of this program begins. Allow participants to gather materials from the designated station, and bring them back to their group to begin constructing their instrument. Encourage the responsible use of consumables, but if using donated or salvaged stock, encourage objects to be taken apart, and so on, and allow participants plenty of time to experiment.

2. At this stage, participants should now have a clear idea about the form and function of their instrument, but assure them that revisions and modifications are allowed, especially if the chosen materials are not working as intended. As participants work through the design process, they will learn about what materials are conductive and what is needed to build an electronic circuit. Their finished product might be totally different from their design blueprint, but that's completely okay.

3. Participants will need to connect various parts of their instrument to their Makey-Makeys to bring their instrument to life and satisfy the project brief. Instructions for connecting the Makey-Makey can be found at http://makey makey.com/how-to/classic/.

4. Once everyone has finished (or within twenty minutes of the project end-time), encourage participants to present their working instrument to the class and share their reflections on the design process and how they overcame any challenges in realizing their design.

5. Invite the R'Orchestra to play together with the volume up loud and celebrate their achievements with awards or gifts for the most inventive instruments.

LEARNING OUTCOMES

At the completion of this program, participants will:

-   Understand the functions of a circuit.
-   Be able to determine which materials are likely to be conductive.
-   Understand programming concepts.
-   Have improved skills surrounding ICT, design-thinking, teamwork, and communication skills.

RECOMMENDED NEXT PROJECTS

You may have a follow-up event in which participants design their own Scratch sound files and/or are challenged to create musical instruments according to a set of predefined criteria or according to a particular theme or genre of music. Numerous project ideas for Makey-Makey kits and music can be found online.

Begin Soldering and Earn a Blinking LED Badge

LAURA BAKER / LIBRARIAN FOR DIGITAL RESEARCH AND LEARNING
Abilene Christian University Library

Type of Library Best Suited for: Any

Cost Estimate: $3–$5 per person in supplies; $25 per soldering station in equipment

Makerspace Necessary? No

PROJECT DESCRIPTION

This project introduces participants to the principles of soldering. Makers solder the components of a badge with a blinking light that they can wear. The badge proudly proclaims that they have mastered the basics of soldering while giving them a tangible product that they make themselves.

OVERVIEW

Soldering is the foundation of many electronics and electricity projects. It is a skill that requires teaching but that can be learned quickly with just a little practice. This badge activity provides that practice and is a good springboard for launching more advanced projects. It works well with ages eight and up. The only room needed is an area with several electrical outlets, uncrowded tables, and good ventilation.

MATERIALS LIST

- Solder badge kits, one per person (with a few extra kits in case of mistakes)
  - Sources: https://www.tindie.com/products/PartFusion/i-can-solder -badge-v1/ (not branded); www.makershed.com/products/learn-to-solder -skill-badge-kit (branded from manufacturer)
- Roll of solder (60/40 alloy mix is common)

NECESSARY EQUIPMENT

- Soldering station (includes pencil-type soldering iron with 25 watts minimum, iron holder, and sponge wipe)
- Note: one station for every 2–4 people
- Small wire cutters
- Optional: solder sucker for removing solder

STEP-BY-STEP INSTRUCTIONS

If doing this with a group, have tables with the soldering stations and equipment already set up. One soldering station can serve four people, although two stations per four people would be better. If working with younger makers, plan to have one adult helper per each group of four kids, in addition to the activity director.

Soldering is not an unduly dangerous activity, but everyone should observe some general safety guidelines. Soldering irons get extremely hot and should be handled carefully. Have plenty of room at each table to work so that no one gets bumped accidentally. Always put the hot iron into the holder when finished. Instead of passing the iron to the next person, put it back into the holder and let that person pick it up. It is possible for solder to drip, so use it over a protected surface and not over bare skin. Soldering creates irritating fumes, so solder in a well-ventilated area.

Preparation

1. Turn on the solder irons and let them fully heat. If your soldering iron shows the temperature, it should be set to about 600–700 degrees F, or medium-high to high.
2. Dampen the sponge that came with the soldering stations. The sponge is used to clean the tip of the soldering iron.
3. Tin the tip. Soldering irons can get dirty with built-up oxidation and slag from melted solder. Tinning is the process of cleaning the tip and coating it with fresh solder so it works better. Unwind a bit of solder and hold it with one hand. Hold the solder iron in the other hand. Push the solder against the iron so it starts to

melt. Turn the iron as you go so that about ⅛ to ¼ inch back from the tip gets completely coated in solder. Wipe the tip immediately on the damp sponge to clean it. Your iron should now have a shiny tip and is ready to go.

Tips for Making a Good Solder Joint

Hold the iron in the same hand you use to write with. Hold it by the handle as if it were a thick pencil.

Unwind a short length of solder and hold it with the other hand.

Heat the joint. Touch the iron against the surfaces you want to stick. Let the tip touch both the component board and the wire or piece that needs to stick. Hold the iron there for about three seconds to heat it up.

Apply the solder. Bring the solder against the tip and push until it melts. There will be some smoke. Let the solder flow into the joint like a drop of water. If the surfaces are heated properly, the heat will draw the solder into the hole and seal it. Pull the solder away, and then pull the iron away, in that order.

Notice that you hold the iron still against the surface and daub with the solder, not the other way around. Sometimes people want to brush at the solder with the iron. This causes solder to stick to the iron and not to the surface. Heat the joint, not the solder. Remember the "3–3-solder out-iron out" mantra:

- Touch the iron to the surface for a count of three
- Push the solder in for count of three
- Remove solder
- Remove iron

FIGURE 27.1 ....

Soldering a connection

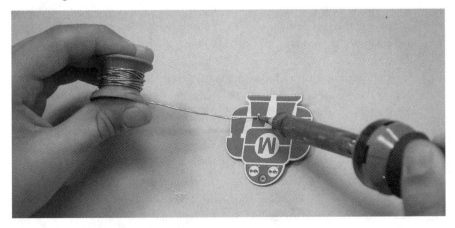

The whole process takes less than ten seconds. A good solder joint has a tiny dome of solder and completely fills the hole. The elements should be secure and not wobble.

Making the Badge

1. *Explain what soldering is.* Soldering is the process of gluing wires and circuits together, only instead of using glue, we use a melted soft metal called solder. Since solder is metal, it lets electricity flow through it. Once you know how to solder, you can do all sorts of things with electricity and electronics.

2. *Pass out the badge kits.* Consider distributing the badge one part at a time so groups do not lose the pieces or try to get ahead of the process. The list of equipment suggests sources for badge kits. Regardless of which one you use, they have similar components.

3. *Solder the battery holder to the circuit board.* The circuit board is the big piece that forms the badge. It has a place that shows where the battery will go. Position the battery holder from the back so that the clips in the holder line up with the holes in the circuit board. The holder will not lie flat against the board but will remain raised to accommodate a battery eventually. Carefully lay the board flat, front side up with the battery holder positioned underneath. You should just barely be able to feel the clips sticking through the holes from the front side. From the front of the board, solder the holes holding the clip. Do one side of the clip and then the other side. Let it cool a few seconds. When finished, the battery clip should not be loose.

4. *Solder the badge pin.* The pin passes through the front to the back. Lay the board front side down so the pin sticks up. Solder the pin from the back.

5. *Solder the LEDs.* Your badge may have one or more LEDs, depending on which badge kit you use. Each LED has two wire leads coming from it: a short lead and a long lead. The long lead is the positive one. It goes into the hole in the circuit board with the plus sign. The short lead is the negative one and goes into the hole with the negative sign. Make sure you get the leads in the correct holes, or the LED will not light up. Insert the leads from the front of the board and solder them from the back. Bend the leads outward a bit so they stay in place while you solder. Solder each lead, but be very careful not to let the solder flow between the leads and make a bridge between them. Position the iron on the outside edges of each lead circuit, and let the solder flow around the connection. After soldering, the LED should feel solid and not move if you try to wiggle it from the front. This is the trickiest joint to solder, so use your experience from the previous joints.

6. *Insert the battery.* The battery slides under the clip on the back. Be sure to insert it with the correct side against the board. Make sure everything lights up. If it does not, check these things:

— Are all the joints smoothly soldered, especially the LEDs? If wiggling an LED makes it flicker, you do not have a good solder and need to do that connection over.

— Check the polarity of the LED. Is the long lead in the positive hole?

— Is the battery facing the right way? Is it held tightly against the board by the battery clip? If you have to mash the battery clip against the battery to make the lights come on, you need to remove the battery and re-solder the clip in place.

If you need to re-solder a joint, heat the old solder with the iron, and remove it with a solder sucker.

7. Trim the excess LED leads with a wire cutter so they do not stick out.

Your badge is now ready to wear to proclaim your soldering competence!

FIGURE 27.2 ⋯⋯⋯⋯⋯⋯⋯⋯⋯⋯⋯⋯⋯⋯⋯⋯⋯⋯⋯⋯⋯⋯⋯⋯⋯⋯

Completed solder badge

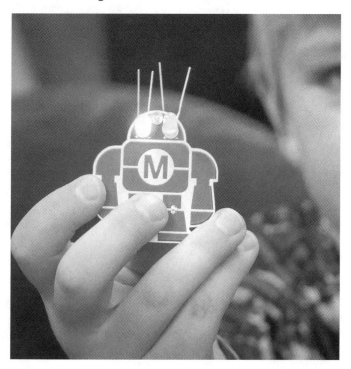

LEARNING OUTCOMES

- Participants gain skill in soldering basic electronic components.
- Participants learn fundamental principles of LEDs and electricity.
- Participants learn safe handling of tools like soldering irons, solder, and wire cutters.

RECOMMENDED NEXT PROJECTS

The "Scribble Droid" project described later in this book is a natural extension of this solder project.

Milling, Soldering, and Cutting Projects

Create a Wooden Maze with a CNC Mill Machine

ERIK CARLSON / LIBRARIAN I
White Plains Public Library

Type of Library Best Suited for: Any

Cost Estimate: CNC: about $2,000; Materials: about $30 for 8 projects

Makerspace Necessary? Yes (this could get messy)

PROJECT DESCRIPTION

Creating a wooden maze is a simple way to get people interested in computer numerical control (CNC) milling. It gives them an opportunity to design their own project and use basic computer-aided manufacturing (CAM) software to create toolpaths and operate the CNC machine. Although this is a basic project, participants in the program need to be able to control the mouse and have intermediate-level computer skills.

One of the greatest difficulties I had when I started developing programs around a CNC machine was how to interest people in the machines. Using acronyms like "CNC" and "CAM" mean nothing to the library users, and the machine itself is not very attractive. Everyone wants 3D printing, but CNC milling can be just as great. My first projects were pretty basic and uninspired. I had people engrave their initials or a simple design into wood or cork. Then I decided to complement the 3D printing program with the CNC machine, which helped. I still needed to think of something that would challenge people, something they would be motivated to make and show

FIGURE 28.1

Completed CNC maze

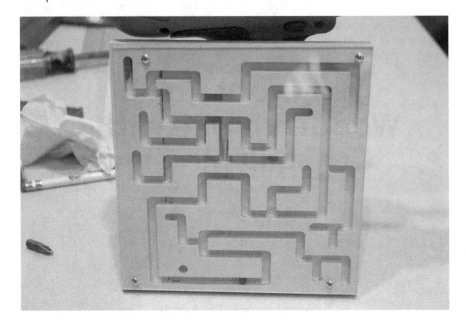

to their friends. What better fits this criterion than a maze? These instructions are for creating a wooden maze using 6.75 × 6.75 × 0.5-inch plywood. You can modify the size depending on the size of maze you want to create.

OVERVIEW

I run this program in two sessions with no more than five participants. The first session runs for 1.5 hours. This is enough time for everyone to design a maze and create toolpaths. I invite the participants to come in between sessions to learn how to run the machine. It takes around two hours to cut out the maze. The second session can take thirty minutes to an hour depending on whether or not you cut the Plexiglass or have the participants cut it. I work mostly with teenagers, so I cut the Plexiglass myself.

MATERIALS LIST

- 6.75 × 0.5-inch squares of plywood
- Plexiglass
- Small wood screws
- 0.25-inch ball

NECESSARY EQUIPMENT

- CNC mill machine with 0.25-inch mill bit (preferably a spiral up-cut bit). (There is an extra step in the outline if you only have 0.125-inch bits)
- Computers for each participant
- Drill and drill bits
- Sandpaper

NECESSARY SOFTWARE

- Inkscape (available for Windows and X11, or other Vector editing software)
- MakerCAM.com (or other CAM program)
- GRBL (or other G-Code software)

STEP-BY-STEP INSTRUCTIONS

Create a new design with Inkscape, an open-source, vector graphic software. To start, I like to resize the document to the size of my maze. The work area is one inch less than the block of wood, leaving room to attach the Plexiglass at the end. Go to "File" in the main menu and then click on "Document Properties." In the new window find "Custom Size." Change the "Units" to inches, then change the "Width" and "Height" to 5.75 and hit enter. Then close out of the window. I also like to add the "Grid" to help guide my design. To do this, go to "View" in the main menu and then click on "Grid." Now we are ready to plot out our mazes.

There are a variety of designs, shapes, and objectives that go into creating a maze. The simplest to design is a linear maze, starting at one point and ending at another. This is the type of maze that we are going to design. (If you would like to add curves, please see my instructions for the cardboard plane cutout. There I show how to curve and round out angles in Inkscape. Project #30, "Laser Cut a Cardboard Glider Plane.")

To get started, click on the tool "Draw bezier curves and straight lines" on the left side of the screen and plot out the course of your maze.

Next we can start adding our dead ends to the maze, the more the merrier. Keep in mind that the actual maze lines will be much thicker, so try not to make the lines too close together. When our designs are complete, select all (Ctrl + A), then click on "Object" in the main menu and then choose "Group" (Ctrl + G).

Next widen the lines to 0.25 inch. Click on "Object," then "Fill and Stroke." This will add a Dialog Box on the right of your screen. Click on the "Stroke Style" tab and change "px" to "Inches," and then change the width to "0.25." If these options appear grey, make sure you select your drawing/maze, so that a dotted line appears around your design. Then try again.

FIGURE 28.2 ....

Inkscape fill and stroke settings

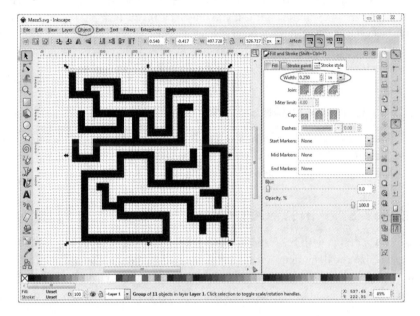

Now our maze should be the thickness that will be produced, and we can see if we made any mistakes by drawing our lines too close. If any of the lines are overlapped, ungroup your maze and select the lines that need to be modified. Remember to regroup when you are finished editing. My personal rule is to keep a minimum of two grid squares between the lines as much as I can.

If you do not have a 0.25-inch mill bit and use 0.125-inch bits, do not despair. You will have to take an extra step in Inkscape and draw an outline (using "Draw bezier curves and straight lines") of the entire maze, then delete the original maze (the thick 0.25-inch maze) so only the outline remains.

Once we are happy with our designs, we are ready to save and export them into a CAM program. I use MakerCAM.com because it is free and easy to use. Save your design by clicking on "File," then "Save-as." Change the file to "Plain SVG."

Open MakerCAM and import your design by clicking on "File" in the main menu, and then choose "Open SVG File." Add a 6.75-inch square by clicking on "Insert" in the main menu and then choose "Rectangle." Make the width and height 6.75 and click "Ok." Move the square to the intersection of the X-Y axis. Then center your maze in the square. You may have to resize your design after importing it to the CAM program. To do this, highlight your maze in red, click on "Edit" in the main

FIGURE 28.3

Maze design in MakerCAM

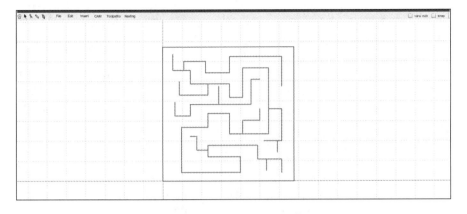

menu, and then choose "Scale Selected." Go little by little when scaling (down or up), subtract by increments of "5". This will give us a better visual of what our finished projects will look like.

Next we can create our toolpath. In MakerCAM, be sure that only your maze is highlighted in red by drawing a selection box around the maze. When highlighted, click on "CAM" in the main menu and then choose "Follow Path Operation." This will open a new window to input our toolpath parameters.

I use a 0.25-inch mill bit. I set the "Target Depth" to −0.3125 so that there is room for the ball to move without touching the Plexiglass. I generally use a very small "Step Down Rate," so I set it to 0.015625. I find that there are fewer mistakes made this way. I set the "Feedrate" to 30 and the "Plunge Rate" to 10.

Next click on the check box to "View Cuts," then go back to "CAM" and click on "Calculate All." This will show the path that the machine will take to cut out your maze. Now we can export the g-code by clicking on "CAM" again and selecting "Export Gcode."

After it is saved you can open GRBL, a motion-control software, and import your project. Clamp your piece of plywood and set up your CNC machine to run the program.

When the machine is finished, sand any rough areas and remove any burr. Remember to sand the edges and corners as well to make them smooth. For some strange reason my machine decided to add a hole towards the bottom.

Now we are ready to fit our Plexiglass over the top. The cleanest way to cut Plexiglass is to score it with a utility knife (I score it about 25 times just in case). I put the Plexiglass between two boards, lining up the scored line in the Plexiglass between the edges of the two boards. Depending on the size of the Plexiglass, I will use a ruler to help distribute the pressure. With a smaller piece I hold the Plexiglass wearing a glove. I give the Plexiglass a strong push to break it along the score. If you have a table saw and don't mind the dust, then you can cut that way. Remember to sand only the edges of the Plexiglass and remove any burr left over from the cuts. Also try to sand the corners down a bit so they are not sharp either.

I cut the Plexiglass about 0.25 inch smaller than the piece of wood and check it by lining it up with my maze. Alternately, you can measure the Plexiglass so that it is flush to the sides of your wood. Drill four holes in the corners to attach it to your piece of wood. Be sure to use a backer to drill into; it is easy to accidentally break off a corner of Plexiglass. Also be sure to check that your holes will not interfere with the maze. With the design I used for this I was not very careful to keep the corners clear, so my screws were not evenly placed in the corners. If you want the object of the maze to be to get the ball out, drill holes to put the ball in at the start and/or end.

Next you can add your ball. I found a small bead that fit in my maze perfectly. You can 3D print a ball, but ball bearings are the best way to go. Once the ball is moving smoothly, you can screw the Plexiglass onto the top. You can also paint or stain the wood to make it look nicer, or engrave your name on the back. Now you should have a nice maze to challenge your friends or give as a gift.

LEARNING OUTCOMES

Through this project participants will . . .

- Learn to use vector graphics software.
- Learn to create toolpaths with CAM software.
- Learn to set up and operate a CNC mill machine.
- Learn problem-solving skills and trickery.

RECOMMENDED NEXT PROJECTS

Once you feel comfortable creating and teaching how to create this maze, you can try more difficult designs, like a more circular maze or taking a design like a logo and turning it into a maze. You can also make a larger maze, depending on the size of your CNC machine. Also, see my project in this section on how to "Build a Six-Piece Interlocking Burr Puzzle" as well as others in this section on milling and cutting.

Create Your Own Catapults

LAURA BAKER / LIBRARIAN FOR DIGITAL RESEARCH AND LEARNING
Abilene Christian University Library

Type of Library Best Suited for: School, Public

Cost Estimate: $20 supplies per catapult; $500–$5,000 equipment

Makerspace Necessary? Yes

PROJECT DESCRIPTION

In this project, makers assemble a small catapult from precut pieces. They design how they will hold the projectile on the catapult and how the rubber bands will connect. After some shooting practice, groups see who can launch something the highest, the farthest, and the most accurately by landing an object into an empty box target. By tweaking the design and the way they launch an object, they discover how small alterations affect overall performance.

OVERVIEW

This is a project the Abilene Christian University Library does for its middle-school maker camp during the summer. It is a variation on the Angry Birds launchers that are popular with college engineering departments. By assembling and experimenting with a small catapult, kids learn about design and the trajectories of different objects.

Some parts of the catapult are precut, but other pieces require decisions, a combination that works well with this age group of middle school students.

Kids can work on the catapults in groups of three or four to encourage collaboration. Have a large room or outside space available for test launching and for the final contest.

MATERIALS LIST (PER CATAPULT)

- Catapult pattern (available at tiny.cc/catapults)
- Sheet of plywood, ¾-inch thick
- Two pieces of wooden dowel, each 5 inches long and ¼ inch diameter
- Four screws (1.5-inch length)
- Projectile (wooden bead, dried bean, piece of hard candy, etc.)
- Box or trash can
- Decorating supplies (markers, stickers, glue, crepe paper, etc.)

NECESSARY EQUIPMENT

- Power drill/driver
- Sandpaper
- Band saw or CNC router (to precut catapult pieces)

STEP-BY-STEP INSTRUCTIONS

Preparation

Precut the pieces of the catapult using the pattern provided. Cut the pieces using a band saw or a CNC router. The circles inside the shapes indicate where a hole should go. Use a ⅝-inch drill bit (or something slightly larger than the wooden dowels) to make a hole completely through the pieces in the places indicated.

Assembling the Catapult

Use the photographs of the completed catapults to help you assemble the pieces. Have a completed catapult ready to show the makers how the parts fit together.

1. Distribute the pieces of the catapult. Have makers sand all the pieces to make them smooth.
2. Assemble and screw the sides. Insert the sides in the notches of the base and screw them in place using one screw in each notch.

FIGURE 29.1

Decorated catapult showing sides screwed at the base

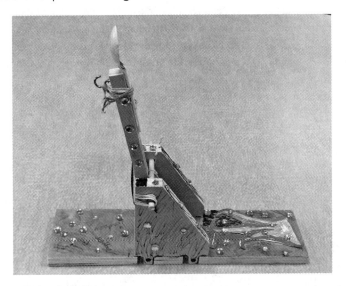

FIGURE 29.2

Catapult arm mechanism

3. Assemble the arm. Insert one of the wooden dowel pieces into the lower hole on the side piece, through the hole in the catapult arm, and out the lower hole on the other side piece. This creates a hinge that lets the arm swing up and down.

4. Assemble the arm stop. Insert the other wooden dowel through the upper holes of the side pieces. This piece does not go through the arm. It acts as a stop for the arm to slam against when launching an object. About ½ inch of dowel should stick out on each side at the top.

5. Add the rubber bands. Hold the arm up so it rests against the stop. Thread a rubber band around the protruding outer end of the stop, stretch it past the back of the arm, and loop it around the other end of the stop. Have extra rubber bands for makers to experiment with tension.

6. Ask makers to decide how they will hold the projectile on the arm to launch it. Have cups, plastic spoons, cardboard, paper, and scissors ready to let them devise something. Some groups will want to decorate their catapults, too.

Shooting Practice

Go outside or to an empty hallway or long room.

Explain that you will test the catapults in three categories: height (measured vertically against a wall), distance (measured from the shooting line to where the projectile lands), and accuracy (whether a projectile can land in the target box or trash can in three attempts). Let the groups practice and make adjustments before doing actual trials. Keep it fun with lots of cheering on each attempt.

A key component of the activity is getting makers to realize how small changes in the design of the catapult affect how it performs. Encourage them to make informed decisions, not merely random ones. Leave plenty of time for the practice sessions, and ask them what they did and if it worked better or worse as a result.

Final Shots

Each group gets three rounds in each category of height, distance, and accuracy. Let people in each group take turns shooting, and have someone record the best of each attempt. Ask everyone to look at the catapults and try to guess what made the difference in that machine's performance.

Catapult practice

Teacher's Tips

- The placement of the projectile on the arm makes a difference. Things on the tip of the arm shoot better than things farther down the arm. A projectile that sits low in the bottom of the holder might not go as far as one that sits high on the edge.
- How far back someone pulls the arm before launching affects trajectory. There is an optimum angle. Anything farther than optimum wastes energy by launching upward instead of forward.
- Invariably, people will try to increase power by adding more rubber bands. It is possible to add so many rubber bands that it will break the arm or the wooden dowel that the arm hits against. Explain that every device has mechanical limitations that cannot be exceeded without damaging the machine. Either live within the limits, or modify the machine. Can you add padding to the arm or the dowel to absorb the shock? Can you use different material, like a metal rod instead of a wooden one, that will not break as easily?
- What happens if you extend the length of the arm with another piece of wood or by attaching a plastic spoon along the arm? The extra length affects distance.

LEARNING OUTCOMES

Through this project participants will . . .

- Learn to use hand tools, like drills and screws.
- Practice the scientific method of hypothesis, testing, and observation.
- Discover the relationships between mechanical design and energy, motion, and trajectory.

RECOMMENDED NEXT PROJECTS

This is a great project to accompany a history lesson about medieval machines, castles, and real catapults used for storming a castle. Partner with a history class in school or have lots of books ready about castles and catapults so makers can see how their object connects with history.

Laser-Cut a Cardboard Glider Plane

ERIK CARLSON / LIBRARIAN I
White Plains Public Library

Type of Library Best Suited for: Public, School

Cost Estimate: Laser cutter about $10,000–$30,000; Materials $0.01–$0.02

Makerspace Necessary? Yes

PROJECT DESCRIPTION

This project will teach participants design skills as well as basic concepts of aeronautics. The best part is that you will sound like a genius explaining to them how to make something glide. I used the Trotec Speedy 300 laser cutter, at Fat Cat Fab Lab in New York City, to cut out my plane. You can also use a CNC machine with either an engraving bit or a small mill bit, or you can cut it out by hand with a utility knife. I am using cardboard, but any other light, thin material like balsa wood or Styrofoam could work as well.

OVERVIEW

This program can be done in two 90-minute sessions. Participants should schedule time between sessions to cut the plane out with the laser cutter. It only takes a few minutes to cut. To start, find a design for a glider to use as a guide. Participants will design their own parts. You can search for templates on the Internet. Here is a template image of the plane I designed for this tutorial:

FIGURE 30.1 ....

Plane template created in Inkscape

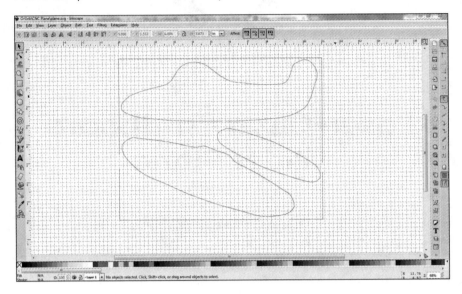

MATERIALS LIST

- Cardboard
- Balsa wood
- Styrofoam or any light, thin material
- Decorations like stickers and markers
- One or two pennies

EQUIPMENT LIST

- Laser cutter and accompanying software
- Utility knife

SOFTWARE NEEDED

Inkscape (open-source vector graphics software available for PC and Mac with X11), Adobe Illustrator (if needed)

STEP-BY-STEP INSTRUCTIONS

To start, we are going to use Inkscape, an open-source vector graphics design program, to design the parts of the plane. After you open Inkscape, resize the Art Board area by going to "File" in the main menu, then click on "Document Properties." In the new window click on "Custom Size." Change the "Units" to millimeters, then change the "Width" to 304.8 mm and the "Height" to 241.3 mm, then hit enter and close out of the window. I also like to add the "Grid" to help guide my design. To do this go to "View" in the main menu, then click on "Grid."

Use the "draw Bezier curves and straight lines" tool, found on the left side toolbar, to draw your outline. I suggest starting with the stabilizer (small piece that goes in the back of the plane) since it is the smallest part. Only draw half of the stabilizer. When you have finished drawing, use the "edit paths and nodes" tool, found on the left side toolbar, to round out the sharp corners. Click on a node and then click on the "make selected nodes smooth" button in the top menu to give it a curve. Do this with all of the nodes. You can select all of the nodes with "CTRL + A" to speed up the process. You can also push and pull the nodes to edit your design. To make the stabilizer symmetrical, go to "Edit" in the main menu, "copy" your half-stabilizer, then choose "paste in place." Now choose "flip horizontally" on the top menu, and move the copy so that the ends meet. I recommend using the arrow keys to move the piece, and to zoom in to see exactly where the ends come together. When the ends meet, select both objects (using the Shift key), click on "Object" in the main menu, and then "Group" them together and save it as a Plain SVG file. This will make your stabilizer perfectly symmetrical.

FIGURE 30.2 ....

Plane stabilizer

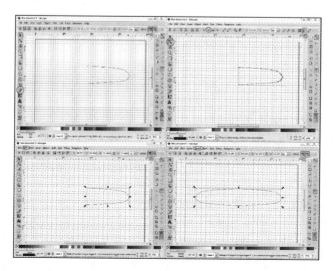

Repeat these steps to design the wing and the plane's body. Be sure to only design half of the wing and copy it to make it symmetrical. The body should be a little longer than the wing. You will resize all of the parts next.

Once you have designed all three pieces, we need to make sure that they are all in correct proportion to each other. Let's create a new project and resize the Art Board to the same dimensions as before. Now copy and paste each piece to the new project. Fix the proportions by selecting a piece and changing the width and height using the arrows. Once you are happy with your design, save it as a "Plain SVG" file.

Now you can set up your design to be cut. The next instructions are for sending a design to be cut with a Trotec Speedy 300 laser cutter with JobControl software. If you use different software for laser cutting, follow the instructions for that software to send your file.

With JobCreator software you need to save your design as an .Ai file. Open your design in Adobe Illustrator and change the color of your pieces to true red. Since we used Inkscape to create the design, and it is only an outline, it should already be a Vector Graphic. If it is not, then select each piece of your plane and click on "Trace Vector," which should be on the menu at the top. We also need to change the size of the lines to 0.001 pt. You will find this setting at the top of the page. Now you are ready to send your design to be cut. Go to "File," then select "Print." Go to "Print Preferences," change the measurement to millimeters, and set the size of the Art Board. Illustrator saves the last settings used, so be sure to change this. Change the material to cardboard, or whichever material you decide to use. Send the file to JobControl (JC). I am using the default settings for cutting cardboard on JC, so I select my job, add it to the cut area, and select cardboard for the material. Now it is ready to be cut. Check that the bottom of the laser cutter and lens are clean. Set your cardboard in the upper-left corner, adjust the focus of the laser, and move the laser to the corner of the cardboard and run the job. When it is finished, remove the pieces and clean the bottom of the laser cutter.

When all of the pieces are cut, you can add openings in the plane's body to fit the wing and stabilizer. You should also make small cuts, about 0.75 inch long, in the center-back of the stabilizer and wing to help slide them into the body. The stabilizer just needs to fit in the back. The wing needs to be placed so that the center of gravity of your plane is roughly in the middle of the plane. You can have your participants play with this in their designs, having them move the wing at different points on the plane's body. Add a penny or two to the nose of your plane so that when you hold the plane by the side of the wings it is perfectly balanced.

Now you can decorate your plane with stickers and color it in with markers. Do not use any electrical tape or duct tape because this will affect the balance of your glider. If you want, you could use some duct tape to attach the pennies to the front of the plane. Once you are finished decorating, your plane is ready to fly. Hold it by the side of the wings, make sure it is level and that the tip is not pointing up, and let it fly.

FIGURE 30.3 ....

Assembled plane

LEARNING OUTCOMES

Participants will gain . . .

- Experience with graphic design tools
- A basic understanding of aeronautics
- Safe practices using a laser cutter

RECOMMENDED NEXT PROJECTS

From here you can try to improve your design to make a glider that goes farther, faster, or that can do flips.

Create a Custom Sign Using a Silhouette Vinyl Cutter

LYSSA TROEMEL / MAKER LAB GUIDE

Allen County Public Library–Georgetown Branch

Type of Library Best Suited for: Any

Cost Estimate: $20–$50, depending on cost of wood

Makerspace Necessary? No

PROJECT DESCRIPTION

In this project, participants will learn how to make custom signs using vinyl and a vinyl cutter to make a stencil. This is a new program that we have worked into the rotation at the Georgetown Branch. It introduces patrons to using the vinyl cutter and also involves measurement, the principles of computer design, and the idea of positive and negative space in art.

OVERVIEW

This is a project that we offer to all ages. It has a typical run time of two hours and is offered multiple times every month. Typically, we only offer it to 3–6 participants because of our room size and equipment availability, but it could definitely be done with more people.

FIGURE 31.1 ···

Example of some signs that have been made

MATERIALS LIST

- Precut wood
- Paint
- Vinyl (typically either Oracal 631 or Silhouette; needs to be removable)
- Transfer paper

NECESSARY EQUIPMENT

- Silhouette Vinyl Cutter and computer with software
- Paintbrushes
- Pick tool or tweezers
- Scraper or old gift card
- Optional: fan and hair dryer
- Optional: cutting mat (usually comes with Silhouette)

STEP-BY-STEP INSTRUCTIONS

Step 1

Paint the wood in a base color. I usually do two coats. If you find the wood is absorbing a lot of paint, I would advise finding a white primer to paint on first. Gesso can be found in most craft and art supply stores and works well. Almost any kind of paint will work; I've used both latex and acrylic paints for this type of project and they hold up.

Step 2

While the paint is drying, design what you want the sign to say or look like. In Silhouette, there should be preloaded designs from when you connected the cutter via USB the first time. You can also find free designs on various websites, trace an image found on the Internet or draw something in Sharpie by hand, take a picture, and trace the image. There are also drawing tools in the Silhouette software that allow you to use shapes, lines, and curves. If a trace has problem spots, you can use the anchor point tool to fix those spots. If you are using text, it is strongly advisable not to do anything that has really tight curls on the end of the letters. The machine tends to have problems cutting the tight loops and catches on the vinyl, resulting in loops that are not cut and torn vinyl.

Step 3

Load the vinyl into the Silhouette. To do this, slide the vinyl under the bar and make sure it is under the white rollers. If you have to, gently pull up on the bar to get the vinyl under the left roller. You will not need a cutting mat if the vinyl is at least nine inches wide. If you are using scraps, place the vinyl on the cutting mat and use that to feed it in.

Step 4

Plug the Silhouette into the computer via USB and check the settings for vinyl. Adjust the blade accordingly by using the tool that came with the blade or the hole in the machine in front of the material bar. After making any necessary adjustments, send the design to the Silhouette and it should start cutting right away.

Step 5

Remove the inner lettering or design carefully using the pick tool or tweezers. This is how the stencil is made. If any inner parts of the letters (the insides of *a*'s and *o*'s, for example) come away and you can't place them back where they were, don't worry about it. This can be touched up later, and in many cases isn't worth the effort of putting back on there. Then use the transfer paper to pick it up. To do this, place the sticky side on top of the vinyl and smooth using a scraper, gift card, or credit card. This is to make sure all the air bubbles are out and all the little details will be picked up. Take the back off the vinyl side and place on the wood. Repeat the process with the scraper and then peel off the gridded transfer paper.

Step 6

Paint the stencil in broad strokes. If you are doing one color, there isn't much need to pay attention to where the paint goes. If you are doing multiple colors, watch where the paint is going and change brush sizes as necessary. In either case, try not to go over the edge of the stencil.

Let dry and add a second coat if necessary. This all depends on the person making the sign. If they feel the need, allow them to add a second coat.

Step 7

After it is all dry, peel away the stencil and touch up as necessary. If paint has gotten outside of the stencil, paint over it with the paint used for the background. If you missed the middle of letters, take a small brush and paint in the insides. Mostly pay attention to the big areas. If there were large bleeds, take care of those, but don't worry too much about some of the smaller ones if there are any.

If you find that it is taking too long for the paint to dry, place the sign in front of a fan or use a hair dryer. If using a hair dryer, try to find one that has a cool setting; the paint seems to cure better when using cool air.

LEARNING OUTCOMES

Patrons should learn about:

- Measurement
- Designing on a computer
- Positive and negative space

Measurement will be learned when it comes time to measure the sign to make sure the design will fit on the piece of wood. Computer design comes into play when making the design in the software. The differences between positive and negative space can be discussed when working on taking out the inner parts of the stencil.

RECOMMENDED NEXT PROJECTS

A good next step to this project would be to use the vinyl as a decal. You can do this by finding other objects like drink tumblers, ornaments, cutting boards, and other things to personalize. If using the vinyl as a decal doesn't appeal to participants, this can be scaled up to larger and more complex signs, or participants can use stencil material to make a reusable stencil. If participants are more interested in using a computer to design, a good next step would be to use Adobe Illustrator or Inkscape to design SVG files. If you would like to move on to fabric-based projects, heat transfer vinyl can also be cut using this process and the vinyl cutter machine. The application instructions are a little different, but they are still easy to use.

Laser-Cut Your Own Greeting Card

JACQUELINE R. MITCHELL / CREATIVE PRODUCTION LAB MANAGER
University of Nebraska at Omaha Criss Library

Type of Library Best Suited for: Any

Cost Estimate: $20 plus cost of software ($0–$400) and laser cutter ($5,000–$10,000)

Makerspace Necessary? Yes

PROJECT DESCRIPTION

This project reviews the process of designing and laser cutting a greeting card. If you already have access to software and a laser cutter, this is an inexpensive project for your library. With a little software knowledge, designs are relatively simple to build and prepare to cut. The end result is a unique card with a personal touch.

OVERVIEW

In this project, patrons will design their card using a vector software. The design will involve text and clip art. Elements of cutting will be discussed to ensure the project is completed as envisioned. Both pieces of the card will be prepared for a laser cutter and cut. Finally, the two pieces of cardstock will be glued together to form the final result.

MATERIALS LIST

- Cardstock or construction paper
- Glue

NECESSARY EQUIPMENT

- Computer
- Laser cutter
- Vector software—Adobe Illustrator, Corel Draw, or Inkscape (free)
- 123D Make (123dapp.com/ make) (As of 2017, 123D Make has changed to Slicer for Fusion 360. This tutorial is still applicable to the new software. Download here: http://tinyurl .com/yay7gsp8.)

FIGURE 32.1 ....

Finished laser-cut greeting card

STEP-BY-STEP INSTRUCTIONS

1. Design your file. You want to design your file for cutting with no etching. The way you assign the laser to cut will vary depending on your software and machine, so you will want to make sure you are familiar with that process before attempting this project. I will proceed using Adobe Illustrator to design and an Epilog brand cutter, in which you want to assign strokes to .001 point in black.

2. To begin, you will want to create an outside file and inside file. You will glue the outside and inside pieces together later. Create each file in different tabs to be 11 inches wide and 8.5 inches tall, the size of your cardstock. Add text and designs in the traditional format, so each of your designs will be on the right sides of your documents.

3. Add your text to the document. There are two ways to do this. You can cut out the letters or you can cut out the space around the letters. In Photo 1, you can see the difference. The blue circle is an example of the space around the letters being cut. This allows for the most variety of fonts to be used, but be mindful of using lowercase letters. The tittle on letters such as "i" and "j" will completely fall out if they are not connected in some way to the piece. The red circle in Photo 1 represents what happens when you cut out the letters instead. Letters like "A" and "O" look less complete. If using this method, I recommend you stay away from closed letters (CNGTULTINS!) or use a stencil font that connects to the center of those letters. See the photo for more details.

FIGURE 32.2 ···

Stencil differences

For this project, we will go with the first method for adding text to the document. Begin by typing your text out the way you want it in white. Next, use the shape tool to make black boxes around each of the sets of letters. If you prefer to begin in black text with white boxes, that's fine; just make sure to convert the colors over before you proceed to the next step. Make sure every piece of the text is attached to an edge of the boxes in some way. The more attachments, the more secure your design will be. As you can see from Photo 2, the text now looks like it is part of the page.

4. Import your images and designs. This process works best with images that have the background already removed. Single-color clip art would work well for this step. Just make sure the images follow the same rules as your text. White pieces will represent the paper, black pieces will represent what is cut out. Connect your pieces as much as possible so you aren't left with fragile structures or pieces that unintentionally fall out.

5. Convert your images. Once you get everything where you would like it and you are confident in the ways the pieces connect, you will want to convert your image to a bitmap. This eliminates any stroke lines that may throw off the way your cutter wants your image to cut. You can do this in Illustrator by selecting all of the content and going to Object > Rasterize. I choose Bitmap as my Color Model and 600 for the DPI.

6. Trace. Next, you want to trace the image, which will trace the black pieces, leaving us with only the lines we need to cut and no extras. You can do this by going to Window > Image Trace. The default settings should be okay, but select Preview and change the View to Outlines to get a closer look at your image. Make sure

"Ignore White" is checked so we don't get duplicate lines. If everything looks okay, click "Expand" at the top of the window in the control panel. You should now see anchor points along all of your black pieces.

7. Adjust lines for your laser cutter. This is where you will assign settings to your outlines to tell your laser where to cut. It will vary based on your specific machine. With our Epilog, we assign the strokes to .001 point and then choose the vector settings in our printer driver. We type in settings for cardstock. Most lasers will come with default settings for materials, so check your manual for that information.

8. Get cutting! Place your cardstock in your machine and cut away! It's okay if things don't go as planned the first time around. Just tweak it and try again. Fortunately, cardstock/construction paper is relatively cheap compared to other laser cutting materials, so do-overs will be relatively inexpensive.

9. Repeat steps 1–5 for the inside sheet of the card. In addition to repeating these steps, I like to draw a box 10.5 inches wide by 8 inches high (a tad smaller than my cardstock) and center it on my inside sheet. I apply the settings for cutting to the box so when I'm ready to glue, I will have a nice colorful margin on the inside of the card.

10. Remove any excess pieces of paper, then glue together and fold in half. Voilà! Your very own greeting card!

LEARNING OUTCOMES

- Patrons learn about popular vector design software used in the industry.
- Basic principles of design are explored.
- Patrons gain an understanding of the limitations of designs when using a laser cutter or similar equipment.

RECOMMENDED NEXT PROJECTS

This project discussed a very basic design. Future projects can focus on creating more complex shapes and text to increase patron design skills and push the boundaries of what is possible with this technology. Additional projects can experiment with different materials, such as using fabric and cellophane as inserts within the card. These steps would also be helpful when designing with materials such as wood or acrylic that can be used for boxes, signs, and more.

Build a Six-Piece
Interlocking Burr Puzzle

ERIK CARLSON / LIBRARIAN I
White Plains Public Library

Type of Library Best Suited for: Any

Cost Estimate: CNC: about $2,000; Materials: about $4 per project

Makerspace Necessary? Yes (this could get messy)

PROJECT DESCRIPTION

The six-piece burr puzzle will get your makers to think more about how a CNC mill machine cuts, and how to draft out a diagram. There are some small challenges involved, and participants will use some problem-solving skills to cut the pieces out. It may take milling two or three puzzles before it comes out just right. Of course, you can lay it out for them, but that's no fun. This program can be a bit nostalgic for older library users who used to play with wooden puzzles like these when they were younger, and interesting to younger people who enjoy puzzles and want to try making one of their own.

You can find diagrams online to download at www.craftsmanspace.com/free -projects/six-piece-burr-puzzles.html. These diagrams range from simple to complex. You can also find larger puzzles with more interlocking pieces if you and your makers are up for a bigger challenge. If you do not have access to a CNC mill machine, you can 3D print these pieces. The design process is fairly easy, but you can create some really colorful puzzles this way.

OVERVIEW

I teach this class in one 1.5-hour session with no more than five participants. By the end of the class, each person should be able to create the toolpaths for each of the puzzle pieces. A CNC mill machine will be able to cut out each puzzle piece fairly quickly. I ask participants to schedule time with me to run the machine. Alternatively, you can schedule a second session to mill the puzzle pieces.

MATERIALS LIST

- 48 × ½-inch square dowels
- Diagrams of burr puzzles
- Graph paper

NECESSARY EQUIPMENT

- CNC mill machine
- One computer for each participant
- Sandpaper
- Handsaw or table saw
- Chisel

NECESSARY SOFTWARE

- Basic CAM program, such as MakerCAM.com

FIGURE 33.1

Completed CNC burr puzzle

STEP-BY-STEP INSTRUCTIONS

To get started, let's cut our square dowels. Each participant will need six 3-inch pieces, but we should have a couple of extra pieces cut just in case.

Choose a diagram to design and use graph paper to draw out the puzzle pieces. Here is the design that I am using for these instructions. For the complete puzzle there are two pieces for Parts 1 and 2, and one piece for Part 3. Part 4, the sixth piece, is left uncut and is used for solving the puzzle.

There are no measurements in this diagram, since the size of the cuts depends on the size of the dowels you are using. I cut the dowels into 3 inches to make the conversion simple since each piece can be broken down to three equal sections. So for Part 1, the first and third inches will be left uncut, and the middle inch will have a quarter-inch cut out of it. I draw out all three pieces on graph paper with the correct measurements.

Next, open MakerCAM.com. MakerCAM is free to use and runs off your browser, so you don't need to download anything or create accounts. It is mainly used to create g-code, which is the program language that tells your CNC machine what to do. It has some simple design features that we are going to use to cut out our puzzle pieces with. There is a tutorial on the MakerCAM.com website that shows how to use the software.

We are going to use MakerCAM.com to add rectangles to the work plane. First find the intersection of the X-Y axis by using the "Hand" tool found at the top of the page. Each square on the grid is "1." Click on "Insert" in the main menu and then choose "Rectangle." Set the Width to 0.5" and the Height to 3" and click on "Ok." This will give us the dimensions of the piece of wood we are going to cut. Next, place the Rectangle on the intersection of the X-Y axis. You can move pieces by highlighting them in

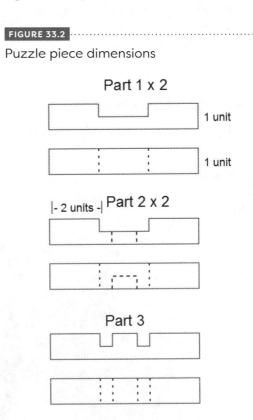

Puzzle piece dimensions

Part 1 x 2

1 unit

1 unit

|- 2 units -| Part 2 x 2

Part 3

red, then clicking and holding the mouse when it is placed on one of the lines. Make sure to zoom in on the grid so that the rectangle is placed right on the X-Y axis.

Now try to figure out how to add the first cut. You need to be able to see all of the negative space (area you are cutting out) as a shape, namely a rectangle. The first cut is a one-inch rectangle in the middle of the dowel. You will probably add a rectangle with a Width of 0.5 inch and a Height of 1 inch. This is fine, but the trick is to have the cut wider than the dowel in order to have a clean cut when the machine is finished. The dowel is 0.5 inch wide, so the cut should be 0.75 inch wide. When you teach a class this, you can have them discover this for themselves after they mill the first piece.

Now we will add the toolpath. Click on "CAM" on the main menu and then choose "Pocket Operation." Here is where they will add the depth, "0.25." I set the "Step Down Rate" to 0.03125" and I am using a 0.125" mill bit. I also change the "Feedrate" to 30, and the "Plungerate" to 10. Click on the "View Cuts" box in the upper right of the screen. Then go back to "CAM" and select "Calculate All." You should see the cuts that the machine will make. Go back to "CAM" and select "Export Gcode" to save your work.

Go through this process to create the toolpaths for the next two pieces. The trick to Part 2 is using the same toolpath from Part 1 and then adding a toolpath for a smaller rectangle that is 0.25 × 0.5 × 0.25 inches. You will also need to figure out which toolpath to run first: the large rectangle from Part 1, or the small rectangle that they added for Part 2. The first time I tried to cut Part 2, I had to draw out the negative space on the piece of wood. This is a good way to visualize the cut. Depending on how you place the piece of wood, you may need to chisel out the corners so they come out square. This will be another learning experience for you, and you may choose to recut an extra piece.

FIGURE 33.3 ....

Finished puzzle pieces

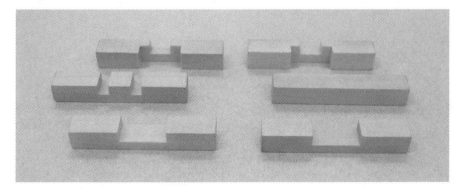

For Part 3 you will add a rectangle 1 inch up from the bottom and 1 inch down from the top. Both cuts are $0.75 \times 0.25 \times 0.25$ inches (make the width wider than the piece of wood by 0.25 inch to get a clean cut across).

When you have finished creating the toolpaths and saved them, you are ready to cut the pieces. Clamp the wood down, set up your CNC machine, and show them how to send their g-code to your CNC machine. I use a Shapeoko 2, so to operate the machine I use GRBL software.

When all five pieces have been cut, follow the instructions to assemble the puzzle. These can be great gifts or a fun way for participants to challenge their friends.

LEARNING OUTCOMES

Participants will learn:

- To create toolpaths with CAM software
- To set up and operate a CNC mill machine
- Problem solving-skills
- Drafting and proportions

RECOMMENDED NEXT PROJECTS

Once you are comfortable with this design, you can challenge yourself to cut out more pieces for a more complicated puzzle, and then try a nine-piece puzzle.

Create a Cardboard Sculpture Using a Laser Cutter

JACQUELINE R. MITCHELL / CREATIVE PRODUCTION LAB MANAGER
University of Nebraska at Omaha Criss Library

Type of Library Best Suited for: Any

Cost Estimate: $20–$30 ($5,000–$10,000 for laser cutting method)

Makerspace Necessary? No

PROJECT DESCRIPTION

This project guides you through the process of converting a 3D file to a physical 3D model using a flat medium such as cardboard. The best way to complete this project is to use a laser cutter within a makerspace. However, if you have patience and a knack for cutting, you can use a box cutter or X-ACTO knife and a cutting mat. This may limit you in how intricate you can get with your model and it is more time-consuming. If you are using this method, I highly recommend starting with very basic shapes. A laser cutter may be a worthwhile investment if you plan to conduct many of these types of projects in the future.

OVERVIEW

Patrons find a 3D model, then import the model into the recommended software. They assign their build settings according to their preferences and the limitations of their medium.

FIGURE 34.1 ....

Laser-cut cardboard sculpture

MATERIALS LIST

- Cardboard
- Glue

NECESSARY EQUIPMENT

- Computer
- Laser cutter, if available. If unavailable, follow box cutter method.
- 123D Make (123dapp.com/make) (As of 2017, 123D Make has changed to Slicer for Fusion 360. This tutorial is still applicable to the new software. Download here: http://tinyurl.com/yay7gsp8.)
- Calipers (if needed to measure depth of cardboard)
- X-ACTO blade or box cutter, if not using a laser cutter

STEP-BY-STEP INSTRUCTIONS

1. Find your 3D model. You can build a 3D model with free software like Tinkercad or Sketchup. You can also find creative commons models on sites like Yeggi.com. For your first project, I recommend a simple model.

2. Open up 123D Make and go to "Import" in the upper left-hand corner and select your design. You should be able to see the full model in the preview window.
3. Take a look at the settings to the left of the object. Here you can set the object size. The bigger you make your object, the more details you will see in the final design. However, you want to make sure your object will fit the size of your cardboard and laser cutter or paper, so be careful not to exceed those dimensions.
4. Set your "medium size." This option is located right above "object size." You can select an option from the list or create your own by clicking the pencil. If you choose the box cutter method for this project, you will want to set this size to the size of your printer paper. For the laser cutter, set the size to your cardboard pieces, making sure those pieces will fit into the bed of your laser. Use the calipers to measure the thickness of your cardboard material if needed, and enter that into the space for thickness. You can also adjust the margins here as well.
5. Take a look at all of the construction techniques listed below "object size." For this one, we will use stacked slices. Go to Assembly Steps, select "cardboard" at the bottom, and use the slider to slide through the object layer by layer. When the slider reaches a certain layer, you will see it become highlighted in the Assembly Reference to the right. In these settings, you can also add dowels for easier assembly, change the slicing direction, and modify the form.

FIGURE 34.2

123D Make assembly reference

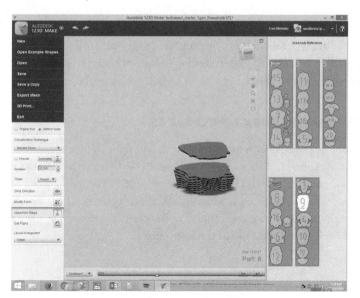

6. If everything looks okay, go to Get Plans on the bottom left. If you plan on using a box cutter, PDF will be fine to use. For the laser cutter, select either EPS or DXF. This is based on personal preference and the requirements of your machine.

7. Cut your pieces. For the box cutter/X-ACTO method, you will have to print each of the PDFs that are generated. You can cut out the individual pieces, then trace them onto the cardboard. Use the box cutter to cut them out. You will want to copy the numbers of the individual pieces on the new piece to prevent confusion when assembling. For the laser cutter, simply open the EPS or DXF and change the settings to match your laser cutter's requirements. This will vary per machine, so it is important to have a good understanding of how your machine operates when attempting this project. If you selected dowels, use a sturdier material such as wood to make them. You can still use cardboard for the layers. If you can, keep the pieces contained within the cardboard because it is easier to assemble later.

8. Assemble the pieces. I like to assemble the pieces prior to gluing, so I make sure everything looks okay before the real deal. This is when your software really comes in handy. Reference the assembly steps from your model in 123D Make to have a layer-by-layer guide. Follow the software and numbers and you will have it together in no time! When you feel confident in your assembly, glue the pieces together. Now you have a 3D object you created on your own!

LEARNING OUTCOMES

- Patrons learn how software can slice 3D models into layers.
- The project provides a great visualization and conceptualization tool showing how virtual 3D models can be translated to the physical world.
- Patrons now have an understanding of how 3D printers interpret 3D models in order to print them.

RECOMMENDED NEXT PROJECTS

Patrons can experiment with more complicated designs they model on their own or find online. Additionally, they can test different construction techniques to see how they compare with the method used in this example. If your library has capabilities for 3D scanning, patrons could scan objects, then replicate them with cardboard. Though not as cost-effective, media such as wood and acrylic can be used in place of cardboard for future projects with the laser cutter.

Create Hidden Treasure Boxes

AMANDA KRAMER AND BRIAN PALMER
Miller Library, Washington College

Type of Library Best Suited for: Any

Cost estimate: Approximately $10 per student

Makerspace Necessary? Yes

PROJECT DESCRIPTION

Participants create tiny treasure boxes in this maker project that teaches basic laser-cutting skills. They hide the boxes with a note that instructs the finder to share the impact of their find on Instagram.

OVERVIEW

Sometimes a small gesture can prove to be incredibly powerful.

Students in the Washington College "Cultivating a Maker Mindset Course" learned this when they had the chance to Skype with artist Danika Brubaker during the semester. Brubaker is the Madison (Wisconsin) founder of the social art movement #fortheonewhofindsme. She encourages people of all ages to create tiny flower bouquets and hide them in public locales. When the finders locate the bouquets—which are labeled with instructions—they take a selfie and post their treasure on Instagram with the hashtag #fortheonewhofindsme.

This is a similar project that is simple and inexpensive and will give your patrons the chance to learn about the power of kindness. And it also seamlessly connects your patrons to a larger creative movement via social media. Check out http://fortheone whofindsme.com/ and www.instagram.com/fortheonewhofindsme/.

MATERIALS LIST

- 12 pieces of 3-mm Baltic birch plywood
- Minwax polyurethane spray
- 5-pack of 150 grit sandpaper
- 1-gallon bottle of wood glue
- 1-inch-wide roll of blue painters tape

NECESSARY EQUIPMENT

- Laser cutter
- Air compressor, brush, or paper towels to clean dust
- Space to spread out and work

STEP-BY-STEP INSTRUCTIONS

Day 1 of Project

1. Start by creating the individual wood components using your makerspace's laser cutter. We've included Adobe Illustrator files in the "Additional Online Resources" link (at the end of this chapter) with plans for a single box and plans for a batch to maximize the use of a full sheet of 12 × 24-inch 3-mm plywood, which fits in our laser. *Note:* Depending on the power of your laser, the cutting can take a little time. On our laser, etching the message on a set of 6 boxes filling a 12 × 24-inch sheet of plywood took about 40 minutes, followed by another few minutes to cut the pieces out. As teachers, we wanted to share the experience of the laser cutting and etching with our students who helped design the boxes in a previous class. Rather than making them wait through the whole process to prepare the wood for the boxes, we prepared most of the wood in advance.

2. Before gluing the boxes together, instruct a group of participants to take each piece of wood and clean up any burn/smoke marks from the laser cutter with sandpaper. *Note:* It's easy to do this before the boxes are glued up, but difficult to sand the insides of the outer casing and removable drawer once the boxes are assembled.

3. With sanding complete, use an air compressor to dust off the wood, or simply wipe the wood clean with a brush or paper towel to help the glue adhere.

4. Apply glue to the tabs on all the pieces of the boxes, and assemble the five sides of the drawer and the pull handle, using blue painters tape to hold the joints tight while the glue dries. Use the same method to assemble the five pieces that comprise the outer casing. Use a damp paper towel to remove glue squeeze-out now while it's easy to clean up.

Day 2 of Project

1. With the gift boxes dry, instruct the participants to remove all the blue painter's tape and sand the boxes smooth and clean. Participants need to be sure the drawers slide easily into the outer casings, because the fit will be even tighter once the boxes are sprayed with polyurethane.

2. When the sanding is complete, use an air compressor, a brush, or paper towels to dust off the wood, and then take the boxes to a location where you can spray polyurethane on them. Apply a light spray coat to each set of drawer and outer casing and set it aside to dry.

3. Fill your treasure boxes with a fun trinket from the local dollar store, or slip a motivational quote inside. It will be fun for the "finder" to open the small box and see the surprise inside.

FIGURE 35.1

Finished treasure box

LEARNING OUTCOMES

- Participants are encouraged to develop their own artistic "eye."
- Participants learn how to use a laser cutter.
- Participants learn how to participate in an art movement through social media.

RECOMMENDED NEXT PROJECTS

Invite participants to continue the goodwill. Hiding small projects you create in your makerspace at your school or library serves as a fabulous way to get the word out about your space, and more importantly, can go a long way toward brightening someone's day. Here are some suggestions for little projects to hide:

- Laser etch small pieces of leather with your library or school logo and attach them to small key rings for a keychain.
- Create mini-terrariums with plants and dirt packed inside small fishbowls.
- Additional Online Resources for this project: https://goo.gl/ZTzBEA.

36

Build
Bluetooth Speakers

BRIAN PALMER / DIRECTOR, DIGITAL MEDIA SERVICES
Library and Academic Technology at Washington College

Type of Library Best Suited for: Any

Cost Estimate: $114 per participant

Makerspace Necessary? Yes

PROJECT DESCRIPTION

As a society, we've generally grown beyond the days of the mid-twentieth-century Heathkit, when the economical solution to owning electronic devices was to build one from a kit. We live in a disposable world, where most people don't know what's inside the devices they use, and when those devices stop working, we discard them. This is where makerspaces play a crucial role in educating our youth and adults alike, helping people realize they can make many of the things they want, and even create new tools and toys the world may never have seen before.

The Bluetooth Stereo Speaker project is designed to increase maker confidence, enabling students to create something useful with their hands from components and raw materials, instead of buying a sealed product with no understanding of what makes it tick. During the build sessions explained here, instructors can draw parallels to related real-world component-based systems, like electric vehicles and personal computers, thereby helping students to become active participants in solving problems as makers.

FIGURE 36.1 ....

Bluetooth Speaker build components

OVERVIEW

Building Bluetooth Speakers introduces makers to a number of different technical, design, and fabrication concepts. This project was designed as the final project in our "Cultivating a Maker Mindset" first-year research and writing class at Washington College, but it also encourages students to be makers outside the classroom and as part of our Makers Union student club. At the college level, we encourage students to make the project their own. This optional customization starts as individual consultations with any students who express a desire to customize their speakers. Instructors then steer them to be prepared to make those customizations, whether it means adding or changing electronics or considering different materials and methods of construction.

The Bluetooth Speakers can be as unique and interesting as the students who build them, and can be as much an expressive extension of themselves in visual appearance as the choice of music they play. The speakers also serve as a fantastic advertisement for the library or makerspace, sparking conversations about their origins.

Although a kit can be purchased online, like those from Kitables (https://goo.gl/zCkPmM), we decided to design our own kits for our students, allowing us to choose specific components for what we feel is a much better finished product. This also allows us to take into account the customization interests of each student. In addition to the instruction in this project, we encourage you to reference the "Additional Online Resources" collection of files we've curated just for this book (https://goo.gl/

KVN65W). This includes the Illustrator designs we created for our laser cutter, our wiring diagrams, and updates to specific hardware and components we found useful.

MATERIALS LIST

Required parts for building each kit

Quantity	Price Each	Item	
1	$24.99	Rockler—DIY speaker kit, 5-inch woofer	https://goo.gl/x5Qfxt
1	$39.90	Wondom AA-AC11162 Bluetooth amplifier	https://goo.gl/y9486w
1	$7.99	Wondom AA-JA11113 battery board	https://goo.gl/Mvhqhh
1	$4.99	Wondom AA-JA11112 interface board	https://goo.gl/u10SKO
1	$1.31	5.5 mm x 2.5 mm DC power jack	https://goo.gl/3r015e
1	$7.90	15-volt AC to DC power supply	https://goo.gl/qXeszG
1	$9.00	½ pack of 6 EBL 18650 lithium batteries	https://goo.gl/pjf7g5
1	$0.35	1/20th pack of power switches	https://goo.gl/ZJnfhG
1	$1.78	1/5th pack of M3 nylon standoffs	https://goo.gl/t7Tew1
1	$7.50	¼-inch thick 5 x 5-foot Baltic birch plywood, from local supplier	1
8	$0.08	#4 x ¾-inch pan head screws (buy a box of 100 for discount)	8
1	$4.00–$8.00	Finish of your choice (we used clear and black spray paint)	1

NECESSARY EQUIPMENT

- Laser cutter (can be substituted by saws)
- Random orbit sander and paper
- Wood glue (purchase by the gallon to refill small containers)
- Hot glue gun (high-temp glue works best for this, but requires caution)

- Clamps (masking tape can be substituted)
- Soldering iron and solder
- Screwdrivers
- Wire stripper/crimper and spare spade connectors

STEP-BY-STEP INSTRUCTIONS

1.5–2 Months before Build Day 1

Buy all the necessary components well in advance. It's best to purchase an extra set for the instructor to use while demonstrating the assembly and one or more extra sets of parts in case someone breaks something. In a pinch, the instructor can give up his parts as well in order to keep a student's project moving forward. *Note:* We chose these stereo components for their great quality and price value, but at that time their manufacturers were often short of stock. Order these well in advance. Use the "Additional Online Resources" link for recommended substitutions if necessary.

1 Month before Build Day 1–Optional

Meet with the students who will build these speakers and give them an overview of what the project will entail. This is a good chance to explain where they may be able to customize and alter the plans, which will be greatly enabled/limited by your makerspace's equipment and support. If there are additional supplies the students will need, order them now. We had students customize parts such as the type of wood used, decorative laser etching, and even the integration of electronics for sound-reactive LED lighting. You can see examples of some of the students' creations in the "Additional Online Resources" link.

Make sure it is clear to the students that they will need to put in additional time outside of the scheduled build sessions if they wish to customize their speakers. As the instructor, be sure you can support and steer what they are asking to try if they are new to these technologies.

1 Month before Build Day 1

We wanted to tackle the soldering for the DC power jack and the power switch in advance of the build days in order to simplify the project. We did the soldering for them and supplied the finished DC jack cable and DC power button cable as part of their kits to prevent a project build bottleneck.

Now is a good time to laser cut the plywood enclosure pieces. Each speaker has six flat sides, four thin internal brackets, and three small pieces for a volume knob. Since there are two enclosures per kit you are building, this totals 23 pieces per student.

This cutting will take time! On our laser it took about 25 minutes of cutting time per kit with ¼-inch Baltic birch.

In the "Additional Online Resources" link, you will find an Adobe Illustrator file that has the design layout for a set of speakers to be cut from ¼-inch Baltic birch. We used the free www.makercase.com utility to create a finger-jointed box with the interior dimensions of 9¾ × 5¾ × 7 inches, then modified it as needed in Illustrator to fit all the components. You can use our designs as is, but you may find that a little more preparation work will save you materials and time in creating multiple kits. Considering the bed size of the laser cutter in your makerspace (or in your local makerspace if you don't have a laser in your library), create an Illustrator document the maximum size the laser can use. Copy the pieces from our design and lay out the parts in order to best fit them and to minimize wasted material and unnecessary pre-cutting of the plywood into laser cutter-friendly sized sections from the 5 × 5-foot original sheets. Once you have a game plan for your cutting, purchase the appropriate number of 5 × 5-foot sheets of Baltic birch. Often you can have the lumber yard make the major dividing cuts, which will make the wood easier to transport with a typical car and save you some cutting time later.

After laser cutting all the wood pieces, organize the wood, various electronic components, and speakers into individual kits for the students. We used recycled cardboard boxes for each student.

FIGURE 36.2 ....

Cutting the wood pieces

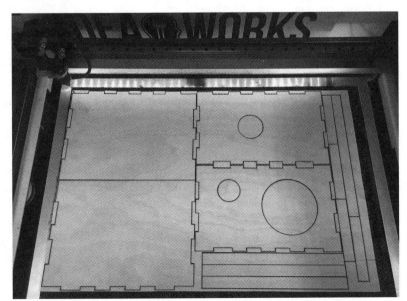

Build Day 1: Overview of Components and Enclosure Assembly

1. Start with an overview of the project and the components used. Explain what each component does. Have students open their kits and follow along with their own parts in hand for a closer examination. You can tailor this discussion's depth to the ability level of the group.

2. Next, take the wood pieces for one enclosure and lay out the front piece face down on a worktable. Align the top, bottom, and sides all facing down so the finger joints mesh up like a big plus symbol. Apply glue to the finger joints and assemble the pieces into a rectangular box, leaving off the back panel for now. Use clamps or blue tape to hold them together while they dry. Glue the four thin internal support brackets around the inside perimeter of the rear opening, leaving enough depth for the rear panel to sit flush when it is screwed on later.

3. *Important:* Use a damp paper towel to clean off glue squeeze-out now while it's easy to remove. Repeat the glue-up assembly process for the second speaker enclosure and set them both aside to dry.

Build Day 2: Finish the Enclosures and Build Speaker-Wiring Harnesses

1. Begin the second day by removing the clamps or blue tape from the enclosures. Each student should use a sander or hand sand the wood enclosures to prepare the surface for paint or clear polyurethane. Before painting, clean off the sanding dust. We used an air compressor to blow the dust off the pieces. Don't forget to prepare the rear panel as well!

2. Take the enclosures and rear panels to a location where you can spray or brush on your paint or clear polyurethane. If you don't have a good location due to fumes and overspray, consider using a low-odor water-based wipe-on polyurethane or water-based paint and brushes. Give the enclosures a light first finish coat and leave them to dry.

3. Returning to the worktables, lead the students through the diagram for building the two wiring harnesses for the speakers within each case (provided in the "Additional Online Resources"). There are differences between the harnesses in the powered and the passive speakers, so be sure the students follow the wiring diagram carefully. It is likely some students will poorly crimp some wires, which will easily pull apart. Have them test their crimps by gently pulling at the connections. Have a pack of similarly sized crimp-on connectors ready to allow them a second try at crimping any bad connections.

4. To finish up the day, return to the enclosures and give a second light coat of spray-on finish. It should be dry enough for a second coat if they didn't apply the first coat too heavily. Tell them the first coat is not fully dried yet, so they

should be careful not to handle the speakers between coats or they may get fingerprints in the finish. Leave the speakers to dry until the next build day.

Build Day 3: Installing the Components and First Test of the Speakers

FIGURE 36.3 ·

Wiring the speakers

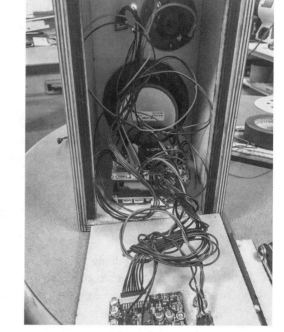

1. Begin by reviewing the electronic components with the students, and walk them through connecting the main Bluetooth amp with the interface board and the 18650 battery board with the supplied ribbon cables. Be sure to point out that the cables only fit properly in one direction (make reference to one side of the connector having ridges or however you best identify the cables in your kit if they happen to look slightly different).

2. Continue by following the wiring diagram we supply in the "Additional Online Resources" link. It outlines the connections between the components, as well as the LEDs, volume knob, DC power jack, speakers, and other parts that are mounted on the front and rear panels of the powered speaker. Stack the 18650 battery board on top of the Bluetooth amp using 3-mm standoffs, which also provide legs to support the stack in the bottom of the powered speaker. A generous blob of hot glue will secure these feet to the bottom inside of the powered speaker. As shown in the wiring diagram, the passive speaker is much simpler, getting its audio feed out of the terminal cup on the powered speaker and into the terminal cup on the passive speaker.

3. Before you close up the two speakers, each with four #4 ¾-inch screws, loosely stuff half the acoustic insulation from the speaker kit into each of the speakers, which will improve the low-frequency performance of the speakers. Finally, you can connect the speakers with the remaining foot of speaker wire, or use

other speaker wire you provide to separate the speakers further on a desk or across a bookshelf or room. With the speaker's power on, you'll notice your Bluetooth-connected phone can control the volume, as can the wired volume knob on the face of the powered speaker. It is great fun to see the students' faces light up as they reach the moment when they can play music from their own phones on their speakers.

LEARNING OUTCOMES

As a result of this project, students will:

- Gain a working knowledge of Bluetooth Speaker system components, including multicell lithium battery management systems.
- Gain a basic understanding of the acoustic properties in the design of the enclosures.
- Understand from a high level how a 3D design can be broken into 2D parts, and how Adobe Illustrator can be used to control a CNC laser cutter with extreme precision.
- Gain comfort in assembling and finishing a project made from wood.
- Become comfortable reading a simple wiring diagram, connecting the printed circuit boards and components using the supplied cables, and making their own wiring harnesses using a wire stripper/crimper tool.

RECOMMENDED NEXT PROJECTS

There are several projects that can stem from what was learned in the Bluetooth Speaker build project. Here are a few suggestions using some of the same tools and types of components:

- Basics of design using Adobe Illustrator for cutting and etching with a CO_2 laser cutter
- Build your own PC from components, including a custom laser-cut wood or acrylic case
- Build a portable all-in-one computer using a Raspberry Pi, a scavenged laptop screen, 18650 lithium batteries, and a custom laser-cut enclosure

Create Stamps to Tell Stories

LIZZIE NOLAN / LIBRARIAN
San Jose Public Library

Type of Library Best Suited for: Any

Cost Estimate: $10 per participant

Makerspace Necessary? Yes

PROJECT DESCRIPTION

Make a mark! Learn about Ghanaian culture by creating Adinkra stamps that then serve as inspiration for creative short stories. This two-part project for tweens combines textile arts, creative writing skills, and cultural awareness. A makerspace with a vinyl cutter is useful to create the stamps, but a scissors or box cutter can also be used instead.

OVERVIEW

Adinkra are traditional printed or stamped symbols on clothing and artwork made by the Ashanti people in Ghana, West Africa. Adinkra (pronounced ah-DEENK-rah) symbols date back to the nineteenth century when King Adinkra was a king from what is now the Ivory Coast. Each one of these symbols has a specific meaning such as jealousy, wisdom, hope, and so on. Strung together on a piece of fabric or artwork, the different symbols can tell a story, or offer a word of advice or warning. Depending on the tools available, tweens can draw or trace the established symbols, or they can design their own onto a sponge cloth or foam pieces directly and cut those out with a scissors or a box cutter. Or middle schoolers can use a computer design program and a vinyl cutter, such as Silhouette Cameo or Cricut cutter, for more intricate designs. Inspired by these symbols, tweens can explore Western story structure to create their own short stories.

MATERIALS LIST

- Craft foam pieces/sponge cloth
- Sticky notes for tracing
- Tempera paint, fabric paint (depends on your choice of medium)
- White butcher's paper, or fabric, or bags, or muslin bags, pillowcase, or notebooks
- Craft glue
- Chopsticks or cardboard

NECESSARY EQUIPMENT

- Vinyl cutter
- Computer(s)
- Scissors/box cutters (if no vinyl cutter)
- Sharpie markers
- Pencils

STEP-BY-STEP INSTRUCTIONS

Welcome

Explain to students the origins of Adinkra stamps.[1] Explore examples[2] and watch online[3] videos to understand the traditional creation process.

Creating Symbols

Just as in traditional processes, each artist has his or her own take on a symbol. (*Note:* The creation process will differ if a vinyl cutter is available.) Have students draw a design on a sticky note. You can use a traditional Adinkra design or design your own. If making an original, be sure to assign it a meaning. If going the high-tech route, teens can design their symbol in simple programs like Microsoft Paint or even Microsoft PowerPoint by inserting shapes and playing with their placement, size, and thickness.

Students can upload their designs into the vinyl cutter web applications and follow the instructions for cutting into craft foam, cardboard, and so on.

For the low-tech route, tweens can stick their sticky note directly onto the sponge cloth and cut out the negative space with scissors or a box cutter (with adult help.) Once the stamps are created, make a stamp backer or handles with large foam pieces (use craft glue) or chopsticks. Stamp your stamp on your fabric, bag, and so on.

Storytelling

When people in Ghana make Adinkra cloth, they often create several different designs. By alternating stamps or using different stamps on different parts of the cloth, these designs can tell a story. Often stories in the Western part of the world follow this "story spine" or outline for the basic plot of the story:

Once upon a time there was _____.

Every day, _____.

Until one day _____.

Because of that, _____.

Because of that, _____.

Until finally _____.

So for example, the movie Frozen's Outline or "Story Spine" would look a little like this:

Once upon a time there were **two happy princesses, Elsa and Ana.**

Every day, **Elsa would make magical winter creations for Ana.**

Until one day, **Elsa accidentally hurt Ana.**

Until one day, **Elsa and Ana's parents die in a shipwreck.**

Because of that, **Elsa disguises her powers.**

Because of that, **Elsa gets upset and blankets the town in snow because of a magic curse.**

Because of that, **Elsa disappears into a frozen castle. And Ana searches to find her.**

Until finally, **Ana and Elsa reunite and break the magic curse.**

FIGURE 37.1 ···

Word association brainstorm

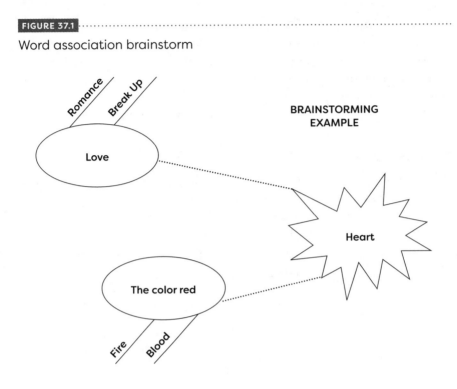

Have students use the symbols they choose to brainstorm story ideas. Here is an example of word association brainstorming:

After the word association example, ask students to brainstorm characters and settings by asking them the questions listed below. Since students are writing "short stories," have them only develop two or three characters with one or two settings.

Characters	Settings
What is their name?	Does this place have a name?
What do they look like?	What does it look like?
How old are they?	What does it sound like?
Where were they born?	What does it smell like?
How do they dress?	Are there any furniture or objects?
How do they walk?	Is this place real or imaginary?
How do they talk?	What kind of people live here?
How do they act with . . . their family? Their friends? Strangers?	

Characters	Settings
What do they love?	
What do they dislike?	
What do they believe?	
Who do they care most about in the world?	

Once students have enough to work off of, have them sketch out the story by filling in the story spine. From there have them start writing! If time allows, share the stories with the class.

LEARNING OUTCOMES

○ Participants will have designed their own stamps using the vinyl cutter and have completed a unique short story using these designs.

This program aligns with the following Common Core Standard

○ CCSS.ELA-LITERACY.W.6.3 Write narratives to develop real or imagined experiences or events using effective technique, relevant descriptive details, and well-structured event sequences.

RECOMMENDED NEXT PROJECTS

○ Enjoy more creative writing games and props. Try a modified version of the Exquisite Corpse game but with the Story Spine as the inspiration instead of drawings.
○ There are also many different options for the stamp material and different kinds of fabrics, paper, and so on.
○ Learn more about other aspects of Ghanaian culture such as hiplife music, games, and food recipes on the "Australia to Zimbabwe" website.[4]

Notes
1. Adinkra orgins, http://kidworldcitizen.org/2011/12/17/adinkra-fabric-printing -from-ghana/.
2. Adinkra symbol examples, www.adinkra.org/htmls/adinkra_index.htm.
3. Adrinkra online background, https://www.youtube.com/watch?v=6CdCrjUiEVk &feature=youtu.be&t=1m27s.
4. "Australia to Zimbabwe" website: www.australiatozimbabwe.com/ghana/.

Scribble Droid: Making a Robot out of Found Objects

LAURA BAKER / LIBRARIAN FOR DIGITAL RESEARCH AND LEARNING
Abilene Christian University Library

Type of Library Best Suited for: Public, School

Cost Estimate: $40–$50 per group of 10 makers (not including optional solder equipment)

Makerspace Necessary? No, unless using solder

PROJECT DESCRIPTION

In this project, makers will use a combination of new and recycled objects to create a motorized device that scribbles by itself as it moves across a flat surface. Makers will take apart a small toy to reveal the motor inside. Repurposing the motor, they will wire it to a battery to make a complete circuit and will modify the motor to make it vibrate as it spins. The droid's body is made from cups, cardboard tubes, and other items from the recycle bin. The legs are made from felt-tipped markers. When the offset motor is attached to the droid's body, the vibration causes the droid to bounce and spin in a unique pattern, leaving a colorful marker design in its wake.

FIGURE 38.1 ··

Scribble Android video at youtu.be/KVR-ac04qjc

OVERVIEW

During the summer, the Abilene Christian University Library holds a 2–3 day Maker Camp for kids. This activity is geared toward 4th–6th grade kids and middle schoolers, but we have also involved adult teachers and college students who want a fun way to learn basic circuitry. The activity can take 4–8 hours depending on how much kids decorate and tweak their androids.

This project is an interesting combination of new and recycled objects. It also combines the mechanics of circuitry with the aesthetics of decorating the android's exterior, creating a fun merging of engineering and art.

For the toy to take apart, we have used inexpensive objects like battery-powered toy cars or pocket fans from the dollar store. Instead of repurposing a toy motor, however, the library can buy motors in advance.

MATERIALS LIST (PER MAKER)

- Mechanical toy for repurposing *or* buy a motor:
    - https://www.amazon.com/dp/B01HQH36AK (with wires)
    - www.mcmelectronics.com/product/28–12811 (no wires)
- Two AA batteries
- Thick rubber bands
- Felt-tipped markers

- Strong tape such as duct tape, painters tape, or even book tape (masking tape can work if used generously)
- Clean recycled containers (water bottles, empty yogurt containers, cardboard mailing tube cut into four-inch sections, packing foam chunks, etc.)
- Paper for the android to draw on
- Decorating supplies: crayons, markers, stickers, cardboard scraps, pipe cleaners, bits of fabric, yarn, wooden craft sticks, and so on

NECESSARY EQUIPMENT

- Hot glue gun
- Scissors
- Screwdrivers
- Optional: soldering irons and solder, extra wire, wire cutters or knife for stripping wire

STEP-BY-STEP INSTRUCTIONS

1. Use screwdrivers and scissors to take apart a small mechanical toy. Find and remove the motor inside. The motor will have two wires coming from it. You may need to re-solder the wires to the motor or replace them with newer, longer wire for more room later on. If the library purchased a motor, you can skip this step.
2. Connect the AA batteries to each other. Place two AA batteries side by side with the positive end of one battery up and the negative end of the other battery up. Tape them together so they form a pack. Cut a small piece of new wire about two inches long. Using a knife or wire strippers, remove the insulation from both ends of the wire. Solder one end to the positive node of the first battery and the other end to the negative end of the second battery. You should now have a battery pack with a small loop of wire joining the batteries at one end.
3. Connect the motor to the battery pack. Attach the wires coming from the motor to the free ends of the batteries, the ends that are not connected by the loop of wire. Solder one motor wire to the free positive end of one battery. If not using solder, hold the wires in place with tape or a wide rubber band. Connect the other motor wire to the free negative end of the second battery. As soon as the second wire touches the battery, the motor should run. Secure this second wire with tape or a rubber band so you can remove and reconnect it at will to turn the motor off and on. Congratulations! You have just made a complete circuit.

FIGURE 38.2

Wires connecting motor and batteries

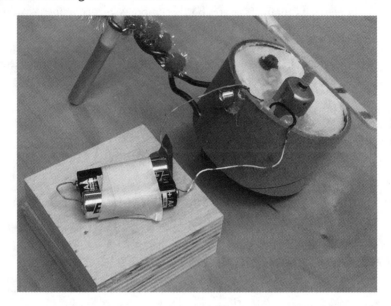

4. Add something to the motor shaft to offset the motor. The motor needs to spin something off balanced so it will vibrate enough to move the droid. Wads of tape, craft sticks, or a small washer work well. If gluing, be sure not to get glue inside the motor.
5. Build the android body. Empty water bottles, upside-down plastic cups, and portions of mailing tubes work well. Have fun decorating the droid with stickers, pipe cleaners, and other supplies.
6. Attach the felt-tipped markers for legs or arms. Make sure the android can stand by itself.
7. Strap the motor and battery pack onto the android. Make sure the propeller has enough room to turn without hitting the robot.
8. Connect the wires to turn on the motor. The vibration should cause the android to bounce along on its marker legs and draw interesting patterns on a piece of paper.
9. Experiment with different placements for the motor, different heights of the marker legs, and different weights of propellers. Each change will create a new scribble pattern.
10. For extra fun, unroll a long length of butcher paper and tape it to the floor. Have several of the scribble droids drawing at the same time. Be sure to display the finished artwork in the library to showcase what your makers did.

FIGURE 38.3

Scribble art display

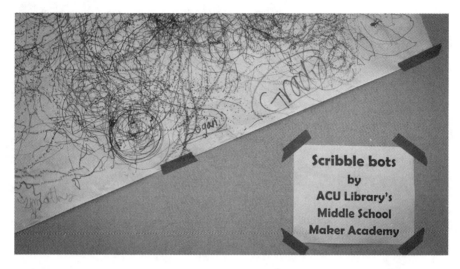

LEARNING OUTCOMES

- Explore new uses for everyday objects.
- Combine low technology with high technology to form new objects.
- Learn how to wire a complete circuit and to fix broken circuits.
- Investigate variables of balance, motion, weight, speed, and direction upon movement patterns.
- Appreciate how both art and mechanics work together to make a pleasing design.

RECOMMENDED NEXT PROJECTS

Add a switch to the motor/battery circuit to make it easier to turn on and off. The switch goes between one of the wires going from the motor to the battery. You can buy a switch from an electronics store or make your own using a paper clip or other metal object that you clip or unclip to the wire to complete the connection.

Build Solar Robots

JESSICA LOGAN / BRANCH MANAGER
Hamilton Mill Branch, Gwinnett County Public Library

Type of Library Best Suited for: Any

Cost Estimate: $25 per group of 2–4

Makerspace Necessary? No

PROJECT DESCRIPTION

Desiring to host a program that challenges youth to learn about the benefits and uses of solar energy, the Gwinnett County Public Library purchased several "14 in 1" Educational Solar Robot kits from OWI Robots (owirobot.com) to be shared among the system's fifteen branches. With renewable energy playing such a pivotal role in sustainability, now is the perfect time to start children on the path to learning the basic concepts behind these technologies. The OWI Robots kits were evaluated by the Gwinnett County Public Library and were determined to be both an educational and fun method for youth to learn about alternative energy concepts.

The Solar Robot program is a stand-alone event that can easily be held at any time during the year and is designed for middle school and high school students. Given the nature of solar energy, you may wish to have an alternate project available should the weather not cooperate on the date of your program. The kits allow for fourteen different configurations, so it is possible to reuse the kits repeatedly with several different outcomes. The pieces can be quite small, so we find that the assembly of the robots does not work well as an activity for participants younger than middle school, without the assistance of parents.

OVERVIEW

Solar Robots is a program that works well with teens and tweens, ages 12–18. We find that this age range should be strictly adhered to because the fourteen different configurations provided in the kit vary in difficulty and some of the pieces can be quite small. Most participants work in small groups for assembly and are generally able to complete this process in 30–45 minutes. Plan to start your participants off by initiating a group discussion about solar energy. Distribute the OWI Robot kits and allow the participants to form groups for assembling the kits. Many of our students tend to form sibling groups or pair with friends; we also have had groups form over a shared interest in the assembly of a particular robot configuration. We find that groups of 2–4 individuals are ideal.

FIGURE 39.1 ....

Solar robot kit

Allow participants time to work together to assemble their robots based on the instructions provided in the kits. You will want to remain available for those who may have questions or need assistance during the project. Once the groups begin to finish putting their robots together, allow them to go outside and test whether or not they have assembled all the components correctly. If there is enough sunlight available and the robot has been assembled properly, it will begin to move almost immediately.

MATERIALS LIST

- OWI 14-in-1 Robot Kits (participants can work in groups of 2–4 to cut down on cost)

NECESSARY EQUIPMENT

- Tables on which to assemble the robots
- Sunlight

STEP-BY-STEP INSTRUCTIONS

Prior to the start of the event, make sure to open each kit and remove the individual pieces from the plastic framing. This step is essential because many of the pieces will have extraneous sharp, plastic bits left behind from the removal of the framing. These plastic pieces will need to be filed down prior to use by the students—both for safety and proper assembly of the robots. This process can be tedious, time-consuming, and requires those handling the kits to keep all the pieces organized and separated by kit. That being said, we have found this step to be important prior to first use and essential to the success of your Solar Robot programs. Once the kits have been prepped for use, they can be assembled and disassembled repeatedly to allow for experimentation with various configurations and usage at various locations.

Begin the program with a discussion on solar energy, including its environmental benefits and applications. For example, you may wish to explain that solar power converts energy from the sun into electricity or heat. Because of this, it can replace facilities powered by oil, coal, and other nonrenewable fuels. Solar panels which are used to capture the energy in sunlight are becoming an increasingly common sight. Encourage the students to share places where they have noticed solar panels in action, including on rooftops, in calculators, and . . . robots, of course!

Once the participants have had an opportunity to read over the instructions and ask any related questions, distribute the OWI 14-in-1 Robot Kits—one per group. Together each group must decide which configuration they would like to attempt for the program.

As each group starts completing the assembly of its robot, invite them to take it outside into the sunlight to determine whether or not they have completed the process correctly. If there is enough sunlight available and the robot has been assembled properly, it will begin to come alive almost immediately. While the OWI Kit states that indoor halogen lighting will activate the robots, we have found that only bright sunlight really does the trick.

LEARNING OUTCOMES

Through this project, participants will . . .

- Explore the environmental benefits of solar energy.
- Learn about the real-world applications of solar energy and related technologies, including solar panels.
- Gain hands-on experience in robotic construction and assembly.

RECOMMENDED NEXT PROJECTS

The OWI 14-in-1 Solar Robot Kits have been a hit throughout the Gwinnett County Public Library system for several years. In an effort to expand our program offerings related to solar energy, we have also explored the construction of solar ovens. This is a logical next step since the participants are able to build an oven of their own design rather than following the set instructions provided in a kit. DIY Solar Ovens are also a hit program with children because they tend to involve food, obviously. S'mores are our go-to solar oven treat and the children inevitably go wild with excitement when they learn what we will be using the ovens for.

Another program that we recommend as a next project is something we call STEM Academy: LEGO Cityscape. This takes the idea of city planning and engineering and combines it with LEGOs . . . an instant hit, as you can imagine. This program is quite involved and is held over a period of several days. We ask participants to register ahead of time and commit to attending all days of the program because it is a cumulative learning experience. The participants work as a group to design a city from scratch, including all essential buildings, streets, and services. In building upon what our students learn about solar energy from other library programs, we encourage the STEM Academy participants to consider energy resources when making decisions about the layout of their city. More advanced groups of participants may also include programming using basic computers such as Raspberry Pi and/or Arduino for functions such as street lights and electricity needs for their LEGO city.

Robot Biomimicry

MICHAEL CHERRY / TEEN AND YOUTH LIBRARIAN
Evansville Vanderburgh Public Library

Type of Library Best Suited for: School or Public

Cost Estimate: $5,000–$10,000

Makerspace Necessary? No

PROJECT DESCRIPTION

The Robot Biomimicry program explores how engineers are inspired by animals, reptiles, and other living organisms in the design of real-world robots. In addition to exploring companies like Boston Dynamics and Festo, students learn how nature influenced Leonardo da Vinci's designs for flying machines. Students attending the classes build and program Lego Mindstorms and Lego WeDo robots. They must design a robot inspired by an animal, insect, or reptile and describe its form and function for a robot zoo.

OVERVIEW

This program is designed as a robotics camp for grades 2–4 and 5–8. The camp consists of four 90-minute programs and the classes are separated according to age groups. Students attending the 2nd–4th grade camp design and program Lego WeDo robots.

Students attending the 5th–8th grade camp design with Lego Mindstorms. This camp can be modified into a one-day workshop or special program, such as Hour of Code.

MATERIALS LIST

- Lego WeDo 2.0 sixteen-student classroom pack
- Lego Mindstorms EV3 and NXT 2.0
- Lego software and app
- Lego WeDo 2.0 curriculum pack
- Sample videos, books, and websites
- Rechargeable or AA batteries

NECESSARY EQUIPMENT

- iPads (3rd generation or newer)
- Laptops

STEP-BY-STEP INSTRUCTIONS

Day 1: Locomotion

Each day of the camp explores a different theme relating to biomimicry. Day one introduces students to the term *biomimicry* and examines the robotics design company Boston Dynamics. This is one of the leading companies utilizing biomimetic design in the construction of its robots.

Librarians can screen various videos of Boston Dynamics's robots that are accessible via the company's YouTube channel. The videos contain robots influenced by various creatures, including BigDog, Sand Flea, and Wildcat, among others. As students watch the videos, prompt them with discussion questions. For example, can students describe how these robots might aid humans at certain tasks? Are there limitations to the designs that may impede their intended functions? It is important to note that Boston Dynamics receives funding from the Defense Advanced Research Projects Agency (DARPA), an agency of the U.S. Department of Defense responsible for the development of technologies used by the military. Robots like BigDog are designed to aid in the transport of heavy military supplies.

After viewing and discussing the videos, students are tasked with designing their first robot. The 2nd–4th grade class designs the Lego WeDo tadpole from the Lego WeDo 2.0 curriculum. After building the tadpole, students program it to move forward by starting with the sample code Lego provides and then modifying the code with additional blocks. In addition, students transform the tadpole to a frog using Lego bricks and reprogram it. Whereas the tadpole included step-by-step instructions, the frog must be designed by the students.

Similarly, the 5th–8th grade class designs and programs a Lego Mindstorms frog. Step-by-step instructions for building a frog can be found in Fay Rhodes's book *Robots Alive!: Endangered Species*. Pieces can be modified to work with the Lego NXT 2.0 and EV3 kits. Upon completing their designs, students program their robots using the movement, sound, and wait blocks.

Day 2: Flight

Day two explores the use of aerial robots. Students are introduced to the work of Leonardo da Vinci. Da Vinci's drawings of early flying machines illustrate the use of biomimicry throughout history. Compare Da Vinci's sketches to the aerial robots manufactured by the German automation company Festo. Whereas the previous videos demonstrated the use of robots on land, Festo's biomimetic robots explore aerial terrain. The company's website contains a link to their research network called the Bionic Learning Network. The network contains various videos that illustrate aerial robots in the form of birds, butterflies, and dragonflies. Discussion questions may include: What potential uses do aerial robots have today? How can aerial robots aid with agriculture and various industrial applications?

Upon completing the videos, the 2nd–4th grade class designs and programs the Lego WeDo bee and flower from the Lego WeDo 2.0 curriculum. They program the bee to stop at the flower using the motor and motion sensor.

Similarly, the 5th–8th grade class builds and programs a winged creature using Lego Mindstorms. Each creature must be able to move its wings using the programming blocks. Advanced builders can incorporate the ultrasonic (NXT 2.0) or infrared sensor (EV3) to trigger this movement. Yoshihito Isogawa's book *The Lego Mindstorms EV3 Idea Book: 181 Simple Machines and Clever Contraptions* is a great resource for this activity. The chapter titled "Arms, Wings, and Other Movements" contains various wing designs. Additional chapters include designs for four-legged creatures and projects that resemble claws or jaws.

Day 3: Touch

Screen the video featuring Festo's robotic elephant arm from NOVA's television episode "Making Stuff Wilder." Portions of this PBS episode can be accessed via YouTube by searching "Robotic Arm Inspired by the Elephant Trunk." The video features a robotic arm inspired by an elephant trunk and fish fin. Discuss the ways robotic arms can aid in different industries, including aerospace and manufacturing.

Additionally, both classes begin work on their final project. Students must design an original robot for the robot zoo. Their robot can take the form of an animal, reptile, or insect and must aid in human development. Each robot must include a moveable feature, such as a tail, wings, legs, or other body part. Programmable sensors are optional.

FIGURE 40.1 ···

Lego Mindstorms raptor, 5th–8th grade

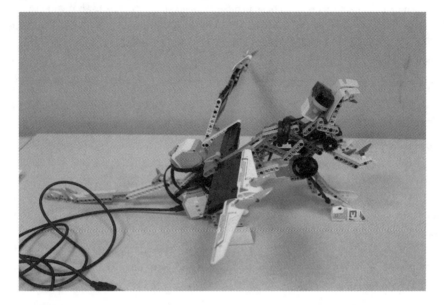

FIGURE 40.2 ···

Lego WeDo beetle, 2nd–4th grade

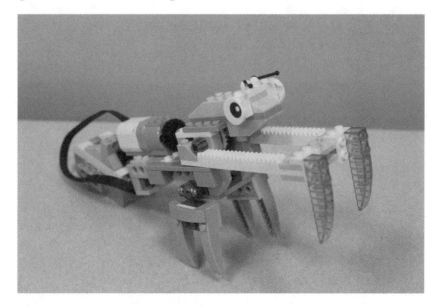

In addition to the books mentioned above, there are a variety of resources students could use to get started. For example, the Lego WeDo 2.0 curriculum contains a section called "open projects." These projects provide base models for building robots that walk, grab, push, wobble, or tilt. Many of the base models can be used to create different creatures. Elsewhere, the website www.nxtprograms.com contains free project instructions for building robots with Lego Mindstorms. Some of these projects include mammals and reptiles that may inspire students to think about their own designs.

Day 4: Health and Medicine

Screen the TEDx Cleveland State University video titled "Robot Biomimicry" featuring Professor Ton van den Bogert. As with the preceding videos, Professor van den Bogert's TED talk can be accessed via YouTube. This fascinating video describes the limits to the aforementioned BigDog and explores the use of robotic exoskeletons in human rehabilitation. Discuss other ways robots can aid with medical disabilities, such as personal assistants.

Finally, students complete their projects for the robot zoo. Each student presents his or her original robot and describes its form and function.

LEARNING OUTCOMES

- Students learn the concept of biomimicry by exploring its applications in engineering, science, and art.
- They discover how engineers are inspired by animals, insects, and reptiles in the design of real-world robots.
- Students explore biomimetic robots from different industries that aid in locomotion, health and medicine, flight, and touch.
- They design and program various biomimetic robots, including one for a robot zoo.

RECOMMENDED NEXT PROJECTS

Libraries can partner with their city zoo to enhance students' understanding of the natural world. Students can design robots based on animal and reptile exhibits at their city zoo. In addition, they can learn how zoo animals adapt to their natural environments and how they may inspire solutions to design challenges. This is a partnership that the Evansville Vanderburgh Public Library is currently exploring with the Mesker Park Zoo in Evansville, Indiana.

3D Printing and Robotics: Hooks and Hammers

MICHAEL CHERRY / TEEN AND YOUTH LIBRARIAN
Evansville Vanderburgh Public Library

Type of Library Best Suited for: School or Public

Cost Estimate: $5,000–$10,000 (less if library has 3D printer)

Makerspace Necessary? No

PROJECT DESCRIPTION

The Hooks and Hammers Challenge requires students to build their own Lego Mindstorms rover. In addition to building the automated vehicle, students are tasked with designing a hook or hammer that can be 3D printed and attached to the vehicle. The robot vehicles are programmed and challenged to complete simple tasks, such as ringing a desk bell with a hammer or picking up an object with a hook. This project requires a combination of engineering, computer programming, and computer-aided design.

OVERVIEW

The Hooks and Hammers Challenge was originally introduced as part of a robotics club at the Evansville (Indiana) Vanderburgh Public Library (EVPL). Over the summer, the EVPL hosts robotics camps at several locations throughout its eight-branch system. During the school year, the library offers a six-week robotics club on a seasonal basis. The Hooks and Hammers Challenge was designed for a robotics club offered to 5th–8th grade students. Students attending the club met once a week for a total of six weeks. This project takes multiple 90-minute sessions to complete and is described below.

MATERIALS LIST

- Desk bell
- Bulls-eye images
- Videos and books

NECESSARY EQUIPMENT

- 3D printer
- PLA filament
- Laptops
- Tinkercad account and Internet connection
- Lego Mindstorms software
- Lego Mindstorms NXT 2.0 and EV3

STEP-BY-STEP INSTRUCTIONS

Day 1

Introduce students to rovers by showing them videos of the Mars rovers *Spirit*, *Opportunity*, and *Curiosity*. Two great videos accessible via YouTube include the Science Channel's "How Does NASA's *Curiosity* Rover Work?" and NASA's "A Tale of Two Rovers." The former describes how the car-sized robotic rover explores the Red Planet. It illustrates how *Curiosity* is engineered, from its computer to its massive arm and eighteen cameras. The latter video explores *Curiosity*'s much smaller predecessors, *Spirit* and *Opportunity*. Additionally, a fascinating book that can accompany these videos is Alexandra Siy's *Cars on Mars: Roving the Red Planet*.

After watching the videos, engage students by prompting them with discussion questions. For example, are there other ways that rovers or unmanned ground vehicles aid at certain tasks? Are there any industries that make use of robotic rovers other than aerospace? Discussion may center on the use of rovers for safety and rescue, surveillance, and other applications. Following the discussion, students are required to build a Lego Mindstorms rover. They can either build one from scratch or follow the building instructions for the 5-Minute Bot on the website www.nxtprograms.com. The chassis and wheels of the robot should be built by the end of the first program.

Day 2

Students engineer an arm that will attach to the chassis of their robot. The arm is controlled by an additional motor and will later include the 3D-printed hook or hammer. It is best to limit students to one additional motor that will control the movement of the arm. Students can also use gears and experiment with different gear ratios that transfer motion and power to the arm. Once the arm is built, it is attached to the base of the robot. Additionally, students may modify the base by adding other features.

Day 3

Students' robots should be completely built by the third program, with the exception of the 3D-printed hook or hammer. Begin class by discussing and comparing the students' designs. For example, compare how each student designed the robotic arm and discuss principles such as weight and balance. Following a brief discussion, introduce students to the Hooks and Hammers Challenge. Students are tasked with designing and 3D printing a hook or hammer that can be attached to their robotic arm.   To facilitate this process, introduce students to Tinkercad and screen the Autodesk "Tinkercad Tutorial" that is accessible via YouTube. This short video describes Tinkercad and demonstrates how to use a set of geometric shapes to create models. The Hooks and Hammers Challenge is a great introductory project involving computer-aided design. It allows students to move and rotate basic shapes, stack solid objects, and use shapes to add or remove material.

Furthermore, describe how engineers use 3D printing as a way to quickly test and fabricate ideas. In this case, students fabricate a machine part that can be added to their robot. It is used to help them test a concept or solve a problem.

Day 4

The hooks and hammers are printed outside of class between the third and fourth week. Each print takes on average sixty minutes to print. Librarians can set up a 3D printer in class to demonstrate how this process works. Once students have attached their 3D prints to their robots, demonstrate how to program the robots using the Lego Mindstorms software. Students who designed a hammer must program the Lego robot to drive forward using the move block and corresponding motors. Upon reaching the desk bell, the arm is programmed to raise and strike down on the bell. Similarly, students completing the hook challenge program their robot to move forward using the move and wait blocks. Upon reaching a small object, the hook lifts the object up and drives toward a bulls-eye, placing the object in the center of the eye.

After mastering these programs, students reprogram their robots by adding additional blocks. For example, students completing the hammer challenge may want to strike the desk bell more than once. Students completing the hook challenge may want to add a sound block indicating victory upon completion. A sample video of the hook challenge can be accessed via YouTube by searching "Hooks and Hammers at the EVPL."

FIGURE 41.1

Robot with 3D-printed hook

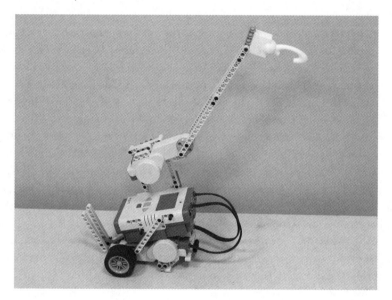

LEARNING OUTCOMES

- Students learn about rovers and design and build a Lego Mindstorms rover of their own.
- They discover how unmanned ground vehicles help with space exploration, safety and rescue, and surveillance, among other applications.
- Students design and 3D print a hook or hammer for their Lego robot.
- They program the robot to successfully complete the Hooks and Hammers Challenge.

RECOMMENDED NEXT PROJECTS

Students can build another Lego Mindstorms robot that requires a 3D-printed part of their choice.

Create a DIY Raspberry Pi Bar Code Scanner

TOM TRAN / SYSTEMS LIBRARIAN, LIBRARY TECHNOLOGY DIRECTOR
Minnesota State University, Mankato Memorial Library

Type of Library Best Suited for: Any

Cost Estimate: $100

Makerspace Necessary? No

PROJECT DESCRIPTION

We will be configuring a Raspberry Pi camera module to read bar codes or QR codes. Libraries use different types of bar codes attached to books and other items. This project is great for students to learn Python programming, LINUX commands, and downloading and installing software.

OVERVIEW

In order to use the camera as a bar code scanner, you will learn how to configure the camera for the Pi. Participants will learn some general concepts of downloading LINUX software and installing it on the Pi. Participants will learn LINUX commands to configure software to read and translate bar codes and/or QR codes.

For this project, participants will be installing the SimpleCV software. SimpleCV is an image-processing software to perform image manipulation and recognition. Its

FIGURE 42.1 ....

Raspberry Pi bar code scanner

scanner can read bar codes and QR codes. Participants will also be installing the ZBar library. ZBar is a module that provides an interface to the bar code reading library. And finally, participants will be installing User space VideO4LINUX (UV4L), which is a collection of modules for cross-platform drivers for audio and video streaming and output devices.

The programming language we will be working with is Python, which is an easy-to-learn programming language. It can be used to create web pages, apps, and games. The Python script takes in the video feed from the camera and then compares it against the installed libraries to translate and display the bar code or QR code. The output will be displayed onto the screen

MATERIALS LIST

- Sample bar codes and QR codes

NECESSARY EQUIPMENT

- Raspberry Pi 3 model B running Raspbian OS (Debian Jessie version)
- Camera module v2 (Sony IMX219 8-megapixel sensor)
- Internet connection or Wi-Fi
- Monitor, keyboard, mouse, and cables

STEP-BY-STEP INSTRUCTIONS

1. Enable the camera on the Pi
   a. Connect the camera to the Pi (see your owner's manual)
   b. Boot up Pi
   c. Open the terminal window
   d. Type the following command at the prompt: **sudo raspi-config**

```
pi@raspberrypi:~ $ sudo raspi-config
```

   e. The raspi-config window will pop up. Select **Enable Camera**
   f. On the next screen, "Would you like the camera interface to be enabled?" Enable the camera by selecting **<Yes>**
   g. The camera interface is enabled. Select **<OK>**
   h. Select **<Finish>**. The system will prompt you to reboot the Pi. Go ahead and reboot.

2. Installing SimpleCV on the Raspberry Pi
   a. Open the terminal window
   b. Type the following commands in the terminal window to download the necessary updates and dependencies

```
pi@raspberrypi:~ $ sudo apt-get update
pi@raspberrypi:~ $ sudo apt-get install ipython python-opencv python-scipy
python-numpy python-setuptools python-pip
```

You will be prompted to continue [Y/n], enter Y
This will take a few minutes to install.

   c. Installing SimpleCV from github

```
pi@raspberrypi:~ $ sudo pip install
https://github.com/sightmachine/SimpleCV/zipball/master
```

   d. Installing svgwrite:

```
pi@raspberrypi:~ $ sudo pip install svgwrite
```

3. Installing the ZBar library
   a. Open the terminal window
   b. Install updates and install python-zbar

```
pi@raspberrypi:~ $ sudo apt-get update
pi@raspberrypi:~ $ sudo apt-get install python-zbar
```

4. Installing uv41

```
pi@raspberrypi:~ $ curl http://www.linux-projects.org/listing/uv41_repo/lrkey.asc |
sudo apt-key add -
Add a repository to your OS updates.
(Use the pico editor to edit the file sources.list)
pi@raspberrypi:~ $ sudo pico /etc/apt/sources.list
(Add the following line to sources.list)
deb http://www.linux-projects.org/listing/uv41_repo/raspbian/ jessie main
(Save the file and exit)
^O WriteOut
^X Exit
pi@raspberrypi:~ $ sudo apt-get update
pi@raspberrypi:~ $ sudo apt-get install uv41 uv41-raspicam
pi@raspberrypi:~ $ sudo apt-get install uv41-server
(Load the driver at boot)
pi@raspberrypi:~ $ sudo apt-get install uv41-raspicam-extras
(Restart the driver without rebooting.)
pi@raspberrypi:~ $ sudo service uv41_raspicam restart or reboot Pi
```

5. Create your Python file, read.py
   You will use the pico editor to create a Python file called read.py
   Type the programming codes and save the file

```
pi@raspberrypi:~ $ pico read.py
from SimpleCV import Color,Camera,Display
cam = Camera() #initializes the camera
display = Display()
while(display.isNotDone()):
img = cam.getImage() #gets image from the camera
barcode = img.findBarcode() #finds barcode data from image
if(barcode is not None): #if there is data to be processed
barcode = barcode[0] #initialize array and set to zero
result = str(barcode.data)
print result #display barcode or QR code in python shell
barcode = [] #reset barcode data to empty set
img.save(display) #shows the image on the screen
```

Save the file and exit
^O WriteOut
^X Exit

6. Running the program
   a. Open the terminal window
   b. One way to run a Python script in the terminal window is to type the
      following command: **python read.py**

```
pi@raspberrypi:~ $ python read.py
```

Place the bar code or QR code you want to scan in front of the camera. The bar code data or QR code will be displayed.

FIGURE 42.2 ·

Sample QR code

LEARNING OUTCOMES

Through this project, participants will . . .

- Learn to use some LINUX commands to download and install updates and software.
- Learn about different bar codes used in libraries.
- Create and execute a Python script to read bar codes and QR codes.

RECOMMENDED NEXT PROJECTS

- A follow-up project to this might be to have participants 3D print cases for Raspberry Pi, a camera enclosure, and the mount stand for the Pi.

Sonic Pi for Creative Coders

KATE LOMAX / COFOUNDER, ARTEFACTO

Type of Library Best Suited for: Any

Cost Estimate: $0

Makerspace Necessary? No

PROJECT DESCRIPTION

Many learn-to-code tools forget to bring the creativity and so they can be a little dry for beginners. Creative computing tools offer a way for people to learn new coding and computer science skills while also creating new and interesting things.

Sonic Pi is a great new resource for learning to code *and* for composing music. Think of it as a new kind of musical instrument. You can write code to create your own music, including using samples and different instruments.

OVERVIEW

Sonic Pi is a live coding environment that was developed by Sam Aaron at the University of Cambridge Computer Laboratory. It was created specifically to support both music and computing lessons in schools. Sonic Pi was created to work with the Raspberry Pi computer and comes preinstalled on the Raspbian operating system, but you can install and use Sonic Pi on PC and Mac computers as well.

With Sonic Pi, you can compose music by writing text-based code. It's based on the Ruby programming language and helps users learn computer science concepts such as debugging, loops, conditionals, data structures, and more. Plus, you can code music along the way. This is a great, engaging tool for learn-to-code programs as well as for music lessons. It's suitable for a wide range of ages.

In this workshop we introduce learners to the Sonic Pi software, learn about the main features, and start composing music by writing code. You can start with simple melodies, but you can also use Sonic Pi with more advanced learners to work on soundtracking or Foley projects. This workshop can be adapted to suit the age (and music preferences) of the learners.

MATERIALS LIST

It's a good idea to have some simple song notations printed out for workshop attendees to use when they're first getting started. You can find music scores from sites like Jellynote at https://www.jellynote.com.

NECESSARY EQUIPMENT

- Computers with speakers (or headphones)
- Sonic Pi installed

STEP-BY-STEP INSTRUCTIONS

Start with simple melodies to pick up the syntax and then gradually introduce different instruments, beats, and code structures.

1. Introducing the Sonic Pi Interface

Give an overview of the user interface. Sonic Pi comes with a comprehensive tutorial that you can let users work through at their own pace, or you can demonstrate the main areas of the interface (as below) and then jump right into writing notes and basic melodies.

2. Introducing the Syntax

Once users are familiar with the different parts of the application, you can start introducing the syntax of the Sonic Pi coding environment. The main concepts to introduce at this early stage are the different ways you can write notes, how to set rests between notes using the sleep command, and how to combine notes to form chords.

FIGURE 43.1 ···

The Sonic Pi interface

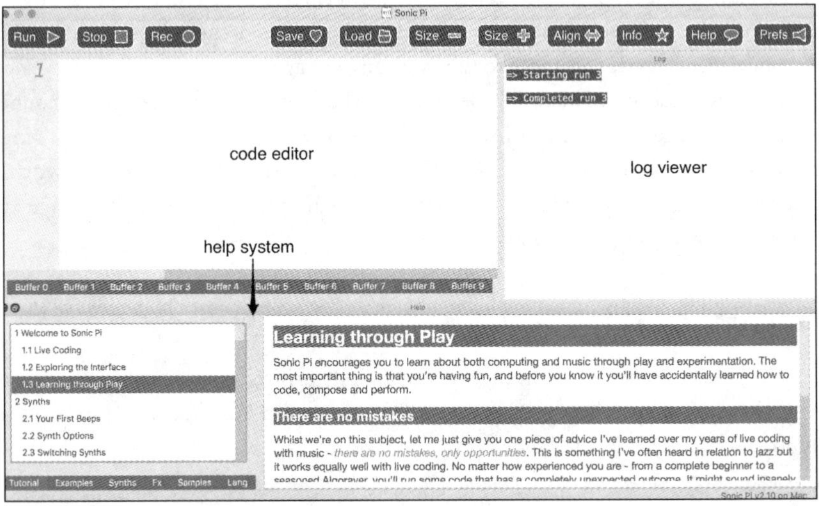

Demonstrate the two different ways to write notes in Sonic Pi—using the name of the note or its MIDI note number. A simple Google search for "MIDI note numbers" will return many charts as results.

It can help to describe the way the numbers align with a MIDI or piano keyboard—the lower the number, the lower the note that is played. Higher notes on the keyboard will play higher-pitched sounds.

But you can also use the name of the note preceded by a semicolon and indicate whether notes are sharp or flat using *s* or *b* after the note respectively.

Chords are when you play more than one note at a time without a rest between them.

3. Playing Simple Melodies

Once everyone is comfortable with the basic syntax, you can start creating simple melodies. You can pick a well-known nursery rhyme or theme song or let the users suggest a starter song.

Demonstrate how to code a melody by combining the keys or notes using the "sleep" command with a number parameter to designate rests between the notes (in seconds).

You can pick a simple melody from songs that the students might recognize. If you can't think of any, you can't really go wrong with "Frère Jacques" or "The Imperial March" (Darth Vader's theme).

4. Debugging and Refactoring

A key principle of coding and developing software is *Don't Repeat Yourself,* or *DRY.* So next, we want the learners to *DRY* their code up by rewriting it in a cleaner way that removes unnecessary repetition.

You can run a task a specific number of times using the *times* method (e.g., *2.times do . . . end* will run the code in-between twice). Give everyone time to rewrite any code that repeats using a loop and the *times* method. Also, show students how to add comments to their code and why commenting your code can be useful.

You can also store values that are going to be used more than once (like sleep statements, for example) using variables.

Once everyone has had a chance to refactor their code, ask them to rerun it and check that everything is okay.

If anyone gets an error when they run their code (such as missing a semicolon from before a note or forgetting to include an *end* after a *do* statement), show them the error log—it will spit out a whole bunch of stuff, but somewhere among all of that will be some useful information about the error, including the line number.

5. Changing the Sounds

Now that everyone has a handle on writing clean code to create melodies, they can start experimenting with different instruments and samples.

Sonic Pi also comes with a plethora of synthesizers you can use—everything from a piano synth to "blade" (*Blade Runner*-style strings). Thankfully, it also has autocomplete, so you can try out some random synths to find out one that works best.

Demonstrate how to change from the default synth by adding a *use_synth :name of synth* statement at the top of the code. You can also show how to specify a sample by typing *sample :name of sample.*

Give students a chance to try a few of the included synths and samples using either the autocomplete or by checking the list of synths and samples available in the help panel. There are also some additional parameters that can be introduced at this point, including how to alter the duration and amplitude of samples.

6. Composition Playtime

Once everyone has had a chance to play with different synths and samples, it's a good time to introduce *code blocks* that let you combine beats, sounds, and melodies into a more complex tune. Next, demonstrate how to combine different sounds, beats, and melodies at the same time using loops and threads.

You can then give everyone a chance to play and to compose something of their own by trying out different aspects of Sonic Pi coding. One way to do this is to create a theme or a challenge to prompt users to create their own music. For example, you could ask everyone to write a summery tune, or to write a theme song for an imaginary TV spy show. These can be individual or group projects.

LEARNING OUTCOMES

Through this project, participants learn . . .

- To write code statements to give instructions to a computer
- Basic coding concepts such as variables and loops
- To create simple music compositions by writing code using Sonic Pi
- To refactor code to make it clean and readable
- To troubleshoot errors in code by reading and responding to error messages

RECOMMENDED NEXT PROJECTS

There are different ways you can enable and support learners in exploring the more advanced coding potential of Sonic Pi, including:

- Composing and trading tracks in groups
- Soundtracking a film using external samples from free sound effects libraries such as the NASA sound library[1] and British Library Sounds[2]
- Live coding performances

A follow-up program might be to teach participants to use Sonic Pi on Raspberry Pi computers.

Notes
1. NASA sounds on Soundcloud, https://soundcloud.com/nasa.
2. British Library Sounds, http://sounds.bl.uk/.

Create an Ultrasonic Speed Detector

JOE STEWART, JAMES BETTKE, ANNIE STEWART, AND SHANE MANN
SubProto

Type of Library Best Suited for: Any

Cost Estimate: $30–$50 each

Makerspace Necessary? Yes

PROJECT DESCRIPTION

If you've ever wanted to know how fast fellow librarians are going when they're racing their book carts through the stacks, then this is the project for you!

The ultrasonic speed detector uses ultrasonic sound to measure speed. The project is intended to be an affordable exercise that will introduce participants to the worlds of electronics, software development, computer-aided design (CAD), and 3D printing. This is a great advanced workshop for more experienced makers to create something extraordinary. Although this may sound daunting, we have done all the hard work for you. All you have to do is follow the instructions and put it all together!

OVERVIEW

The ultrasonic speed detector measures speed. To do so, it must first measure two distances. The first distance is how far it is to an object. The radar waits 50 milliseconds (that's 50 thousandths of a second!) and then performs another distance measurement.

FIGURE 44.1

Ultrasonic speed detector

If the object is moving, there will be a difference in the two measurements. That information, combined with the amount of time taken between measurements, can be used to calculate how fast an object is moving.

In essence, this is like a radar gun except for one key difference. A radar gun uses the Doppler shift of reflected radio waves. The ultrasonic speed detector uses successive distance measurements to a moving object to calculate that object's speed.

MATERIALS LIST

- Project files—download at http://subproto.com/ultrasonic.zip
- Arduino Uno rev 3 or equivalent
- Adafruit 0.56" 7-segment LED HT16K33 Backpack
- HC-SR04 Ultrasonic Distance Sensor Module
- 9-volt battery
- 9-volt battery clip/snap connector
- 8 jumper wires, male to female
- One W jumper wire, male female male (see picture of red wire with three ends)

NECESSARY EQUIPMENT

- 3D printer
- 3D printer software such as Cura or Simplify3D

STEP-BY-STEP INSTRUCTIONS

To begin, download all the files from http://subproto.com/ultrasonic.zip.

3D Print the Frame

1. If you don't have a 3D printer, search your community for a makerspace. A makerspace will surely have a 3D printer you could use to print the frame of your snazzy ultrasonic speed detector.
2. Load Cura, Simplify3D, or your favorite 3D printer software.
3. It may depend on which 3D printer software you have, but each will offer some way to load a model, usually under File -> Load or similar. Locate the right option and load the file "ultrasonicx.stl" from the files you downloaded.
4. Make sure you have configured the 3D printer properly for the type of material you're using before you begin your print. If you aren't sure, ask your local makerspace for help.
5. Once you've kicked off the 3D print for the frame, you can start working on the electronics.

FIGURE 44.2

Parts List, Top Right: HC-SR04 Ultrasonic Distance Sensor Module, Right Middle: Arduino Rev 3, Right Bottom: Adafruit 0.56" 7-segment LED HT16K33 Backpack

FIGURE 44.3 ···
All wired and ready to go!

Electronics

1. Make sure you have all the required parts first.
2. Lay out all the parts on a nonmetallic surface. Why yes, you are right, a *breadboard* would be a great tool for this project!

Connect the HC-SR04 Ultrasonic Sensor to the Arduino

1. Use one male-to-female jumper wire to connect pin 7 of the Arduino to the pin labeled "Trig" on the HC-SR04.
2. Use one male-to-female jumper wire to connect pin 8 of the Arduino to the pin labeled "Echo" on the HC-SR04.
3. Use one male-to-female jumper wire to connect the 5V output pin of the Arduino to the pin labeled "VCC" on the HC-SR04.
4. Use one male-to-female jumper wire to connect a GND pin (GROUND) of the Arduino to the pin labeled GND on the HC-SR04.
5. The HC-SR04 is now connected to the Arduino!

Connect the Seven-Segment LED Backpack to the Arduino

1. Connect one male-to-female jumper wire to a free GND pin of the Arduino and the GND pin of the LED backpack.
2. Connect one male-to-female jumper wire to pin A4 on the Arduino and to pin SDL on the LED backpack.
3. Connect one male-to-female jumper wire to pin A5 on the Arduino and to pin SCL on the LED backpack.
4. The LED backpack is now wired to the Arduino!

Hook Up Your 9-Volt Battery Connector

1. Connect the red wire (positive lead) of the 9-volt snap connector to the female lead of the W jumper wire. Plug one male end of the W jumper wire to the VIN pin of the Arduino. Plug one male end of the W jumper wire to a female-to-female jumper wire that is connected to the VCC pin of the LED backpack.
2. Connect the black wire (negative lead) of the 9-volt snap connector to the last free GND pin of the Arduino.
3. Congratulations, you are all done with wiring!

Load the Software onto the Arduino

1. Open your Arduino IDE and import the file "main.cpp." Arduino IDE will likely ask to create a new project folder. Click yes.
2. Use the library manager to add the following libraries to the project:
   a. Wire
   b. Adafruit LED Backpack
   c. Adafruit GFX
   d. NewPing
3. Verify that the code compiles.
4. Plug the Arduino into your computer.
5. Upload the code to the Arduino by pressing the upload button in the Arduino IDE.
6. Plug in the 9-volt battery to the 9-volt battery snap connector. The LED backpack should be displaying numbers at this point. If not, make sure all your wire connections are good, or try resetting the Arduino.
7. Is your speed detector 3D-printed frame done printing yet? If everything is working, you are ready to mount the electronics into the 3D-printed frame.

Once you've mounted the electronics into the frame and attached a battery, you are ready to measure speed. Just aim the detector head-on in the direction of the moving object to be measured and wait for your reading.

LEARNING OUTCOMES

Through this project, makers will . . .

- Learn about an electronics prototyping platform called Arduino. This includes basic Arduino operation, how to write code to control one, and how to upload that code to one.
- Learn how 3D printing utilizes computer-aided design models to make physical copies of virtual objects.

RECOMMENDED NEXT PROJECTS

The ultrasonic speed detector is by no means the perfect, final version of this project. As an exercise for the maker, consider refining or improving the project, perhaps with a trigger to start measurement or with a memory to store speeds.

Privacy and Security Awareness Training with Raspberry Pi

KATE LOMAX / COFOUNDER, ARTEFACTO

Type of Library Best Suited for: Any

Cost Estimate: $250–$500

Makerspace Necessary? No

PROJECT DESCRIPTION

Raspberry Pi is a small, stand-alone computer that makes a great learning environment for demonstrating and experimenting with different tools. This includes privacy and awareness tools that can't always be accessed or installed on school, university, or other library computers.

By providing a separate, customizable learning environment, both the risk and the fear of "getting things wrong" are alleviated. You also remove users from their familiar web environment, which helps make people more aware of their usage and behavior. Raspberry Pi provides a kind of low-powered neutral territory.

In this workshop, we use the Raspberry Pi to show users how to protect their information online and to show some best practices for safeguarding their online privacy.

OVERVIEW

Protecting your privacy and security online doesn't have to be a massive inconvenience, but there are some things that you can do and steps you can take to keep yourself safe. This workshop demonstrates some practical ways that people can protect their data and privacy online. It is designed as a gentle introduction to online privacy and security and to demonstrate some of the key concepts and best practices. It's aimed at beginners.

This can be run as a series of workshops or can be modified to suit a particular theme or age group of learners. It also works as part of a general digital literacy series curriculum or as part of a series of Raspberry Pi workshops.

MATERIALS LIST

Online Privacy Checklist Bookmark[1]

NECESSARY EQUIPMENT

- Raspberry Pi with monitor, keyboard, and mouse (one per user + instructor)
- SD card with New Out Of the Box Software (NOOBS) and KeePass2 or KeePassX password management software installed (one per user + instructor)
- Projector with HDMI port

STEP-BY-STEP INSTRUCTIONS

1. Introduction

If this is the first session using the Raspberry Pi, you can introduce the Raspberry Pi and the Raspbian operating system.

A good way to start the workshop is by opening up a discussion about online privacy and security.

- Do workshop attendees currently use any privacy tools online?
- What messaging applications do people use?
- What about different search engines?

You can then get everyone logged into their Raspberry Pi and with the default browser open. This is Chromium at the time of writing, the open-source web browser that provides the source code for Google Chrome.

2. The How and Why of Online Tracking

In this part of the workshop, you can introduce the topic of online tracking—how it's used by different sites (e.g., online stores, social networks, and search engines) and how this impacts our web browsing. For example, online tracking is responsible for the way advertisements on websites will start looking eerily familiar based on your recent browsing history.

The best tool for demonstrating online tracking is Lightbeam, but it is only available for Firefox (or IceWeasal, depending on what you have installed). Lightbeam visualizes the trackers and provides a connections graph. If you have a projector, then you can use this to demonstrate Lightbeam's visualization of tracking, but otherwise participants can use a Chromium-compatible plug-in like Privacy Badger or Adblock Plus (installed by default on Chromium) that shows a list of online trackers without the connections visualization.

Demonstrate how to view and install browser plug-ins via the "Settings" menu and using the Chrome web store. Then give everyone a chance to visit a few different sites and see what tracking is in place on different pages. Some good websites to try are online newspapers and other advertising-heavy sites.

You can also explain the role of cookies, the bits of information that websites you visit store in your browser (or on your computer), and show users how they can view or clear their cookies.

It's also worth noting here the difference between blocking trackers with browser add-ons and the limited provisions of "private" or "incognito" browsing modes.

FIGURE 45.1 ....

Chromium with Privacy Badger installed

3. Search Engines and Privacy

Search engines use your browsing history (and other stored data) to "personalize" results. This means that your search results will be different from those of other people based on your previous browsing and search results that you've clicked on.

Give students a chance to try out a privacy-aware search engine such as DuckDuckGo to compare search results from different tools and devices.

4. Strong Passwords

What makes a strong and secure password? Explain some of the best practices for strong passwords (including passphrases and avoiding using place names or people's names that can be easily linked to you).

A lot of online sites and services (including Google and Facebook) now offer two-factor authentication, which means that you're not just relying on your user name and password to access these sites. This makes it harder for anyone to hack into your account.

Show students how a Password Manager can help by storing passwords in an encrypted form and helping generate secure random passwords. Demonstrate using KeePass and setting a master password and creating a database. Then give everyone a chance to try it out (with the caveat that all data will be cleared at the end of the session).

5. HTTPS and Encryption Online

Another way you can keep yourself a bit safer online is by using HTTPS wherever possible. In a (very small) nutshell, the Web works by sending data between a client and a server each time you make a request to the server by typing in a web address or clicking on a link. The protocol that is used to send this to the server is called HTTP. HTTPS is an encrypted (S is for "secure") version of this protocol. If you're interested in finding out more, the Electronic Frontier Foundation (EFF) has a guide to HTTPS for librarians.[2]

Demonstrate how to see whether a website is using HTTPS by finding the little lock icon next to the left of the address bar (though there's some variation here between browsers)—shopping and banking sites are good examples here.

You can also introduce the HTTPS Everywhere plug-in. HTTPS Everywhere is another tool from the EFF—it's a browser extension available for Firefox, Chrome, and Opera and it encrypts your communications with many major websites, which makes your browsing more secure.

SUMMARY

Online privacy and security awareness is a constantly evolving space, but the main thing is to help people be more aware of what and how they share information online and how this is used by third parties. Give everyone a copy of the Privacy Checklist Bookmark to take home with them as a guide.

Don't forget to reformat the SD cards at the end of the session to clear everyone's data from the previous session.

LEARNING OUTCOMES

- How to install and use some of the main privacy browser plug-ins.
- Understand what Hyper Text Transfer Protocol Secure (HTTPS) is and how to identify secure connections.
- Understand how online tracking impacts web browsing and how it works.
- Best practices for protecting your privacy online.

RECOMMENDED NEXT PROJECTS

This introductory workshop is a little light on encryption, so for a future session, you can introduce additional encryption tools such as Signal or CryptoCat and some more advanced tools for protecting personal data tools online.

Other possible future extensions are Onion Pi Tor Proxy[3] or hosting a crypto-party in the library.[4]

Notes

1. "Privacy Checklist Bookmark," http://librarymakers.net/resource-privacy -checklist-bookmark https://www.lockdownyourlogin.com/.
2. "What Every Librarian Needs to Know about HTTPS," Electronic Frontier Foundation, https://www.eff.org/deeplinks/2015/05/what-every-librarian -needs-know-about-https.
3. "Onion Pi—Make a Raspberry Pi into an Anonymizing Tor Proxy!" Adafruit, https://learn. adafruit.com/onion-pi?view=all.
4. CryptoParty, www.cryptoparty.in/.

Make a Movie in Four Hours

NICK MADSEN / YOUTH SERVICES SPECIALIST
Community Library Network: Kootenai and Shoshone Counties

Type of Library Best Suited for: Any

Cost Estimate: $0–$200

Makerspace Necessary? No

PROJECT DESCRIPTION

Our library has found that students love the process of making movies. Several years ago, a grant required a promotional video, and several teen volunteers were asked to assist in its creation. After some brief comments and ideas from a library staff member, the students quickly made the idea their own. Bringing props, costumes, and their positive attitudes, they brainstormed a story, decided who would fill each role (director, camera person, actors), and gathered some great footage. Later that month, a librarian edited the footage together, found some music online, and posted the video on YouTube as "Library: After Hours." After this first successful experience, several "Make a Movie" events have taken place at our library.

OVERVIEW

Each of the Make a Movie events has been run informally. They can be run as simply (a point-and-shoot camera with no costumes) or as complex (lighting and green screens) as you would like. The events included brainstorming the elements of the movie, delegating what role each participant would play, and shooting the footage. After the event, a librarian or the participants would edit the footage.

For the purposes of this chapter, several different ideas on how to implement the program will be offered. Mix and match these ideas, and find what will work best for your participants. In addition to this guide, a Pinterest board has been created with moviemaking ideas, tips, and resources. The Pinterest board can be accessed at www .pinterest.com/cln4nextgen/movie-making/.

MATERIALS LIST

- Whiteboard
- Sticky notes
- Pens/pencils/markers
- Props
- Costumes

NECESSARY EQUIPMENT

- Video camera
- Editing software
- Studio lights
- Microphones
- Green screen

STEP-BY-STEP INSTRUCTIONS

1. Brainstorm

At the conclusion of this step, students will have their overall plan for the movie they want to create. This plan should include the genre, plot, characters, and scenes required to make the movie, and what needs to happen in each scene. Students can take into account what props and equipment are available, the size of the venue where filming will take place, and what technological expertise the team editing the film needs to possess.

Giving students the best possible experience in sharing their ideas is the key to a successful brainstorming session. With a smaller group of participants (5–10), have a staff member guide the discussions as a group. With a larger group of participants (11 or more), break the participants into teams, no larger than four people each, ask them to brainstorm in their teams, and then share their ideas with the larger group. Whatever method is chosen, ensure that all ideas from all groups are heard and that a final decision is reached by consensus, or a vote. Keeping track of the discussions will also be beneficial. A whiteboard, sticky notes, or pen and paper can be used.

Discussions can begin with general ideas for a short movie—for example, cowboys beat up a horde of zombies—and should become more specific as the discussions continue. Discussions could include favorite TV shows or movies, genres, basic plot structure, basic movie plots, and basic characters. Participants should be able to compile a list of many ideas, then whittle this down to the ideas they want included in their short film.

2. Delegate

At the conclusion of this step, students will have decided who will be filling each role in the short movie. Participants can now decide what roles and tasks are going to be required to carry out the film. These roles and tasks should be listed, for example: good guy, bad guy, speechless robot, camera people, microphone operator, assistant to director, and so on.

While filming, having an individual who has the final say such as a director will be helpful. An experienced participant or the staff member should most likely fill this role. For other roles, let participants choose what they would like to do. If multiple participants are interested in the same roles or tasks, let them audition, or split the responsibilities, for example, have two camera operators take turns. For acting roles that require an audition, let the participants who did not audition decide who will embody that role in the film.

3. Shoot

At the conclusion of this step, the primary filming will have been completed for the short movie. Before each scene commences, several groups of participants can quickly make specific decisions based on the brainstorming session. The actors can discuss what exact dialogue and actions will be taken. The camera people can decide what kinds of shots and angles will be best for this scene. The prop and lighting team can prepare the set while these discussions continue. Each participant has a role to play, and the director can ensure that the groups are working together to bring about the vision established in the brainstorming session.

4. Edit

At the conclusion of this step, a finished product will be compiled on editing software or an application using the gathered footage, music, and sound effects. Typically, this step was conducted after the Make a Movie event ended by the staff member or a participant. But this step could also be included in the event. Team members could be entrusted with editing different scenes, and the final product of each team could be combined into the final project. During a four-hour event, enough footage was typically gathered for a five-minute short movie. If editing is going to be included in the event, the final product might need to be shortened or the event might need to be lengthened. Our library has used Windows Movie Maker for editing software, SoundCloud for music, and Freesound for sound effects. For further suggestions on

···

Moviemaking in action

movie-editing software and free resources for music and sound effects, check out the Pinterest board: www.pinterest.com/cln4nextgen/movie-making/.

5. Post

Once your masterpiece has been created, make sure to share it far and wide. Put the movie on social media, share it on your e-mail lists, create a display in your library, and give it to your board of trustees and/or administration. The finished project could also be entered into a state or local teen film festival or contest.

LEARNING OUTCOMES

- Participants share their ideas and collaborate to create a singular vision for a story.
- Participants learn about the basic elements of a movie and make decisions on their own movie.
- Participants are able to take on roles and create a movie.
- Participants learn about editing a film and combining footage with sound effects and music.

RECOMMENDED NEXT PROJECTS

- Stop-motion animation with Legos, sticky notes, or clay
- Screenwriting workshop
- Creating a computer animated film using scratch.mit.edu or Blender.org

Light Painting

EMILY STRATFORD / TEEN LIBRARIAN
San Jose Public Library

Type of Library Best Suited for: Public, School

Cost Estimate: $0.50 per participant plus equipment

Makerspace Necessary? No

PROJECT DESCRIPTION

Make the world your canvas! Light painting, made famous by Pablo Picasso, is the process of drawing designs in the air using light-emitting objects like flashlights, LEDs, or cell phones and capturing it with a long-exposure photo. This is a great project for teens in a public or school library, with or without a makerspace. This project costs about $0.50 per flashlight plus the cost of equipment.

OVERVIEW

Light painting is a fun (and Instagram-worthy) program that sneaks in some learning, too. Teens will learn how circuits work, creating Popsicle stick flashlights using conductive materials, an LED light, and a power source. Next, they will "paint" with their light in a dark room, or outside at night, and capture each other's creations using a digital camera with a long exposure setting. If you don't have access to a digital camera, you can also use a phone or mobile device with a long exposure app. The result is striking, unique, shareable photos.

FIGURE 47.1

Students drawing with their flashlights

MATERIALS LIST

- Jumbo craft sticks
- Metal binder clips (medium size)
- Copper wire (22 gauge, solid)
- 3-volt coin cell batteries (CR 2032)
- LED (10-mm LED, or standard LED)
- Copper tape or tinfoil
- Nonconductive tape (masking, electrical, scotch, duct, etc.)
- Hot glue sticks

NECESSARY EQUIPMENT

- Hot glue gun
- Scissors
- Camera with long shutter exposure option, or mobile device with a long exposure app
- Tripod
- Dark room (or do outside at night)
- Optional: other light sources, like flashlights, toys with lights, cell phones, and so on
- Computer(s) to upload images

STEP-BY-STEP INSTRUCTIONS

Make the LED Flashlight

- Remove one leg of the metal binder clip. Simply pinch the sides together near the top of the clip and wiggle it out.
- Using a little hot glue, adhere the metal binder clip flat onto the Popsicle stick, about 1.5 inches from one end. Make sure not to use too much hot glue or the copper wire won't fit through the binder's hole.
- Next, cut (and strip if necessary) about four inches of copper wire. Feed the wire through the two holes of the binder clip. Previously, these holes were holding the leg we removed. Twist the wire around the back of the Popsicle stick and try to make it lay flat.
- Take one strip of copper tape (or tinfoil) and place it on the back of the Popsicle stick. It should cover the twisted copper wire and go almost to the end, leaving about 0.25 to 0.5 of an inch at the other end of the Popsicle stick free.
- Flip your Popsicle stick back over, so the metal binder clip is facing up.
- Lay another piece of copper tape (or tinfoil) down the front of the Popsicle stick. It should run from one end to about 0.5 inch from the metal clip. Make sure it doesn't touch the metal clip or your flashlight won't work (because positive and negative will be touching).
- Bend the extra bit of copper tape back so the sticky side is up, place the positive side of the battery (the smooth side) down onto the sticky copper tape, and press it firmly down so it touches and lays flat against the Popsicle stick.
- Flip the metal leg down. It should touch the negative side of the battery.
- Add the LED. If you've followed the steps thus far, the positive side is the top (or the side with the metal clip) and the negative side is the bottom (or the side with the twisted wire).
- The LED's cathode (long lead) goes on top, and its anode (short lead) goes on the bottom. Affix your LED in place with some nonconductive tape. Make sure both leads are touching their respective copper tape sides. If you want to test that your light works before taping it in place, just flip the switch.

Take the Photo

- Affix the digital camera to the tripod. Designate a certain area (perhaps with tape on the floor) that will fit in the camera's viewfinder.
- Set the exposure to a relatively long value. If you are inside, turn off the lights.
- Make the click. Once the shutter is open, use your flashlight to light the areas that you want to paint. You can use the flashlight as a brush or pen to paint the light or draw precise objects. Areas where you go slowly will be more brightly lit than others.
- Communicate with the photographer about when you are starting and stopping.

Tips

- Offer challenges like writing your name (teens found this pretty difficult because you have to write backwards), having two people each draw half a face, playing a game of tic-tac-toe, or adding a person or other objects to the painting. Teens really enjoyed doing group painting. Try painting with other light sources such as flashlights, toys with lights, or cell phones.
- As the program leader, you may want to be the main person behind the camera so you can adjust the shutter speed properly—if the painter is writing out a word, leave the shutter open longer, whereas simple designs only need a few seconds.
- Making the light sources is relatively simple, but having needle-nose pliers might be helpful in twisting the wire and making sure it lies flat against the copper tape. The most difficult part is attaching the binder clip with hot glue—it seems to secure well, but then while putting the wire on, the clip can sometimes detach from the glue. If the light doesn't turn on, or flickers, adjust where the copper wire touches the tape and make sure the clip is tight against the battery.

LEARNING OUTCOMES

- Participants will create a light source and demonstrate how a digital camera can capture a trace of light.

This program aligns with the following Next Generation Science Standards: Science and Engineering Practices—Constructing Explanations and Designing Solutions.[1]

RECOMMENDED NEXT PROJECTS

To expand upon this program, you may want to try other circuitry projects next, like wearable LED fashions (i.e., a skirt that lights up when you move), or an LED light-up greeting card. The Exploratorium Museum in San Francisco has some great ideas for experimenting with light, like a Poking Fun at Art[2] experiment, which involves creating a pinhole viewer and exploring colorful mixtures of light; the Polarized Light Mosaic,[3] where you use transparent tape and polarizing material to make and project colored patterns reminiscent of stained-glass windows; and Glow Up,[4] a chemistry experiment that uses different types of light to study life.

Notes

1. Next Generation Science Standards, Web, www.nextgenscience.org.
2. "Poking Fun at Art," Exploratorium, https://www.exploratorium.edu/snacks/poking-fun-at-art.
3. "Polarized Light Mosaic," Exploratorium, https://www.exploratorium.edu/snacks/polarized-light-mosaic.
4. "Glow Up," Exploratorium, https://www.exploratorium.edu/snacks/glow-up.

Storyboarding to Create Films without Celluloid

ANDY HORBAL / HEAD OF LEARNING COMMONS
University of Maryland Libraries
LEALIN QUEEN / PRODUCTION SPECIALIST
University of Maryland Libraries

Type of Library Best Suited for: Any

Cost Estimate: Less than $25

Makerspace Necessary? No

PROJECT DESCRIPTION

When called upon to support a class or group working on a video production project or to teach novices the basics of filmmaking, it can be difficult to know where to start. There's a temptation to focus on technology: even though it has never been easier to make a movie, many students don't have experience with any camera other than the one on their phone (assuming they have one) or with the kinds of accessories like tripods, lights, and sound recording equipment that are largely responsible for the "professional" look that first-time filmmakers are typically going for. In our experience, though, the biggest bang for your buck is found in *pre*-production support.

Just as most good term papers start with an outline, most successful video projects start with a storyboard. By making sure that students understand the basic principles of visual storytelling, where to position their camera and actors to achieve the effect they want, and how to stay organized and on schedule, you will ensure that they can construct a coherent narrative and capture it on video, which is far more important than slick special effects.

As a bonus, this activity doesn't require any expensive filmmaking equipment, and thus is ideal for makerspaces that aren't able to invest heavily in this area. Our inspiration for it was a group of Soviet film students who, lacking film stock and equipment in the aftermath of World War I, taught themselves how to make movies by acting out scenes as if they were before a camera, sketching the resulting "shots" out on paper, and then rearranging these papers into finished "films."[1] Just like them, we're happy to save money; we've also found that this approach is a great way to get students up out of their seats and moving around; moreover, the approach fosters collaboration, and prevents technology from distracting students from the core visual/media literacy skills that we are trying to teach them.

OVERVIEW

This project was designed to be utilized in "one-shot" library instruction sessions that are approximately one hour long, but it can be adapted for shorter sessions. Students begin by learning about the elements of a storyboard, then complete two storyboards of their own individually and a third working in groups. The session ends with a "film festival" whereby each group performs their third storyboard for the other students.

MATERIALS LIST

- Blank storyboards (three per participant)
- Printed letters "A," "B," and "C"
- Tape

NECESSARY EQUIPMENT

- Whiteboard or chalkboard

STEP-BY-STEP INSTRUCTIONS

1. Draw a sample storyboard on the whiteboard or chalkboard before the students arrive and tape the letter "B" to it. The sample storyboard should depict how you spent your morning. Begin the session by taping the printed letter "A" to the wall somewhere else in the room where the activity is taking place. Walk from the letter "A" to the whiteboard or chalkboard, then use the sample storyboard to introduce students to the three basic elements of a storyboard: (1) the setting/location of the scene, (2) where the actors are positioned (also known as "blocking"), and (3) where the camera is positioned. Explain how the function of the storyboard is to help filmmakers determine what shots they need, where

FIGURE 48.1 ....

Sample student storyboard

they need to shoot, and what they need to do with the camera to tell their story as efficiently and effectively as possible. Also explain that artistic ability is secondary to clear organization and planning. Near the end of this portion of the activity, walk slowly to a third location in the room where it is taking place and tape the letter "C" to the wall.

2. Ask the students to take out their first blank storyboard. Explain to them that not only did you just teach them the elements of a storyboard, but you also acted out a scene: the room where the activity is taking place is the setting, the letters "A," "B," and "C" indicate the blocking of the "actor" (you), and they are sitting in the position of the "camera." Give the students 5–10 minutes to storyboard the scene you just acted out. Discuss everyone's storyboards as a group, highlighting the three elements of a storyboard covered at the beginning of the activity as they appear in each one.

3. Ask the students to take out their second blank storyboard. Instruct them to redraw the scene they just storyboarded, but with one or more of the three elements of a storyboard changed: the scene should take place somewhere else, the scene should feature a different character or a character who behaves differently, and/or the camera positioning should be changed. This portion of the activity will reveal whether or not students really understand the connection between storyboards and moviemaking. Briefly discuss everyone's storyboards as a group.

4. Split the students into groups and ask them to take out their third blank storyboard. Using the example storyboard on the whiteboard or chalkboard depicting your morning, talk to the students about the difference between simply listing events (this happened, then this other thing happened) and telling a story (this happened, and it caused this other thing to happen), as well as how to visually represent that story (for example, what is the best way to depict someone oversleeping?). Instruct the students to create a fictionalized account of their morning

in storyboard form. Their storyboards should contain at least ten panels, each group member should be represented as a character, and the cause-and-effect relationship between everything that takes place should be clear. The students should create enough copies of their storyboard to hand one out to each of the other groups.

5. Conclude the activity with a "film festival." Each group should distribute one copy of their storyboard to all of the other groups. They then should perform their storyboard for the other groups, following the actor and camera blocking indicated on the storyboard. At the end of each presentation, ask the other groups to indicate what worked and what changes they would make.

LEARNING OUTCOMES

○ Students learn the principles of storyboarding, which are also the principles of film analysis, film editing, and visual storytelling.

○ Students learn how to use a storyboard to organize a video shoot.

RECOMMENDED NEXT PROJECTS

This activity is an ideal introduction to film production for students who will next create an actual movie using either their phones (the cameras which come included on smartphones are more sophisticated every year) or filmmaking equipment provided by the makerspace. We also use this activity in conjunction with video production assignments that we design in collaboration with the students' professor. In either case, the "Video Editing to Remix Films" project included in this section, which teaches students about post-production techniques, would be a great companion to it! This activity can be used with film studies classes to teach them how to perform a scene analysis as well.

Note
1. David A. Cook and Robert Sklar, "History of the Motion Picture," 2016, www.britannica.com/art/history-of-the-motion-picture.

Video Editing to Remix Films

ANDY HORBAL / HEAD OF LEARNING COMMONS
University of Maryland Libraries
LEALIN QUEEN / PRODUCTION SPECIALIST
University of Maryland Libraries

Type of Library Best Suited for: Any

Cost Estimate: $0–$2,500 (depending on whether or not you choose to purchase film editing software and/or computers)

Makerspace Necessary? No

PROJECT DESCRIPTION

More and more teachers are turning away from traditional paper-writing assignments and are embracing audiovisual projects as an ideal way to accommodate different learning styles, foster deeper engagement with course content, and inspire students to unleash their full creative potential. Often, though, these teachers don't know where to turn for help when instructing their students in the basic film editing skills they need to be successful. This creates a golden opportunity for library makerspaces to step in and save the day!

In 2013, staff in the University of Maryland Libraries' Library Media Services Department created an "8-second video essay" activity as a quick, efficient way to introduce students in the Film Studies Program to basic film editing concepts that they could use to complete video production assignments. Over the years, this activity evolved into a movie remix activity that could easily be adapted into school and public library environments as a library instruction session for a class working on a specific assignment, or as a training session for "walk-ins" into a library makerspace that offers audio and video post-production software.

This activity is designed to help librarians support students working on audio-visual projects, regardless of how much experience they have in this area. Because it assumes no prior knowledge, it is an effective introduction to film editing for students who have never done it before, but it's also open-ended enough to ensure that more advanced students don't get bored.

OVERVIEW

This project was designed to be utilized in "one-shot" library instruction sessions of varying lengths, but it works best when students have at least an hour to work on their project, and the project ideally would be split into two sessions. Students begin by analyzing a film scene, then receive a crash course introduction to a video editing program like Adobe Premiere, iMovie, or Windows Movie Maker. After viewing an example movie "remix," students create a remix of their own using clips from the film they analyzed at the beginning of the session. The session ends with a "film festival" consisting of everyone's remixes. Students can work individually if enough computers equipped with video editing software are available, but we prefer to split classes into groups of 3–5 students. If working in groups, it can be helpful to survey the class about their level of film editing experience so that more advanced students can be evenly distributed.

MATERIALS LIST

- Set of film clips legally obtained from the Internet or a DVD/Blu-Ray. We typically use the shower scene from Alfred Hitchcock's 1960 film *Psycho*.

NECESSARY EQUIPMENT

- Video editing software. We typically use Adobe Premiere, but we have also worked with iMovie and Final Cut X. You should use whatever software you're most comfortable with.
- Computer workstations able to run the software.

STEP-BY-STEP INSTRUCTIONS

1. Begin by showing students a scene from the movie that they'll be working with: you should discuss its meaning and break it down shot by shot so that students can see what editing techniques have been used. When we first created this

activity, we used scenes from the 1940 Howard Hawks film *His Girl Friday*, which is in the public domain and freely available for download from the Internet Archive (https://archive.org/details/HisGirlFriday-1940), but we later switched to the shower scene from Alfred Hitchcock's *Psycho* because it utilizes editing techniques that are easy to explain and demonstrate. Any film that the instructor is familiar with would work, though. Be sure to highlight any specific techniques that you would like the students to incorporate into their projects.

Next, introduce the video editing software that the students will be using, concentrating on features directly relevant to the activity to avoid overwhelming them with too much information. We typically work with Adobe Premiere and discuss the following topics:

— Basic video editing terms that we'll be using, such as *assets* (all media files which will appear in the project, including image, video, and audio files) and *B-roll* (supplemental footage like still images or landscape shots)

— The basic layout of Adobe Premiere, including the tools panel (where students will select which editing tools to use), the timeline panel (where all the actual editing takes place), and the program monitor (where media from the timeline can be previewed)

— How to add audio such as music, ambient noise, and voice-over tracks to a project

— How to add titles to a project

It is important to keep this portion of the activity as brief as possible in order to allow plenty of time for the students to gain hands-on editing experience. Tutorials for most film editing programs can be found on Lynda.com, the manufacturer's website, and elsewhere on the Internet.

FIGURE 49.1 ....

Adobe Premiere standard workspace

2. Introduce the remixing activity. You can either pre-populate the computer work-stations that the students will be using with film clips, or show them how to either rip them from a DVD or Blu-Ray or download them from the Internet (being sure to explain how this is in compliance with the fair use provision of U.S. copyright law or the equivalent local exemption) themselves. Explain that their task is to make a remix of their own by rearranging the clips and/or adding new material so that it tells a different story. You should show the students at least one example of a remix: movie trailer remixes like *Shining* (https://youtu .be/sfout_rgPSA) make effective examples, or you can create one yourself that models what you want the students to do. The final product should:
   — Consist primarily of clips from the example film
   — Be at least thirty seconds long
   — Include a title card with all group members' names
   — Include a title card citing the example film and any other works used to create the remix
   Students should be given as much time as possible to work on their projects. This portion of the activity could also be completed outside of class as a homework assignment, or in a second workshop or instruction session. Near the end of the allotted time, show each group how to export their finished remix into an appropriate file format; if the students will be working on their remixes at home, then this would obviously need to be covered earlier in the session.
   — Conclude the activity with a "film festival," in which each group screens their remix for the others. In addition to being fun and interactive, this also exposes the students to new ideas and techniques that they might not have tried in their own group.

LEARNING OUTCOMES

- Students learn how to analyze a film scene.
- Students learn how to use a video editing program like Adobe Premiere, iMovie, or Windows Movie Maker.
- Students learn basic principles of film editing.
- Students learn about intellectual property concerns related to using audiovisual materials created by others.

FIGURE 49.2 ....

Students working on projects

RECOMMENDED NEXT PROJECTS

We generally use this activity in conjunction with video production assignments that we design in collaboration with the students' professor, but it would also be an ideal way to prepare people to enter a local film festival. In either case, the "Storyboarding to Create Films without Celluloid" project in this section, which teaches students pre-production skills that they need to prepare for a film shoot, would be a great companion to it!

Black History Month Interview Project

SIENNA CITTADINO / TEEN LIBRARIAN

Carnegie Library of Pittsburgh

Developed by Sienna Cittadino and Terrel Williams

Type of Library Best Suited for: Any

Cost Estimate: $2,000–$5,000

Makerspace Necessary? No

PROJECT DESCRIPTION

These days, information comes from everywhere and everyone, with the traditional idea of sources becoming ever more muddled. This project offers a means of embracing changes in the information landscape while enforcing the importance of multiple viewpoints. It also introduces participants to contemporary social and political issues, with a focus on the local community.

Participants in this project will craft a plan to capture interviews related to the topic of Black History Month. They will write interview questions, discuss themes, and collectively edit a body of footage to create a real film that they can show to their families, community, or school. Beyond learning about how to operate cameras and microphones, participants will walk away with a clearer understanding of how experiences become stories, stories become information, and people edit information to shape a narrative.

Participants will likely encounter many complicated, ambiguous situations while participating in this project. It is the role of the facilitator(s) to guide participants through these situations with care and attention. Open dialogue, willingness to accept critique, and flexibility are key components of this project. It is a wonderful way to build a sense of community and trust among library patrons and program facilitators.

OVERVIEW

This project utilizes audiovisual equipment in the creation of a 15–30-minute movie showcasing local voices on the topic of Black History Month. Youth lead this project and organize themselves to assign roles, determine the movie's form and tone, set goals, and do the work of capturing interview footage. An important aspect of this project is accompanying dialogue. Holding regular discussions regarding oral history, race in America, and the importance of soft skills is essential to the success of the project. Plan to meet at least five times.

MATERIALS LIST

- Paper and Sharpies

NECESSARY EQUIPMENT

- Computers or laptops
- Cameras that record video
- Shotgun microphones (preferable but not necessary as long as the camera captures sound)
- Tripod (preferable but not necessary)
- Video editing software (i.e., iMovie, Windows Movie Maker, Lightworks)
- Projector and screen

STEP-BY-STEP INSTRUCTIONS

Step 1: Hold Planning Session(s) to Determine Roles and Goals

As much as possible, allow youth to lead the initial planning sessions. If the participants do not know one another well or have never done similar planning work, they may be hesitant to begin the process. One way to start is to tape several different pieces of paper to a wall. Label one paper "Roles," another "Goals," another "Challenges," "Extras," and a final paper titled "Next Steps."

The program facilitator or the youth can lead the discussion around these topics, with participants calling out their ideas for each subject. Someone writes the ideas down, ideally going methodically from one paper to the next, and not all five at once. "Extras" can hold ideas that sound good but aren't matching up with the direction in

FIGURE 50.1

Group planning using paper and markers

which the group is headed. Be sure to be clear about "Roles," possibly listing the roles ahead of time. These can include things like the camera person, interviewer, question writer, editor, and sound person. These roles may not stick, but they give participants a good idea of what the project will involve. Save "Next Steps" for last, and try to focus the conversation on concrete actions the group can take to get started on the project. These might include writing questions, doing research on the neighborhood's history, and learning to use the cameras and microphones.

Step 2: Question Writing and Preparing for Interviews

Writing the questions depends heavily on the goals determined in Step 1. If participants decided that they want to create a movie that causes people to question their assumptions, they may want to write hard-hitting questions that could cause some degree of discomfort. If they are aiming for a movie which seeks to paint a picture of their community and the people who live within it, the questions may have more to do with memories, local history, and relationships between people living in the neighborhood. Respect the choices that participants made in the planning session, and guide them toward questions that best reflect the goals they set out to achieve.

Essential to this step is a discussion about opinions, prejudices, and racism. The facilitator must be comfortable discussing the topic of race on more than a surface level. Especially if you are working with students of color, it is important that participants feel supported when they are going out to do interviews. You should prepare youth to hear things that they may disagree with, but with the full understanding that they can feel safe in expressing how this makes them feel. If any participants feel uncomfortable doing the interviews, help them find other tasks and affirm the importance of this work. Even with pre-selected interviewees, you cannot control what people will say when asked about Black History Month. Instead of denying this reality, face it head-on through discussion, care, and clear antiracist affirmations of support for participants.

Step 3: Hold Interviews

This step is the fun part! Set out in teams or small groups to collect interviews. Interviewees may be patrons in the library (be sure to bring copies of photo and video releases), pre-selected interviewees, or students and faculty in a school. Be sure to practice consent, clearly introducing the topic of the interviews and asking people if they would like to be interviewed. Take time setting up, whether that means getting the camera on a tripod or finding the right location to do the interview. Have one participant ask questions while the other operates the camera. A third participant might ask the interviewee to sign a video release and keep materials organized. Depending on the scope of the project, the program facilitator might be present for the interviews as well. This may be more important or even necessary if the interviewees are strangers.

Step 4: Overview Footage and Acquire More if Necessary

As a group, watch the interviews and start to locate a narrative across them. Refer back to the goals from Step 1. If the existing footage is not enough to meet those goals, reflect on what is missing and collect more footage in a focused manner. This step is another important time for discussion. Be sure to allow participants ample time to share their experiences with one another.

Step 5: Assign Editing Roles and Edit Footage

Much like in Step 1, reconvene to assign editing roles. These roles may include sound adjustment, cutting, transitions, introductory text and credits, and more. Adjust these to the participants' skill levels and the scope of the project. Be sure to also take time to determine the overall arc and tone of the movie. How will it begin, how should the interviews and questions be presented, and what is the tone? These are all important questions. Make sure everyone is on the same page, and then begin the editing process.

Step 6: Group Viewing and Final Edits

Once the editing feels "done," watch the movie as a group. Afterward, solicit comments or hold a discussion, and create a final list of editing action items. Assign roles for who will complete which items, and finish the editing process. If time allows, view the movie one final time as a group to make last-minute changes.

Step 7: Hold a Viewing Party

Invite everyone who had a role in the project, library staff, interviewees, and friends and family to view the final project. Popcorn is recommended! If possible, give participants time to discuss the project with the audience and hold a Q&A session afterward.

LEARNING OUTCOMES

- Participants will learn how to handle audiovisual equipment and basic video editing.
- Interviewing is a fine art that requires patience, listening, and research. Participants will experience a crash course in soft skills as interviews inevitably stray from the pre-selected set of questions and topics.
- This program is all about project management. Participants will collaborate closely, working together to assign roles and set goals, determine the collective tone of the movie, and work to overcome disagreements.
- Participants should feel empowered through this project to openly discuss race and racism in the United States, and acquire a vocabulary for doing so.

RECOMMENDED NEXT PROJECTS

Participants may need some time to cool off after this project is completed, and it may be best to let them determine what should come next. If the movie was the hook that brought everyone together, make more movies and partner with local filmmaking organizations. If the discussion of race and community pulled in participants, consider other ways to bring these concepts into regular programming.

Hack a JPEG Image

....

SIENNA CITTADINO / EEN LIBRARIAN
Carnegie Library of Pittsburgh

Type of Library Best Suited for: Public or School

Cost Estimate: $500–$1,000

Makerspace Necessary? No

PROGRAM DESCRIPTION

Do you ever feel like the photos you see online just aren't . . . weird enough? This may be the project for you! With minimal equipment, an appetite for the unknown, and the willingness to get a little strange, your patrons can take the "guts" of an image into their own hands and change it.

This project is great for quickly capturing the attention of techies who may not know they're techies yet. Tell teenagers they get to "break pictures" and you'll have their attention right away. Then, all you have to do is a little random copy-and-pasting to achieve dramatic visual results. On top of that, this project provides a knowledge of file organization and digital file structure, which is harder and harder to come by in the era of the smartphone and the Cloud.

It all starts with the Internet. Hop online, download photos, and get ready to be confused! This is a project for program facilitators who are comfortable saying "I don't know," and meaning it. The code inside of a JPEG photo is pure gibberish to a human brain—but that doesn't mean you can't make it your own. Follow up with Photoshop or other photo-editing software to take back some of the control in this equation.

OVERVIEW

This program requires minimal equipment and preparation. Participants only need to browse online for a JPEG photo, load the photo into a text editor, and begin randomly altering the contents of the file. Once finished, they reopen the file as an image and see what has changed. Images can be further modified with Photoshop or GIMP to produce eye-catching effects.

MATERIALS LIST

- Paper for printing

NECESSARY EQUIPMENT

- Computer or laptop with Internet connection
- Text editing software
- Image manipulation software (GIMP or Photoshop)

STEP-BY-STEP INSTRUCTIONS

Step 1: Find a JPEG Image

Using a search engine such as Google, participants can search for any image of their choosing. Google allows searchers to specify file type and usage rights, which makes it ideal for this activity. The chosen image must be a JPEG file and available for modification. Images with plenty of color and internal variation lend themselves well to this activity. This activity can also be done with photos taken on a camera or cell phone, so long as they can be saved as JPEG files. An ideal image is a native JPEG, and not an image converted from a PNG or other format.

Step 2: Download the Image and Open with a Text Editor

Download the chosen image to the computer. When opening the image, do so with a simple text editor application as opposed to an image viewer. On a Mac, the default text editor, TextEdit, works well. On a Windows computer, the default application Notepad will also get the job done. External applications will work as well, as long as they have the capability to work in plain text. Especially with TextEdit, be sure to set the application preferences to "open" and save the files in plain text mode. When you open the file, it will look like nonsense with no discernible pattern. This means you've done the right thing.

Step 3: Begin Hacking the Photo—Delete, Copy, and Move Things Around

Now for the fun part. Skipping the first couple chunks of text (you'll figure out where this begins and ends after looking at a few images), start to randomly delete chunks of text. Depending on the size of the image file, deleting text may have a huge effect or almost no effect at all. Additionally, copy large chunks of text and then paste them further down. Interpose regions of texts into other areas, and swap the beginning, middle, and end of the code. In general, don't overthink this process; instead, just go with the flow.

Step 4: Save the File and Reopen as an Image to See What Changes Were Made

Once a satisfactory amount of the JPEG text file has been modified, save the image. The application may prompt you to save the image as a .txt file. Ignore this, and ensure that the file is saved as a JPEG with a .jpeg or .jpg extension. Once saved, close the text editor. Reopen the image file with a normal image-viewing application.

FIGURE 51.1 ....

The gibberish innards of a JPEG file

Preview is the default application on a Mac, and Photo Viewer is available on most Windows computers. The image that opens should resemble the original, but with streaks of color, rearranged areas, and interesting pixilation. If the image was very large (over 500 KB or so), there may only be small changes. Smaller images may be totally unrecognizable.

In some cases, the image will no longer open. Unfortunately, the only option in this case is to repeat steps 1–4. This is part of the process of trial and error that makes this activity both interesting and surprising.

Step 5: Edit the Photo with Image Manipulation Software

While the photos produced up to this point are already unique, they can be further tweaked with image manipulation software. A popular and free option is GIMP, which is available for Mac and Windows. The current industry standard, Photoshop, is more powerful but is pricey. Nevertheless, it is a great option for this kind of work. Any software that allows participants to tweak the contrast, hue, saturation, and levels of the image will work. Software that has features such as layers is even better. Participants can now further edit their images to produce startling colors and effects. They can also crop or repeat portions of the image, or layer effects on top of one another. The idea is simply to be as creative as possible, moving the image ever farther away from its original visual composition. Participants may be tied to the original image to varying degrees, while others may want to wipe away any trace of the original. Others may prefer to riff upon the image, focusing more on patterns and color variation than on blurring the visual landscape. This is an exercise in letting go and trying something new.

Step 6: Load or Print the Final Images

Save the image files in the image manipulation software. Additionally, export them as JPEG files. Next, simply print the files as you would normally, or load them to a shared image-hosting site. In many cases, the images will no longer "work." You may get error messages saying that they can't be printed or uploaded. In these cases, open the image with whatever application still works, and take a screenshot of the image. Both Macs and PCs can take screenshots, but you can also download third-party screenshot software. Then print or upload the screenshot. You and your participants now have a unique image that has been fundamentally altered—a true hack!

FIGURE 51.2 ....

An image of a songbird with an altered JPEG file and additional
manipulation in Photoshop

LEARNING OUTCOMES

- Participants will learn to manipulate files on a traditional computer file system.
  This concept is not as evident in tablets and smartphones, but it is important
  for understanding the underlying mechanisms of computers.
- The project encourages participants to consider the differences between different
  types of files. Would this work with a PNG image file? What about a GIF?
- Participants will gain exposure to image manipulation software such as Adobe
  Photoshop or GIMP.
- JPEG files are gibberish to human eyes. The project encourages participants to
  work with the unknown and to try again when they do not succeed.

RECOMMENDED NEXT PROJECTS

This project serves as a fun and artistic introduction to basic computer concepts. Next
projects should further explore the fundamentals of computing. The Raspberry Pi
offers an affordable and hands-on way to explore computers in library programming.
The Raspberry Pi can be used to create a fully functional computer that serves as
anything from a remote control to a retro game station. Future programs could explore
these types of computers and their capabilities.

Green Screen Photography

AMELIA VANDER HEIDE / LIBRARIAN
San Jose Public Library

Type of Library Best Suited for: Any

Cost Estimate: $200–$500

Makerspace Necessary? No

PROJECT DESCRIPTION

Make photo magic! Participants will learn how to manipulate green screen photos with their very own backgrounds.

Although this project is suitable for almost all patrons aged eight and older, tweens and teens in school and public libraries will probably have the most fun with this program. A makerspace is not necessary for this program, but it does require a well-stocked technology lab or library. The program itself should last about an hour, and twenty participants is the suggested maximum number for this program. It is suggested that project leaders try to manipulate their own photos in advance and watch some YouTube videos about the photo-editing process.

OVERVIEW

In this project participants will work in groups of two to create their own manipulated green screen images. This program will teach participants a simplified technique of

FIGURE 52.1 ···

Space kitties

using chroma key compositing. Chroma key compositing is professional lingo for layering two images based on color hues in post-production. When a photographer or moviemaker uses this technique, they will typically film the subject they want to manipulate against a green or blue screen. These colors are used because they are the furthest from human skin tone.

In order to change a background image, the first layer (or subject photo) will have the green removed from the background and then this first layer will be placed on top of a new background layer. Any background can be added to the first or base layer. This project enables participants to see how some of their favorite images and movies are made.

One of the biggest issues when making a chroma key photo can be shadows. Shadows can make the photos harder to edit and remove the background image. Be sure to avoid and minimize shadows by using proper lighting. Also make sure the background screen is smooth to avoid problems when editing out the background. Additionally, if participants are using props, make sure to limit the reflections.

MATERIALS LIST

- None required
- Recommended materials include fun props and photo paper for printing images

NECESSARY EQUIPMENT

- Laptops equipped with editing software. The instructions in this project are designed for a cost-effective free software: GIMP. GIMP is a free open-source software that works similarly to the much more expensive Photoshop.
- Green screen
- Digital camera or cell phone
- Additional lighting, such as a small spotlight, flash, or table light. A light reflector might also help.
- Optional: color photo printer

STEP-BY-STEP INSTRUCTIONS

1. Introduce participants to the session, and cover concepts such as chroma key compositing.
2. Break participants into groups of two.
3. Once participants are in groups, have them search for a background image using their web browser on their laptop. It is suggested that the librarian pick a theme or type of background for participants to search for such as Niagara Falls or Waikiki. This will make the program go faster and make the participants more focused.
4. Participants will need to save their images onto the computer. It is recommended they either save onto the desktop or into a specially labeled folder to make it easier to find the images again. Make sure participants click on the images to save a full-sized image. If they save directly from the browser search, the image will be too small.
5. Now that participants have found and saved their perfect background image, they will need to take their green screen photos. Participants should go in front of the green screen one at a time and their partner should take the photo. Participants should be encouraged to be as goofy as they would like to be.
6. Once pairs are finished, they will upload their files to the laptop.
7. Now have participants open the GIMP software.
8. Begin by opening the chroma key (green screen) image.
9. Have participants save a copy of the image. This will help in case they make a mistake. Go to FILE and hit SAVE AS COPY.
10. Go to the Layer Window floating on the right-hand side of the screen. Open the Channel Dialog tab and make sure the Alpha Channel is selected for the image.
11. Now go to the Tool Window, which should be open to the left of the image. Select the SELECT BY COLOR tool.

12. Left click the image, selecting the green parts of the background. Hold shift while left clicking to select multiple parts of the image at once.

13. Once the selection process is done, go to EDIT and click CUT. Continue this process until all the green parts of the background are removed. Hit SAVE to save where you are in the process.

....

Removing green screen

14. Go to FILE and select OPEN AS LAYERS. Open the saved background image.

15. Go back to the Layer Window. Move the subject layer back to the top position by dragging it above the background layer.

16. Now the subject layer might be bigger than the background layer. In order to resize the layer, use the SCALE tool located in the tool window.

17. When starting to use the SCALE tool, you will scale the image, but you might not see any change. Check the layer window—it might have created a floating selection layer. All you need to do is left click the layer and select ANCHOR LAYER. You will now be able to scale the subject image smaller. Scale until it fits into the background.

18. Now click on the background layer in the layer window. Go to IMAGE and FIT CANVAS TO LAYER. This will make the entire image one size.

19. Now click on the subject layer in the layer window. Left click the layer and select MERGE DOWN. This will merge the entire image together.

FIGURE 52.3

Merge layers

20. Encourage successful participants to try and manipulate more images and make whatever they can dream up.

LEARNING OUTCOMES

Participants will come away feeling more confident with a piece of technology that seems complex, but is actually quite easy. This program fosters creativity and innovation by having participants use their imagination to create fantastical and complex images. It also fosters initiative and self-direction as participants make their own images once the first photo is edited and try with each iteration to improve.

RECOMMENDED NEXT PROJECTS

- Explore more photo-editing projects by trying to clean up or change the way people look in photos.
- Run a film class with teen students where they make short films that are less than five minutes long.
- Create a photo shoot with teens.

Create Digitized Sketchbooks

INGRID GRACE / LOCAL HISTORY RESEARCH AND ENGAGEMENT OFFICER
Waverley Public Library

Type of Library Best Suited for: Any

Cost Estimate: Australian dollars $3,000 approximately

Makerspace Necessary? No

PROJECT DESCRIPTION

Sketchflash makes traditional hard copy sketchbooks filled with original drawings done by hand of the Waverley Library's culture. The sketchbooks are then digitized to make an e-collection that is accessible to all from the Waverley Library home page.

OVERVIEW

Sketchflash is a drawing group that meets weekly where participants assist and encourage each other with knowledge from their own experience of drawing rather than having a teacher. Instead the facilitator, who ideally has experience in drawing and activities that surround the act of drawing, acts as mediator, guiding and encouraging conversation among the participants, especially during the times when participants are asked to view and comment on each other's work. This is a crucial element in the project, and inviting such criticism can be a little daunting for participants at the beginning, but it is an element that they will get to love. Moreover, at times the participants will need to be reminded to do some more drawing. This conversation reinforces the community-building aspect of the project that is embodied by the concept of "makerspace." The goal is to make drawings of the library's culture in traditional paper sketchbooks that are then digitized into an e-collection and placed on the Waverley Library home page. The drawers get to keep their books as mementos, but they can be assured that their work has a wider audience via electronic access.

No experience of drawing is necessary. The event is about the maker movement and building a community of like-minded individuals to enrich their experience of everyday life and specific interests. The library becomes a meeting place and source of meaningful activity using its traditional and contemporary resources to help in bridging the digital gap. The program shows how things made with our hands can be enlarged via electronic resources without difficulty by collaborating with others and the library.

MATERIALS LIST

- Sketchbooks provided for free by the library; these should be standard A5 size with good-quality cartridge paper. The quality of paper makes a difference, and the participants notice and remark on it.
- Drawing implements such as pencils, pens, brush, ink, or whatever is favored by the drawer. The participants provide these. Make certain this is stated on the promotional material. The library will supply some materials, because inevitably there will be those who do not bring something to draw with. Office pencils and ballpoint pens are good. Encourage participants to draw with whatever is at hand.
- A few drawing implements to spike curiosity; for example, a brush with a water reservoir to use with aquarelle pencils or some other water-soluble medium. Erasers are also useful.
- A pool of volunteer models from the staff and borrowers. They are fully clothed so modest volunteers will not be embarrassed and participants won't be offended.
- A list of items from the library's existing collection that can be brought to the sessions to inspire and inform participants and promote the collection. One of the repeated comments is the exclamation, "I didn't know the library had such a good art collection," followed by "I didn't even know that books like this existed!" Participants fall on the books like hungry birds. Take note of what books might engage particular participants from their conversation or their drawing styles. Participants will start to ask for specific items from the collection to be brought to the sessions, and at this point borrowing can be encouraged. The observation of good art and drawing from the artworks pictured in these art books is a time-honored way of learning drawing skills. Here, it also serves to promote the collection and further stimulate paths of specific interest.

A participant's drawing

NECESSARY EQUIPMENT

- Our Sketchflash event is held in a regular meeting room in the library. It is not a specific makerspace but a room with glass paneling that easily allows other library patrons to view the session, and hopefully be enticed to join in if they want to. Though the room is not closed off from the rest of the library, it does contain some of the noise arising from the lively conversation during share and exchange time.
- The sessions have access to the library's photocopiers and computers. The use of this equipment is encouraged during the drawing session, and it promotes the services available in the library. The equipment allows for enlarging and reducing the scale of drawings quickly or for repeating elements of a drawing for collage.
- Scanner to digitize sketchbooks. The scanner will not need special settings. It is best to have one generalized setting for all drawings in order to minimize the time taken for scanning. The scanner will need the capability to make each sketchbook into one long PDF.

STEP-BY-STEP INSTRUCTIONS

Step 1

Once you have an idea for a program, it is best to write a proposal. Do some research, look at similar projects that are successful, and see how they might be applied to the project in your library. Your proposal doesn't need to be perfect, but it should be worked out well enough for you to be able to explain it and point out the program's benefits to the library and its customers and how the program relates to the organization's goals and objectives. Seek out a management person who is likely to lend her support, and pitch the proposal to her. Her support can be of great assistance in getting your idea off the ground. She can also point out other people in the organization to consult with who may assist with the project.

Step 2

Determine a regular time/pattern framework that will be followed for each session. Build a plan for each session around this generic framework. A workable frame for a session that lasts one and a half hours is as follows:

1. Introduction: take five to ten minutes for announcements, introduction of new participants, and outlining the suggested drawing project for the main part of the session.
2. Two quick warm-up drawings, each of ten minutes' duration, with a five-minute break at the end of each drawing segment for the group to get up walk around the table to view and discuss the drawings made. Always commence with the two warm-up drawings. Participants get to know this and commence these drawings as soon as they arrive; they will eventually instruct participants joining the group for the first time that this is how to get started. This gets the session underway by itself because participants have a sense of knowing what to do and how to start. This builds familiarity and makes a comfortable atmosphere. The two warm-up drawings are of other group participants: the person sitting next to you or across the table.
3. Three drawings interpreting the project introduced for the session, each of fifteen minutes' duration with a five-minute break at the end of each drawing segment for the group to view, discuss, and gather ideas for a possible different approach to the next drawing; during this time they take inspiration from the drawings of the other participants.
4. Close: reinforce the date, time, and location of next week's session, and remind the group of important events coming up such as a group exhibition or the end of the term. Celebrate what has been achieved by participants in the session and thank them for their attendance.

Step 3

Make a list of projects for the term, one for each of the sessions in the term. This will include guest visits by artists in residence and guest tutors.

When devising projects, work with the features of the particular library where the Sketchflash is to be held. The drawings are to make a record of the culture of the library over the duration of the Sketchflash program. The participants should enjoy their time drawing at the library while they extend their skills and help build a community of like-minded individuals.

Participants are not compelled to comply with the suggested project. They simply need to make drawings that relate to the general set theme of Sketchflash, giving the overall project uniformity in the Sketchflash Sketchbook Collection when it is digitized

The following are seven project suggestions, with a description for how to approach each one.

Project 1

A popular project is the construction of a large drawing by all the participants of the group. This project will not be included in the individual sketchbooks. Participants may like to take a photo of the finished image, print it out at A5 size to fit into the standard issue sketchbook, and paste it in.

If a person with little drawing experience was asked to draw a whole complicated scene with people and furniture, they would most likely say that they could not do it, but given a small piece of a large scene, which when enlarged appears as an abstract pattern, participants draw it without too many qualms and are pleasantly surprised at the end result.

Each participant receives a small section of the image and is requested to draw what they see on the small section without referring to the enlargement that it is taken from.

Prepare an enlargement of a photograph of the group using the library photo-copy machine that is approximately A1 in size. It will need to be done in A3 sections because this is usually the largest paper size in a photocopier. Cello tape the enlarged sections together to form one image. Make two copies.

On the back of each enlargement draw a grid equaling the number of participants in the group. Number each piece from one to ten or however many participants are in the group.

Make a small diagram of the grid to note the layout for reassembly.

Cut one enlargement along the grid lines. Keep the other copy of the enlargement in one piece to use as a key for reassembly.

Distribute the cut pieces to the group and have them draw what they see on the piece they have been given on to a piece of paper that is the same dimensions as the piece of the image they have. Use two of the fifteen-minute segments of the main project part of the session to do this.

In the last fifteen-minute segment, get the group to put the big drawing together according to the numbered grid so it will be face down. Appoint one participant to coordinate the assembly and cello tape the pieces firmly together. The group will still not have viewed the enlargement as one image. This stage generates much talk about what pieces should go where. It is an exciting point in the project.

Once all the pieces are together, turn it over!

After their initial surprise, the group will spontaneously make a few corrections to the drawing, and they will be delighted at the construction and the recognition of the total picture. Now have the group compare their reassembled drawing to the photocopy that has been kept as a key.

Project 2

Live model—clothed—from library staff or patrons.

Prepare handouts of the proportions of the human body and face, both male and female. These can be found in books on anatomy for artists. Hand these out during the introduction time, remarking to the group that in drawing, all proportions and sizes of things are relative to one another; for example, an open hand will cover a face, a foot is as long as a head, and the space between the eyes is about one eye width.

Ask for volunteers from the library staff and/or library patrons to pose as models. Make sure that the model knows that if at any time their pose becomes uncomfortable, then they should stop.

In this project, the participants make drawings from the live model, just as artists do in life-drawing classes. Because the models are from the library staff and its patrons, this makes the project very much about the library culture.

Have at least three poses worked out for the model to take and hold, one for each segment of the main project part of the session. Often the person acting as model with have their own ideas for poses.

Have props for the model if appropriate, such as a trolley if the model is the home library service's delivery person.

At the end of the session, give them a round of applause and a small gift of appreciation.

Project 3

Library still life. Gather interesting objects from the library archive room such as shoe lasts, trophies, and costumes, whether they are of a sporting nature or reflect other achievements that are relevant to the local area.

In this session, have the participants look for the large general shapes of the objects, and have them include the shadows that the objects cast. For the adventurous, have them include some of the other participants in the background of the still life, making a complete composition.

Project 4

Invite a guest speaker from the governing body's artist-in-residence program. Engage the speaker well ahead of time, making sure to coordinate the time and date of their appearance.

Discuss with the speaker what their topic might be and how it relates to drawing. Ask them to bring along their own sketchbooks to share with the group, and maybe bring a few larger drawings as well.

Have the speaker tell the participants about their own experiences of drawing; there will always be a funny story that the participants can relate to. Have the speaker tell of their own methods of drawing and how they get themselves started on the task of drawing.

Arrange for there to be enough time for participants to ask questions of the guest speaker and make sure that they are comfortable with this.

If the guest speaker is willing to give a soft critique of the participants' sketchbooks, have them do this. Participants enjoy this engagement with a practicing artist.

The segments of these guest sessions will run according to what the speaker will be delivering. There will be no planned drawing on these days, though participants will start drawing as they arrive and while they are waiting for the guest speaker to begin.

Project 5

A guest tutor from the governing body's artist-in-residence program. The Sketchflash program arranges for the guest tutor to be a regular feature once a month during term time. Participants look forward to this extra value, which introduces new and different drawing techniques as well as various approaches to drawing that were not previously thought of.

Engage the tutor well ahead of time in order to coordinate the time and date of their appearance. Meet with the tutor to discuss possible lesson ideas they may have and would like to present. Outline the skill levels of the group and their possible expectations.

Lessons for these guest tutor sessions might include the technique for the drawing of hands and how to do foreshortening. These are two areas where drawers encounter difficulty and are appreciative of the extra instruction.

Project 6

Locations of interest around the library. A list of four suggested locations:

1. Local studies/museum unit. In this unit there will be objects of local significance to draw, such as scale models of local historical buildings, ceramic pots, surfboards, and life buoys.
2. A seasonal display that is on in the library. For example, Halloween or Library Lovers Day.

3. A special architectural feature of the building such as a colonnade or garden feature.
4. Sculptures in the library that are part of local history owned by the library.

Each of the above items would serve as a main project for one session.

Project 7

Session plans suggested by participants of the existing Sketchflash group. This project becomes feasible when the group becomes more confident and established participants come forward asking to lead a session. A participant may have art teaching skills and a plan prepared to lead a session on a particular drawing idea.

Meet with the participant beforehand in order to discuss their idea. Ascertain if they will need the library to supply items like a whiteboard for demonstrating a drawing to the group, or if there are props needed for their session so that they can be sourced.

During these sessions, take a step back from leading the group but be ready to assist.

Step 4

- Arrange for the digitization and future access of the finished sketchbooks. Discuss with your web team the most appropriate location for the e-collection.
- Collect the group's sketchbooks at the end of the term for digitizing.
- Refer to the instructions for the particular scanning product available to you. It is best not to make adjustments for each drawing or sketchbook, but instead to have a standard setting for all of the sketchbooks, because otherwise time and labor costs become prohibitive.
- When placing the sketchbooks on the bed of the scanner, place the scans vertically or horizontally as makes sense for the drawing. This is for the ease of the end viewer of the sketchbook when it is presented on the library home page.
- Once all the sketchbooks are scanned and saved to a desktop, name each file with the drawer's name. First names are sufficient, and this assists with privacy issues when making the sketchbooks available for wide public viewing.
- Save the sketchbooks to a place on the organization's network that is accessible to yourself and the web team member who will be loading the sketchbooks on to the home page.
- Once the books are loaded, check that they appear as you would like and then encourage participants to view them. To do this, have a segment of a session devoted to where the sketchbooks are located. Have a printed handout of the path to the sketchbooks, a projector screen, and a laptop with Internet access for the viewing of the sketchbooks. Guide the participants through the process

FIGURE 53.2

Group feedback

and look at some of the sketchbooks. For some participants, it is a revelation and a source of enjoyment to see their work on the library home page and a computer screen.

LEARNING OUTCOMES

- Raised awareness of electronic items now becoming available and how hard-copy drawings are digitized and converted into electronic images.
- Raised awareness that electronic technology doesn't necessarily mean something that is hard to understand, make, do, or access.
- Participants discover items in the collection that relate to their specific interest; in this case, art books. If you have hidden parts of the collection, such as closed access stacks or rare books, these can be promoted during the course of the program.
- Raised awareness of how to use the catalog to find those items of specific interest that enhance customers' experience of the library.
- Participants find out how to become library members.
- Cross-promote library events and activities.

- Strengthened sense of community, with the creation of a group of people with similar interests who assist each other in this shared interest. Participants learn and extend their knowledge of drawing techniques.
- Position the library as a center of entertainment, recreation, and lifelong learning.

RECOMMENDED NEXT PROJECTS

The Sketchflash group may like to present a formal exhibition in the library with displays of the group's work, including the hard-copy sketchbooks, a digital loop with a PowerPoint of digitized sketchbooks, and a selection of larger drawings developed from the sketchbook drawings. During the exhibition a Sketchflash session can be held at the exhibition space itself. It works well as a promotion for the exhibition and the Sketchflash program. It further raises the spirit of community among the participants working together to show what they do and how they enjoy it.

Turn Yourself into a Chocolate Lollipop!

SIENNA CITTADINO / TEEN LIBRARIAN
Carnegie Library of Pittsburgh
Developed by Sienna Cittadino, Sondra Hart, and Amalia Tonsor

Type of Library Best Suited for: School or Public

Cost Estimate: $2,000–$4,000 for all equipment and supplies

Makerspace Necessary? No

PROJECT DESCRIPTION

Around Valentine's Day, library patrons are on the lookout for sweet ways to flex their creative muscles! Every participant in this program will walk away with a 3D replica of their head made of chocolate and attached to a lollipop stick. This project satisfies all sugar-related needs while also teaching a whole suite of interesting skills. If your patrons have interests ranging from food science to 3D modeling and you're looking for a way to engage them, this project may be the answer. Depending on your participants' comfort level, the entire process can be hands-on, or you can save some of the more precise procedures for time between program sessions. Be sure to save plenty of time for this program—using food-safe silicone is inspiring, but professional-grade materials require plenty of patience and testing.

OVERVIEW

The program consists of three main sections: capturing and printing the scanned 3D busts, creating the food-safe silicone molds, and making chocolates out of the finished molds. The first and third sections are ideal for drop-in programs, but the mold creation process is best saved for more structured learning environments and older participants. Set aside at least three days of program time. Above all, be ready to experiment and adapt. This program involves a lot of trial and error and has an adventurous spirit.

MATERIALS LIST

- Food-safe silicone mold-making kits
- Chocolate chips (consider allergies)
- Popsicle sticks
- Paper plates and cups

NECESSARY EQUIPMENT

- Computer or laptop
- Xbox Kinect or other 3D scanner
- Skanect software or other software for processing 3D scans
- Autodesk Meshmixer software
- 3D printer and PLA filament
- Laboratory or jewelry scale
- Induction burner and saucepan
- Measuring spoons or cups
- X-ACTO blade

STEP-BY-STEP INSTRUCTIONS

Step 1: Scan the Participants to Create 3D Busts

To capture the 3D scans of participants, you will need equipment that can perform a 3D scan and software that can process and edit the scans. A great option for performing the scans is Xbox Kinect. The accompanying Xbox is not required to use this device, and some libraries may even have one on hand if they bought an Xbox for gaming in recent years.

A popular and affordable option for the software is Skanect. So long as you are utilizing Skanect for noncommercial use, the free version has plenty of power to fuel this project. Simply download Skanect to your computer (Mac and PC versions are available) and create a "New" scan. Most of the default settings are fine, but it's worth setting the "bounding box" to the rough size of the area you'll be scanning.

After that, record the scan of the participant's head. It may take a few tries to get the hang of the scanning process, but participants will likely enjoy figuring this out with the program facilitators. The rest is fairly straightforward, but stay open to experimentation. Be careful with the settings in the "Process" phase, because they can sometimes ruin a perfectly good scan. Export the scan to an .stl file and you should be almost ready to print!

Step 2: Tweak or "Fill in" the Scan

In some cases, the scans from Skanect or similar software end up "hollow." The .stl files will have holes and gaps that make them hard or impossible to print. If this is happening, consider using a free program like Autodesk's Meshmixer to fill in the .stl file. It has straightforward functions and can be used in future 3D printing programs. The "Make Solid" function can do wonders on a troublesome scan. Additionally, using Meshmixer will allow you to cut a flat plane onto the back of the scanned bust (removing the back of the head). While not necessary, this will make the final product neater and easier to remove from the mold.

FIGURE 54.1 ··

A 3D bust with a flattened back plane in Meshmixer

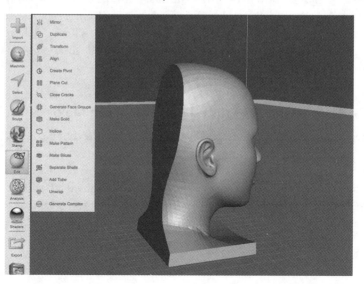

Step 3: Load the .stl Files to the 3D Printer and Print

Once you have a satisfactory .stl file of the scan, load it up to print. Most 3D printers come with software for loading and editing the prints. Be sure to resize the print, if necessary. The silicone molds are pricey, so shoot for smaller busts. About 1.5 inches in height and 1 inch wide works well. The distance from the back of the bust to the tip of the nose should not be much longer than an inch. Once the size is set, print!

Step 4: Mix Silicone Molds

All previous steps must be completed before you begin this step. Depending on the age of your participants, the amount of time you have to do the program, and your ability to accept things going very, very wrong, it may be best to do this step on your own, splitting the program into two sessions. Set aside at least fifteen minutes for each mold.

Create the mold containers with simple paper plates and cups. Cut the wide part (near the mouth) of the cup so you have a piece about two inches tall. Glue the wider end to the plate with hot glue. This is the container for your mold. Hot glue the 3D-printed bust with the nose facing up against the plate as best you can. If you cut off the back of the bust to a flat plane using Meshmixer, this step will be easier.

Closely following the instructions provided with your food-grade silicone, mix the components together. You will need a very precise scale and measuring equipment, as well as plastic spoons for mixing.

Once the mix is ready, pour it over the bust until the bust is *completely covered*. Wait at least a minute to see if some of the mold mix settles and exposes the nose or other parts of the face. Add at least a centimeter or two of silicone mold mix *above* the tip of the nose. Once completely covered, move to a safe location. Allow to dry for at least as long as the instructions specify.

Step 5: Remove the 3D-Printed Busts from the Molds

This step is simple but crucial. Carefully cut the cup and the solidified silicone mold away from the paper plate. Using a small knife or blade, cut away the silicone mold that is covering the 3D bust on the flat side that was against the plate. Then, using plastic utensils or a dull pair of scissors, remove the 3D-printed bust. Once it is out, you should see a very detailed mold of the bust! At this point, you can also notch the mold near the base of the neck or chin to create a slot for a lollipop stick.

FIGURE 54.2

A deceptively firm silicone mold in its paper cup and plate holder

Step 6: Melt the Chocolate and Create the Lollipops

If you chose to do the silicone mold portions of the program on your own, outside of actual program time, this is the step to bring back to the public. Using an induction burner (essentially a hot plate that meets most building safety codes), heat up some chocolate chips in a saucepan. The chocolate will melt very quickly, so have the molds ready, with Popsicle sticks inserted into the notches. Once melted, carefully pour the chocolate into the molds. Have someone take the molds to a refrigerator, and let the molds sit for about thirty minutes. If you have access to a freezer, you can cut this down to about fifteen minutes.

If you incorporated Popsicle sticks, be very gentle while removing the chocolate. Slowly pop the chocolate busts out of the molds, and wonder at the near-perfect likenesses of your participants! Participants can either eat the chocolates right away, or wrap them in cellophane and give them to friends and family. Depending on how much chocolate you're able to buy, the molds can produce chocolate busts over and over.

FIGURE 54.3 ....

A finished lollipop and 3D-printed bust

LEARNING OUTCOMES

- Participants gain a better understanding of interdisciplinary projects. The chocolate lollipops demonstrate how tools and technologies from various industries can come together to create a single end product.
- Participants gain hands-on experience with 3D scanning, 3D printing, and food preparation.
- Participants learn to follow procedures while thinking critically to overcome roadblocks.

RECOMMENDED NEXT PROJECTS

Libraries may want to continue offering 3D scanning as a regular program offering. Try to use the 3D scanner and printer for practical purposes, leading sessions in which participants brainstorm an object that they could scan, modify, and print that would improve the library in some way. The 3D lollipops can also serve as an introduction to entrepreneurial programs. Since the lollipops can be packaged in cellophane and sold, participants can delve deeper into the world of marketing, creating merchandise, and graphic design.

55

3D Print a Bust
of Yourself

ANDY HORBAL / HEAD OF LEARNING COMMONS
University of Maryland Libraries
PRESTON TOBERY / INSTRUCTIONAL TECHNOLOGY COORDINATOR
University of Maryland Libraries
YITZHAK PAUL / MEDIA AND EMERGING TECHNOLOGIES SPECIALIST
University of Maryland Libraries

Type of Library Best Suited for: Any.
We've done this activity with college students, members of the general public
attending university events, and children as young as six.

Cost Estimate: $1,500–$10,000 (depending on how many and what kind of
3D scanners and 3D printers you decide to purchase, and whether or not you decide
to purchase spinning chairs or stools)

Makerspace Necessary? No

PROJECT DESCRIPTION

Handheld 3D scanners are a great resource for generating interest in a library maker-space because they are portable, offer relatively instant gratification (it takes only a few minutes to scan something), are highly interactive, and have an undeniably futuristic feel to them. We use ours at an annual open house for alumni, prospective students, and current students, faculty, and staff called Maryland Day, where it is always a big hit with people of all ages, from six up.

In addition to their appeal for marketing and outreach efforts, 3D scanners can also be used in an ever-expanding range of practical applications. This activity is designed to give library users a quick introduction to the technology that provides them with a fun takeaway, and whets their appetites to learn more.

OVERVIEW

Participants in the activity take turns using a handheld 3D scanner to scan a partner's head and shoulders, resulting in the creation of two digital, 3D "self-portraits." The participants then create 3D-printed busts of themselves from their scans. Because it only takes a few minutes to execute a scan, the first part of this activity scales well: with just one or two scanners, you can accommodate groups of nearly unlimited size, making this activity great for events like fairs and open houses. In a setting such as this, participants can save their scans onto a USB drive and return later to create their 3D prints.

MATERIALS LIST

- Filament for 3D printer
- Micro-shear flush cutter or needle-nose plyers

FIGURE 55.1 ....

Scanning a participant

NECESSARY EQUIPMENT

- Handheld 3D scanner. We use a 3D Systems Sense 3D scanner, but any portable scanner would work.
- 3D printer.
- Laptop or desktop computer. The scanner will typically come with its own software, which can be installed on the computer.
- USB cable for connecting the 3D scanner to the computer. We recommend using an extension cable, which gives you extra freedom of movement.
- Spinning chair or stool for the person being scanned to sit on. The benefit of a spinning chair is that you can spin the subject instead of moving the scanner, which will give you a better result.
- USB drive to save scans on if participants won't be proceeding onto the 3D printing portion of the activity right away.

STEP-BY-STEP INSTRUCTIONS

1. Begin by plugging the 3D scanner into the computer and either installing the software that comes with it if you've never used the scanner before, or starting the software if you have. Follow the prompts until the device is ready to be used.

2. Instruct participants in how to scan their partner: the person being scanned should sit in a spinning chair or on a stool. The person doing the scanning should either slowly spin their partner in the chair or slowly circle them and "paint" them with the scanner by gently waving it back and forth and up and down. The in-progress 3D model will be displayed on the computer in real time, showing where additional scanning is needed. The model is complete when there are no more empty spaces to be filled in.

FIGURE 55.2

Scan in real time

3. Instruct participants on how to edit the model using the options available from the software you are using. The software which accompanies the 3D Systems Sense scanner we use allows you to add color, erase unwanted portions of the scan, remove background "noise," and solidify the image by filling in holes that would be problematic for 3D printing the scan. Tutorials for your scanner can probably be found on Lynda.com, the manufacturer's website, and elsewhere on the Internet.

4. Show participants how to save their models. The software we use automatically saves the image as an .OBJ file, which is compatible with 3D printers. Other options might include files compatible with digital sculpting software or game engines. Participants can either save their models onto a USB drive and return to create their 3D prints at a later date, or proceed directly on to the 3D-printing stage of the activity.

5. Instruct participants on how to import their .OBJ files into the "slicing" software you are using (each 3D printer comes with its own software, and software can also be found online). Show participants how to orient and resize the object, add scaffolding, and select an appropriate level of resolution to ensure a successful print. You can also edit the model here instead of in the software which accompanied your scanner if you prefer.

FIGURE 55.3 ··

Scan in slicing software

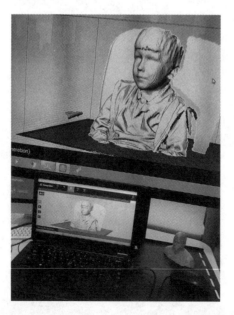

6. Prepare the 3D printer by loading it with filament and ensuring that the build plate is level. Execute the print.

7. After the print is finished, show participants how to safely remove the scaffolding from their print. We use our hands in combination with a micro-shear flush cutter, but needle-nose plyers would also work.

LEARNING OUTCOMES

-   Participants will learn how 3D scanning hardware and software works.
-   Participants will learn how to use a 3D printer.
-   Participants will develop a better understanding of how digital representations of real-world people and objects are created.
-   Participants will gain firsthand knowledge of how to convert a 3D scan into a usable object.

RECOMMENDED NEXT PROJECTS

Instead of instructing participants on how to create a 3D print from their scan, a library makerspace could instead show them how to import their scan into a gaming engine, where participants can convert themselves into a video game character. Alternatively, participants could import their scan into a digital sculpting program, where they can further manipulate the scan by, for instance, creating a portrait of themselves as an animal or some kind of alien, monster, or mythical creature (which is how many Hollywood special effects artists work). Another follow-up project would be to task participants with finding a useful object, scanning it, and creating a replacement. Examples could range from simple handles and gears, to statues and figurines, to prosthetic limbs. 3D scanners can also be used in this way to create movie props, architectural models, and toys (such as furniture for a doll house). You may also choose to run the "Turn Yourself into a Chocolate Lollipop!" project found earlier in this section.

Create Your Own
Board Game

JESSICA LOGAN / BRANCH MANAGER

Hamilton Mill Branch, Gwinnett County Public Library

Type of Library Best Suited for: School or Public

Cost Estimate: $1,000–$5,000 for all supplies and equipment

Makerspace Necessary? No

PROJECT DESCRIPTION

The Gwinnett County Public Library hosts a cumulative board game creation series at the Hamilton Mill Branch called Get Your Game On! that incorporates 3D printing and provides an immersive, collaborative learning experience. Participants learn the history of board games and explore various types of games used for entertainment. They discover the importance of design considerations such as theme and mechanics, and reliance on player skill vs. the element of luck. Participants in the series are presented with tips and tricks for success and are encouraged to establish end goals and outline clear game rules prior to construction.

Additionally, students learn how 3D printing can be used to design and create various game pieces and components. The series is held during the summer months and is geared towards middle school and high school students. After the successful creation of their very own board game, participants invite family and friends to a finale event that provides an opportunity for the students to present their game publicly and then compete in an open game play tournament.

OVERVIEW

Get Your Game On! is a cumulative series that consists of six two-hour meetings. Students attending the series meet one day a week, over the course of six weeks. Participants are initially presented with a brief history of board games and given various considerations to help set them up for a successful outcome. Various activities are used to introduce students to 3D printing, including hands-on demonstrations and the use of both Thingiverse and Tinkercad as computer-aided tools for design and printing. Participants work in groups of 2 to 4 and class size is not limited, but each group is prohibited from relying too much on 3D-printed components due to the amount of time it takes to print a three-dimensional object. While our series incorporates the use of 3D-printed components, it would certainly be possible—and less expensive—to re-create this maker project without the use of a 3D printer.

MATERIALS LIST

- Paper
- Foam board
- Cardstock
- Pens
- Pencils
- Markers
- Paint
- Paintbrushes
- Glue and/or tape
- Tinkercad account

NECESSARY EQUIPMENT

- Projector or TV
- Laptops (and wireless connection)
- 3D printer(s)
- Filament (various colors preferred)
- Scissors
- Rulers

STEP-BY-STEP INSTRUCTIONS

Day 1

Begin by presenting your participants with a brief history of board games illustrating the fact that they have been a source of entertainment for people across the world for thousands of years. Some games that we discuss include the Royal Game of Ur, Chaturanga, Senet, and Mancala. Provide discussion on the various types of board games and the components that will make for a successful final product. Our initial presentation and discussion covers considerations such as theme, mechanics, the number of players the game will accommodate, the desired length of game play, mastery, variance, and randomness.

3D printing

Once the students have been provided with this introductory information, they are encouraged to form groups of 2 to 4 based on their interest in a shared theme or game mechanism. We do not require students to work as part of a group and have occasionally encountered a student who wishes to work on a game concept independently. While this is not encouraged due to the time constraints of the project, it is acceptable for dedicated participants, especially if it helps them to feel comfortable during the series.

After forming groups, the students collaborate to determine a set of shared end goals and a clear outline of their games' rules. A basic concept for the board game and a draft set of rules should be completed by the first day.

Day 2

Groups come back together to share any new ideas that they have thought of during the week and to sketch a diagram of their game. Once the groups have finished their drawing and have come to an agreement on the layout, they then proceed to create a prototype using basic materials such as paper and small objects to represent game pieces. After all of the pieces have been assembled into a rough draft, the participants start testing the game to see how it plays and to determine if there are any alterations that need to be made in either the prototype or the rules.

You may find that some participants initially underestimate the importance of written game rules in favor of board game design and hands-on construction. We provide guidance, but as part of the learning experience, we allow our participants the freedom to follow their own paths to creation. Most quickly learn the value of both preparation and flexibility as their games begin to take shape and eventually evolve through the testing of prototypes.

Day 3

All groups should have a working prototype of their game by the third meeting of the program. Make sure to have your 3D printer set up for this session and familiarize your participants with the equipment by providing a hands-on demonstration. A set of dice makes for a good example because it does not take too long to print, and most groups end up requiring dice for their game. Introduce your participants to Thingiverse and encourage them to search existing designs for desired game components. Commonly requested game pieces include dice, spinner devices, and various small game pieces to represent players; groups can save a considerable amount of time by using existing designs for these. For any group that may wish to design their own game component, have them begin exploring the introductory tutorials on Tinkercad. Make sure that students are aware of common design concerns, such as the need for temporary supports that can be removed after the printing process. Create a list of the desired print jobs from each group and continue printing these between meetings so that everyone has their pieces in time for the finale. This process takes a substantial amount of time, so be sure to plan accordingly and consider limiting the requests per group to a specified amount should the task seem overwhelming or not likely to be completed in time.

While the 3D printing is taking place, the groups begin construction of their final versions of the game by using a foam board to serve as a foundation. We provide a wide range of materials for the groups to use during creation, including cardstock (good for game cards), markers, paint, scissors, rulers, and so on. We also invite the participants to use any recycled materials at their disposal.

Day 4

Participants continue to work together on the construction of game boards and print 3D items as needed. All files for group-designed print jobs are to be submitted by the end of this meeting.

Day 5

Prior to this meeting, library staff review all student 3D print designs to ensure that they will print properly. If changes or alterations are required, staff work with the groups during this final preparation session to finalize the designs. Participants continue to work together on the construction of game boards and to print 3D items as needed. Encourage any group(s) that may have finished early to test their final version thoroughly for any design flaws. Remind participants (and their parents) of the reveal party and open gaming tournament the following week.

Day 6

Give each group the opportunity to introduce and explain the rules of their very own board game. Following the reveal, invite friends, family, and the public to play the newly invented games together. Consider adding to the celebratory atmosphere of the event by providing snacks or an awards ceremony (Best Strategy Game, Best Wild Card, Most Unique Theme, etc.). Don't forget to take lots of pictures and to get a shot of each group with their creation. We find that each finished game ends up having a different theme, mechanism, or twist that makes it unique and intriguing. The games inevitably showcase the creativity of the groups and illustrate their ability to work together and to accomplish goals and objectives . . . all while having fun!

FIGURE 56.2

Finale game event

LEARNING OUTCOMES

Through this project, participants will . . .

- Explore the history of board games and the different types of games commonly used for entertainment.
- Compare popular gaming strategies and consider important concepts such as theme, mechanics, skill, variance, and randomness.
- Determine the beginning elements of design and engineering needed to construct a working game board.
- Learn the basics of operating a 3D printer and develop an understanding of how to use basic computer-aided tools like Thingiverse and Tinkercad to design and/or print small game components.
- Build teamwork and collaborative skills through the successful invention of a new board game.

RECOMMENDED NEXT PROJECTS

Libraries may consider hosting a 3D MakerCamp that can be held over several days or weeks in which participants learn how to design their own 3D prints using Tinkercad and then print them using the library's printer. To further expand upon collaborative programming for this age group, libraries could also consider planning a "Pandemic" or "Mystery Box" game series in which a group of students must work together to solve a problem within a specified time limit.

Create 3D Prints on Fabric

HANNAH POPE / EMERGING TECHNOLOGIES LIBRARIAN

Appalachian State University

Type of Library Best Suited for: Any

Cost Estimate: $50 for 30 people (assuming the library already has a 3D printer)

Makerspace Necessary? No, but a computer lab would be ideal.

PROJECT DESCRIPTION

3D printing is a natural fit for makerspaces, but it can be used for more than just printing out spare parts or action figures. This project looks at 3D modeling and how the combination of 3D printing and sewing can enable libraries to create something that is unique to each library patron.

OVERVIEW

Users will learn the basics of 3D modeling, how to customize a design, and a technique for printing on fabric to accent their clothing. Patrons will be able to design something that they will add to the cuff or collar of their clothing, then learn how to print that onto tulle, lace, or net fabric. This technique can be applied to many other textiles projects including handbags, hats, and shoes. There is no limit to the ways that patrons can incorporate their 3D design work into their clothing, and this project is a great way to introduce participants to the world of e-textiles and wearable electronics.

MATERIALS LIST

- One yard of tulle, lace, or net fabric
- Standard thread of any color
- Large clips or clamps
- Filament—PLA or ABS, any color

NECESSARY EQUIPMENT

- 3D printer with heated print bed
- Standard sewing needles
- Scissors
- Computer lab with Internet access

STEP-BY-STEP INSTRUCTIONS

Step 1: Design

The first step in creating a successful 3D modeling project is to sketch out the intended design on paper. When designing for 3D printing on fabric, it is important to keep in mind a few key things:

- The fabric will be able to conform to the garment, but not necessarily the 3D-printed object on that fabric. Create designs and patterns that leave enough room to allow the fabric to be sewn on without breaking the 3D print. An example of something that would cause breakage would be a vine-like pattern. Non-connecting geometric shapes tend to work best for beginners.
- Design for the garment that you are accenting. Don't create a design that is too big for your cuffs or collar. Make sure that the 3D print will work in the space available. This may mean measuring first.

Librarians can also use some of the premade designs available through this link: https://goo.gl/aLBEAG. Once you have created your design on paper, it is time to make it 3D.

Step 2: 3D Modeling

3D modeling can take time and effort to master, but a good place to start is with AutoDesk's Tinkercad. This program is very useful for teaching patrons the basics of 3D design because it not only is simple to use, but it's web-based. Users will be able to use the Internet in the computer lab to create Tinkercad profiles and start designing. There are also many shortcuts and tutorials available to help patrons learn this program. If you already have knowledge of another 3D modeling program, that can be used to create your design.

For patrons who are new to 3D design and Tinkercad, it may be useful for them to experiment in the program individually. Excellent Tinkercad resources can be found at Tinkercad.com and a shortcut sheet is available at http://bit.ly/2gEJDII.

Librarians also have the option of preparing designs ahead of time, or using the ones available at https://goo.gl/aLBEAG.

Step 3: Create!

Once the patrons have sketched out their designs and begun to learn Tinkercad, have them produce their designs. They can use the premade designs, or "remix" them in Tinkercad, which gives the participants a chance to customize their designs. This will be the area with the biggest learning curve for those who have not used 3D design software before.

Step 4: Print

Those who have a 3D printer know that prints can take a long time. For this activity, participants will want to print their designs right away, but it is best to print them in between sessions. Because of the time involved, librarians and staff should consider breaking this activity into two sections; one for the 3D design of the pattern for their garment, and the other for the sewing portion.

3D printing on the actual fabric is relatively easy. First, make sure that the printer you are using has a heated print bed. This is important because the heat helps the plastic stay malleable while the fabric is being placed onto the bed. Next, if you are comfortable correcting g-code, add a pause after the second layer of the design. If you are not so comfortable, make sure that either the slicing program or the printer itself has a pause option. Then send the design to print. Once the print has completed two full layers, pause the print job.

FIGURE 57.1 ···

Starting the 3D print

Carefully slide the tulle, lace, or net fabric on top of the already printed layers. Make sure that the fabric is smooth, and fasten it with clamps to the print bed. Once the fabric is secure and as wrinkle-free as possible, resume the 3D print.

FIGURE 57.2 ....

Adding the tulle to the 3D print

Voila! You have 3D printed on fabric.

FIGURE 57.3 ....

3D prints on fabric

Quick Things to Keep in Mind

- The fabric that you use must be tulle, lace, net, or another variation that has clear holes in it. This is so that the second layer of the 3D print can fuse with the third layer, creating a bond with the fabric that is in the middle.
- When possible, create hollow geometric shapes. This leads to a shorter print time, less pulling on the fabric, and less weight on the overall garment. An example is the hollow pyramids that are available in the premade examples. Also, try to avoid shapes that may require supports. The fabric layer could damage the results of your print.
- If you have questions about 3D printer settings, consult your printer's suggested temperatures for whichever filament you are using.

Step 5: Finalize

When the 3D designs are printed, it is time for the participants to add them to the clothing item of their choice. It is recommended but not required that the library staff give a brief overview of sewing stitches. A basic running stitch can be used to complete this project.

There are two methods that patrons can use to fasten the 3D-printed fabric onto their garment:

- Cut the fabric with the 3D print into a strip. Sew around the edges of the strip of fabric onto the collar or cuff (or wherever patrons want to sew it). This leaves the tulle/net/lace fabric visible on the garment. Depending on how heavy the 3D print is, stitches can be placed strategically in the middle of the fabric for support.
- Cut out the 3D-printed elements while leaving a ⅓-inch rim of fabric around each shape. Place the 3D-printed objects anywhere on the garment, then sew them into place using the fabric that remains around each element. This method greatly diminishes the visibility of the tulle/net/lace fabric that is used, yet gives focus to the 3D-printed design.
- The use of a sewing machine is not recommended, unless participants are very experienced.

Once all of the sewing is done, admire the completed garments of your participants! If the sewing is unable to be completed before the event time is up, consider having participants use social media to share their final outcome. You can now enhance any fashion choice by adding 3D-printed designs!

LEARNING OUTCOMES

- Participants learn the basics of 3D design using Tinkercad.
- Participants learn and use basic stitches to sew their 3D-printed designs onto fabric.

RECOMMENDED NEXT PROJECTS

This technique can be used to add the 3D printing to any other type of fabric-based project. Other projects include adding 3D prints to handbags, hats, gloves, or other clothing pieces and accessories. Once the technique of 3D printing on fabric is mastered, other e-textiles can be incorporated into the design. Try LEDs and circuitry from the "Create e-Textiles with LilyPad Arduino" project to enhance your 3D-printed fabric design.

3D Print a Marionette

LYSSA TROEMEL / MAKER LAB GUIDE
Allen County Public Library–Georgetown Branch

Type of Library Best Suited for: Public or School
Cost Estimate: $15–$40 plus cost of 3D printer
Makerspace Necessary? No

PROJECT DESCRIPTION

In this project, participants will make a 3D-printed marionette using the Tinkerplay app for iPad and Android or by having participants create their own pieces using Tinkercad. It introduces participants to 3D design, using a 3D printer, and the art form of puppetry.

PROJECT OVERVIEW

This is a program that was offered to all ages, but seemed to be most popular with children and young adults. It introduces them to designing in a 3D or CAD (computer-aided design) workspace and using the 3D printer. With pieces preprinted, it can be done in two hours or less. If pieces are not preprinted, it will take two days on separate weeks to allow for print time. This program was first done in March to coincide with World Puppetry Day, but it can be done at any time during the year. The class is limited to six participants due to room size and equipment.

MATERIALS LIST

- 3D-printed parts
- Fishing line
- Yarn
- Popsicle sticks
- Drinking straw

NECESSARY EQUIPMENT

- 3D printer
- iPad and computer with Internet access
- Hot glue gun
- Dremel Rotary Tool (to clear any supports inside pieces)

FIGURE 58.1

Example of finished marionette

STEP-BY-STEP INSTRUCTIONS

Step 1

Design the marionette in either Tinkerplay or Tinkercad. Tinkerplay has a simple drag-and-drop interface along with templates for several different figures. Tinkercad also uses drag and drop. Tinkercad is set up more like CAD software than the app, so this will allow patrons more freedom to design and size the pieces as they see fit. Everything can be resized using click and drag on the corners, or a number can be typed in for better accuracy. Be sure to add a hole in the pieces to string them to the rest of the puppet.

Step 2

Print the pieces. Tinkerplay will give you an IP address and you can download the pieces from the page it takes you to. Tinkercad allows you to download the file using the export feature. The file format should be .stl or .obj. You may need to add supports for some pieces. Most slicing software will automatically generate supports, but if the software won't, Meshmixer can be used. If you can print pieces separately, I would suggest printing the feet at 100 percent infill to make them heavier and easier to move. If you wish to do this project in one day, I would suggest preprinting the pieces in Tinkerplay. If you wish to do it in multiple days, you can print the pieces after participants have finished designing and arrange them on the buildplate to maximize print time.

Step 3

Use the Dremel to clear out any supports in the middle of the piece. This will allow for the fishing line to go all the way through.

Step 4

After clearing out supports, start to put together the marionette in the following way:

Hot glue the fishing line in the socket and string on the arm pieces, then hot glue the hands to keep them on the fishing line. In the hip joints, run a piece of fishing line through the sockets for the legs and hot glue to keep it in place. String on the legs and then hot glue the ends of the feet. If there is only one hole for the hip joint, hot glue the fishing line in place. String the torso on top of the hip joint and hot glue the neck. Attach the head. If there is a hole through the top of the head, run the fishing line all the way through the top and hot glue at the top.

Step 5

String the marionette to the control bar:

- The control bar should be in a cross formation with a small piece of straw on the end.
- The head should be anchored to the middle to keep it standing up using fishing line. This should be hot glued in place.
- The arms should be tied to the arms of the control bar and hot glued on the hands.
- A string on the hips will allow the marionette to bow. This can also be tied to the back of the control bar using yarn.
- The legs should be on one piece of yarn threaded through the straw on the front. The ends of the yarn should be hot glued to the feet.

The reason for tying the ends of the yarn to the control bar is to allow for easy disentanglement. The yarn will get tangled at some point, but by tying some of the yarn instead of hot gluing it, this makes it easier to take off, and it should be easier to untangle.

LEARNING OUTCOMES

This project teaches

- 3D design
- Using the 3D printer
- Introduction to one of many puppetry forms

FIGURE 58.2

Control bar

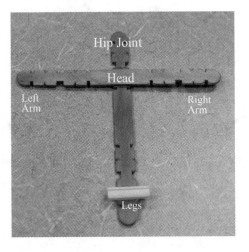

RECOMMENDED NEXT PROJECTS

After this project, experiment with 3D printing. If you used Tinkerplay, try using Tinkercad to design something from scratch like a keychain or maybe another marionette. If you used Tinkercad, try moving on to another CAD software or try to make something more complex. This could be a great way to explore making joints if you don't want to use fishing line inside the pieces. You can also explore different kinds of puppetry and how you would use a 3D printer in the process of making them. Some examples would be to make eyes and eye mechanisms for hand puppets or sock puppets, flat-figured shadow puppets, and rod puppets. If you have a local guild or puppeteer, you may want to see if they would be willing to lead a workshop on operating the puppet.

3D Print Characters for Stop-Motion Films

MICHAEL CHERRY / TEEN AND YOUTH LIBRARIAN
Evansville Vanderburgh Public Library

Type of Library Best Suited for: School or Public

Cost Estimate: $5,000–$10,000 for all supplies and equipment

Makerspace Necessary? No

PROJECT DESCRIPTION

During the summer months, the Evansville Vanderburgh Public Library hosts a 3D Printing and Film Camp at their Central Library. Students attending the camp learn how 3D printing is influencing the Hollywood film industry. They discover how animated films like *Coraline, The Boxtrolls, ParaNorman,* and *Kubo and the Two Strings* utilize 3D printing in the creation of stop-motion characters. Stop motion is an animation technique in which you move a physical object that you're filming very slightly between frames to make it appear to be moving independently.

Additionally, they learn how 3D printing is used for costume and prop fabrication in films like *Star Wars: The Force Awakens* and *Batman vs. Superman: Dawn of Justice,* among others. The camp is geared towards middle school and high school students. In addition to learning about these films, students design and 3D print a character or small prop for a stop-motion movie.

FIGURE 59.1
3D-printed characters

OVERVIEW

The 3D Printing and Film Camp consists of four 90-minute programs. Students attending the camp meet one day a week, over the course of four weeks. Various activities introduce students to 3D design, 3D scanning, and stop-motion filmmaking. In the past, the camp has been divided into two age groups consisting of 5th–8th grade and 6th–12th grade. Each class is limited to the first fifteen students due to the amount of time it takes to print a three-dimensional character.

MATERIALS LIST

- Clay, Legos, cut paper, and action figures
- Giant props for pixilation
- CD or flash drive
- Glue stick or adhesive
- Videos, articles, and books
- PLA filament

NECESSARY EQUIPMENT

- Laptops or iPads
- Cameras
- 3D printer(s)
- Slicing software
- Microsoft Kinect
- Skanect software
- Stop-motion software or app
- Tinkercad account and Internet connection
- X-ACTO blade

FIGURE 59.2 ···

3D prints and designs

STEP-BY-STEP INSTRUCTIONS

Day 1

Show the participants various videos that illustrate the use of 3D printing in stop-motion films, such as *Coraline, The Boxtrolls, ParaNorman,* and *Kubo and the Two Strings.* All four of these films were created by the Portland-based animation studio LAIKA. Videos contained on the DVD extras for these films describe how LAIKA utilizes 3D printing in the creation of stop-motion puppets.

Upon completion of the videos, discuss in further detail how 3D printers work, including computer-aided design, slicing, bed calibration, and other steps in the 3D printing process.

Secondly, have students create a Tinkercad account online. Show the participants Autodesk's "Tinkercad Tutorial," which is accessible via YouTube. This short video explains how to use Tinkercad and guides students through the design process. After watching the tutorial, students are tasked with designing and 3D printing a character for a stop-motion movie. All character designs should be completed by the first day.

Day 2

Introduce students to other aspects of 3D printing and film. For example, show the video *Swipe | Movie Star Body Scans, 3D Printing & The Order: 1886* by Sky News. The video can be accessed via YouTube and describes how actors and actresses are 3D scanned for costume fabrication in Hollywood films. Furthermore, demonstrate how to use a Microsoft Kinect and Skanect software to create a do-it-yourself head scan and 3D print. Anna Kaziunas France's book *Make: 3D Printing* describes how to create a 3D scan and print using a Microsoft Kinect gaming device.

An additional resource includes Scott J. Grunewald's article "How 3D Printing Helped *Star Wars: The Force Awakens* Zoom into Theaters." The article discusses the use of 3D printing for costume and prop fabrication in *Star Wars: The Force Awakens* and *Batman vs. Superman: Dawn of Justice*. It can be retrieved online at 3Dprint.com and contains various images that may be featured in a slide show.

Finally, have the group create a pixilation video demonstrating the process of stop-motion animation. Pixilation is an animation technique whereby people are the subject of the animated film. It resembles human puppetry as live actors repeatedly pose for a sequence of animated frames. This type of animation makes use of large props and other found objects.

Day 3

All 3D prints should be completed and printed by the third program. Characters can be printed outside of class between the first and third weeks. Discuss with students how scaffolding supports arms, legs, and other appendages during the 3D printing process. Scaffolding must be removed with an X-ACTO blade or other sharp tool during post-processing. Show students a video of the printer in action printing supports.

Additionally, students begin work on their final project. They are required to animate their 3D print in a stop-motion movie. Students can use other materials such as action figures, clay, and cut paper in the creation of their final videos.

As students work on their final videos, library staff can show the students other videos related to 3D printing or stop-motion filmmaking. There are many different examples one can use. For example, *The Ray Harryhausen Creature List* video contains a compilation of hand-crafted puppets by the pioneer filmmaker Ray Harryhausen. His stop-motion puppets can be compared to LAIKA's use of 3D printing technology in today's films. Elsewhere, the video by Global News titled *3D Printing: Make Anything You Want* highlights the use of additive manufacturing in aerospace, food, and films like Marvel's *Iron Man*. Both videos can be accessed via YouTube as well.

Day 4

Camp participants complete their final project on the fourth day. Their films are shown and shared with the class. Videos can be saved to a CD or flash drive. Sample videos can be accessed via YouTube by searching "3D Printing at the EVPL."

LEARNING OUTCOMES

- Students learn how 3D printing is influencing the Hollywood film industry by examining various films.
- They learn how to use basic computer-aided design tools like Tinkercad to design and print a three-dimensional character or small prop.
- Students learn the basics of 3D printing, including slicing, scanning, bed calibration, and post-processing.
- They discover various stop-motion formats and create a stop-motion film of their own.

RECOMMENDED NEXT PROJECTS

Libraries may want to partner with a film class at a local high school. The Evansville Vanderburgh Public Library partners with a film class at Harrison High School. Much like the camp, students attending the class learn how 3D printing and scanning is influencing the Hollywood film industry. They learn about many of the films mentioned above and design and print a character or small prop for a stop-motion movie. The program also examines the history of stop-motion filmmaking from the original *King Kong* (1933) to LAIKA's animation today.

60

Hack a 3D Print

SUSAN BARNUM / PUBLIC SERVICES LIBRARIAN @ TEEN TOWN
El Paso Public Library System

Type of Library Best Suited for: Any

Cost Estimate: Free to minimal

Makerspace Necessary? No, but desirable

PROJECT DESCRIPTION

This project will teach participants how to create unique 3D graphics and objects by using existing models and free software.

OVERVIEW

Beginning with 3D modeling is a steep learning curve—and becoming good at it takes both artistic and programming skills. As a librarian, you want to get kids excited right away so that they can enjoy an immediate payoff. This project will help kids to make and use 3D graphics and objects right away. There's no need for everyone to be an artist to make good and often useful 3D objects. This project can also help grab the imagination of budding 3D artists and propel them into a career they never knew existed.

This project uses ready-made 3D objects that others have created and remixes them into something new.

The 3D print hack is a shortcut to unique object creation. It allows participants to have fun, play around with 3D modeling tools, and make something unique. The project uses online software so there is no need to install any programs on your computers, but if you are at a school or library that already has programs like Maya or Blender for 3D modeling, you may want to expand this project to incorporate those as you see fit. You can also do this project even if you don't have your own 3D printer. You can have the kids create the objects, save them to a disk, and then print them out at a local university or makerspace. Alternatively, you can also order prints from a service (at a cost) online.

MATERIALS LIST

- Access to the free websites Thingiverse (https://www.thingiverse.com) and Tinkercad (https://www.tinkercad.com). For participants who are under thirteen, it is suggested that the library set up accounts for Tinkercad ahead of time.

NECESSARY EQUIPMENT

- Computers with Internet connection and modern browsers such as Google Chrome or Firefox
- 3D printer (optional, but awesome to have)

STEP-BY-STEP INSTRUCTIONS

1. Navigate to Thingiverse where there is a huge, searchable repository of open-sourced 3D objects archived. These objects are licensed under various Creative Commons licenses. At the top of the page is a search bar. Have participants find at least two objects that interest them and which they can combine together. They will have to download the files, which should be in .STL format. Often, when you download files from Thingiverse, they will come bundled together in a .ZIP file. This gives you a chance to teach participants how to extract files from an archive. I've chosen the Utah Teapot and Dragon which are in the public domain.

2. Once the files are downloaded and unzipped (if needed), go to Tinkercad and log into, or create, your account. Choose "Create new design." When the Workplane loads, navigate to the right and choose "Import." You will have to import your files one at a time. When you import the files, if they are not loading properly, or not showing up at all, try changing the scale of the model. That often fixes the problem when the model is too small to show up on the Workplane. If the file is too big to fit on the Workplane, adjust the percentage. Rarely, however, a file will be too complex to load, and in these cases a student will have to choose another file.

FIGURE 60.1 ··

Models are loaded into Tinkercad. I am going to "erase" part of the dragon.

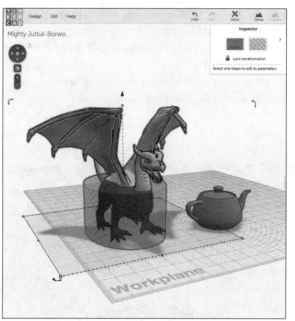

3. Next, participants will resize their files in order to combine them as they see fit. In my simple example, I'm making a flying teapot! In order to accomplish this, I'm going to have to decide which parts of the models to keep, which parts to resize, and which parts to discard. Once your participants have made these kinds of decisions for their creation, have them get started with resizing.

4. For the flying teapot, I'm going to make the teapot a little larger and the dragon a little smaller. In Tinkercad, this is accomplished by selecting the model with a left mouse-click and dragging the mouse on the X, Y, or Z axis. If you hold down the SHIFT key while resizing, it will resize uniformly across each axis.

5. In removing part of a model, you will use the geometric tools that Tinkercad provides. Find a geometric shape that matches the shape of the area you wish to "erase." Drag the shape to the Workplane and resize and move it until it completely covers *only* the area you want to "erase." Once it's where you want it, change the shape to a hole in the "Inspector" area. Then choose both the shape and the 3D model, holding down the SHIFT key to select both and "group" them together. Once they are grouped, it will appear as if you erased the parts you didn't want. Repeat this process as necessary.

6. If participants want to duplicate part of an object, such as adding four wings to my teapot instead of two, you can copy and paste objects within Tinkercad.

7. If you ever find you are having problems erasing everything in Tinkercad, it may be because you are not viewing the file from enough different angles. Always move around your Workplane and view from the top, front, and both sides. You can easily move the Workplane around by holding down the right mouse button and dragging the mouse.

8. When you group objects, sometimes you'll group the wrong ones together. Don't worry. You can undo your mistakes easily.

FIGURE 60.2

The dragon and teapot are merged together by grouping the two objects in Tinkercad

9. Once you have the parts that you want to combine together, move them into place, resize again if need be, and group the shapes together. For this example, I am just grouping the wings with the teapot.

10. The file is ready to download for 3D printing! Navigate to the left side of the screen and click the tab marked "Design." Choose "Download for 3D Printing" from the menu. Most printers use the .STL extension.

11. Once the file is downloaded and you want to print the file, follow the directions for your brand of 3D printer. If your library doesn't have a 3D printer, you can encourage your participants to save the file to print out at a local makerspace or university. If the library wants to pay for prints, you can order the prints online through 3D printing services.

FIGURE 60.3

The final flying teapot, printed out on a Makerbot Mini

LEARNING OUTCOMES

Participants will . . .

- Gain a basic understanding of Creative Commons media and why it is important to respect and understand copyright issues.
- Learn how to download and use different file types and how to unzip an archived file.
- Recognize different common media file types and how to use them.
- Understand and be able to navigate a simple 3D workspace.
- Understand the X, Y, and Z axis used in 3D workspaces.
- Understand the basic concepts of scaling and transforming 3D objects.

RECOMMENDED NEXT PROJECTS

As a next project, you might also check out my project "Turn 2D Graphics into 3D Prints" found in this section (see the next chapter).

Turn 2D Graphics into 3D Prints

SUSAN BARNUM / PUBLIC SERVICES LIBRARIAN @ TEEN TOWN
El Paso Public Library System

Type of Library Best Suited for: Any

Cost Estimate: Free to minimal

Makerspace Necessary? No, but desirable

PROJECT DESCRIPTION

This project will teach participants how to turn a digital "flat" image into a 3D model suitable for printing by using free editing software.

OVERVIEW

Many kids are excited about making their own 3D prints, but they don't know how to get started designing their own unique projects. Learning to create a 3D object from scratch seems intimidating at first, and it's made worse when you realize that many 3D design programs have a steep learning curve. This project is designed to make the process of creation easy and fun for young people (and their instructors.) This project is suitable for any library and can be scaled in detail or interest level to fit your audience.

Making a 2D object into a 3D object involves extruding a flat image into a 3D shape. This project uses free, Internet-based software so there is no cost involved in the creation of the objects and you won't need Information Technology staff to install applications on your computers. While actually printing the final creation is awesome, if your library or school doesn't own a 3D printer or have a makerspace, you can still do this project and have students create the files to print out elsewhere in town. Optionally, you can order 3D prints for participants (usually at a cost) from a third-party service online.

Note: If the free tools used in this chapter are unavailable, this project can still be completed using free, open-source software such as Blender or Inkscape. The drawback here is that these programs must be installed on a computer and participants will need to learn to use them. As an alternative to searching for images on Wikimedia Commons, participants can take photos with their phones or library-owned cameras.

MATERIALS LIST

- Access to the free websites Tinkercad (https://www.tinkercad.com), Wikimedia Commons (https://commons.wikimedia.org/wiki/Main_Page), and PicSVG (http://picsvg.com/). For participants who are under thirteen, it is suggested that the library set up accounts for Tinkercad ahead of time.

NECESSARY EQUIPMENT

- Computers connected to the Internet and using modern browsers such as Google Chrome or Firefox
- 3D printer (optional, but awesome to have)

STEP-BY-STEP INSTRUCTIONS

Navigate to Wikimedia Commons, where there are a huge number of pictures that are licensed for reuse and modification. Pictures with a greater amount of contrast are better for this project than ones that are more "grayed out." You can instruct the students to squint their eyes at the picture. If they can still make out the basic shapes in the picture, then their picture likely has a lot of contrast. Pictures in which the subject is the main focus and the background is rather plain make for good choices. Contrast can, however, be adjusted somewhat in PicSVG. When searching the Commons, most kids like to type in keywords as if they are using Google Search. Wikimedia Commons will often give substandard results using this method. However, you can use this as an opportunity to talk about searching by other methods. The site is best searched by using broad terms or categories. For example, when searching for "Octopus," poor results are returned. By searching for "Octopi" or "Octopuses," the Commons will show more images and also give you image categories that can be explored further. The image I chose comes from the category "Octopuses in Art" and is in the public domain.

FIGURE 61.1 ....

Picture chosen from Wikimedia Commons and loaded into PicSVG

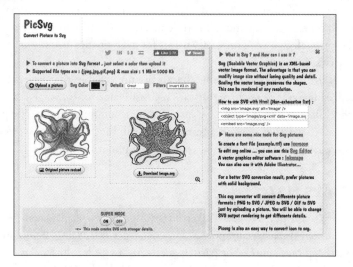

Once participants have chosen a picture that they like, they should download it to the computer. They will need to choose a file that is in the format of a JPEG, GIF, or PNG file type. After the file is downloaded, navigate to the website PicSVG. The front page is where kids will convert their files. Instruct them to "Upload a picture" and then choose the filter they like best. Keep the SVG color black. The area that is black will be "printable." Once they are happy with the SVG file, download the "image.svg." If there are elements of the image that aren't "perfect," we can fix these in Tinkercad.

Next we are going to open Tinkercad. After participants are logged in, choose "Create new design." After the Workplane loads, navigate to the right and choose "Import." Choose the file and import it into Tinkercad. It will prompt you if your file is "too big" and you can scale it as appropriate until it loads. Often the file will still be rather large. You can resize the file in Tinkercad.

Moving the file around, you will notice that it's already been converted in 3D form! At this point, participants can modify their model in many different ways. For example, if there are elements of the background that they don't want to print, you can remove them in Tinkercad by choosing one of the geometric shapes in the menu to the left, engulfing the area to remove and then turning the shape into a "hole" and grouping all of the objects together. This will cause the area to "disappear." Other things participants can do is to change the dimensions of the object. They can also use multiple copies of their object to create a unique 3D shape. Other ways to make the shape unique involve adding letters or creating a loop for a keychain. The tools in Tinkercad make this easy to do. Once participants are happy with their model, you can download the file.

FIGURE 61.2 ···

File loaded into Tinkercad and extruded into a 3D shape

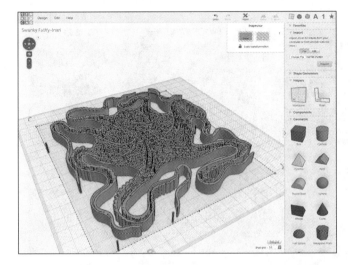

To download, navigate to the left side of the screen and click the tab marked "Design." Choose "Download for 3D Printing" from the menu. You will be presented with several different file types. Most printers use the .STL extension.

Once the file is downloaded and you want to print the file, follow the directions for your brand of 3D printer. Optionally, if you don't have a 3D printer, you can encourage your kids to print the file out at a local makerspace or university. Other ways to print the file include ordering the print online through 3D printing services (these include a cost).

LEARNING OUTCOMES

Participants will . . .

- Gain a basic understanding of Creative Commons media and why it is important to respect and understand copyright issues.
- Learn about different search strategies.
- Recognize different common media file types and how to use them.
- Learn how to download and convert files.
- Understand the basics of the simple extrusion of a 2D shape into a 3D shape.

FIGURE 61.3

The final product printed out from Tinkercad without extra modifications

RECOMMENDED NEXT PROJECTS

As a follow-up project, you might try remixing an object found on Thingiverse; see my project "Hack a 3D Print" earlier in this section.

Create Your Own
3D Designs

....

SAMANTHA TRINH / YOUTH LIBRARIAN
Clearwater Public Library System

Type of Library Best Suited for: School or Public

Cost Estimate: $0–$10,000

Makerspace Necessary? No

PROJECT DESCRIPTION

A fun way to teach kids about 3D design and 3D printing is to teach them how to make computer-aided designs (CADs). Tinkercad is a free online 3D design app that helps people turn model ideas into professional 3D CADs. An intuitive design and ease of use make Tinkercad extremely suitable for kids. This is a program that allows participants to make their own 3D CAD and submit it for printing via the library's 3D printer. The program encourages digital creativity and enhances STEM learning.

OVERVIEW

This is a two hour-long instructional program. It consists of a brief 3D printing presentation, hands-on model building, computer-aided 3D design instruction, and 3D printing. Even though it is best suited for children aged thirteen and older, children as young as eight years old can also learn from the program if they have competent computer skills.

MATERIALS LIST

- Play-Doh/modeling clay
- Handouts (optional)
- Tinkercad free account

NECESSARY EQUIPMENT

- Computer or laptop with Internet access
- 3D printer (optional)
- Projector for presentation (optional)

STEP-BY-STEP INSTRUCTIONS

If your library has a 3D printer and you are planning on allowing participants to print their designs, start the program by showing the participants the 3D printer and allow them to form observations about the way it works. Let them analyze the printing path that the extruder follows and how designs build up. How do the layers and fill affect the structure of the model? Ask participants about the purpose of supports and platforms and how they might alter the way a design is printed. Finally, have them brainstorm what design qualities make a model print successfully.

Next, challenge participants to make their own 3D designs using Play-Doh or modeling clay. Have them use only geometric shapes and remind them of what qualities would make a good design. It may be easier to give them a theme to work with. For example, tell them to make something holiday-related, or something that represents a favorite hobby. Limit the design-building time to 10–15 minutes. If your library does not have a 3D printer, or you will not have participants print their designs, start the program by introducing CADs and then make Play-Doh models. Relate the CAD use of vector graphics to the geometric Play-Doh models that the participants made.

Ask participants how CADs are used in architectural design, engineering, and computer animation for movies. For example, Andrew Tarantola's article "Six Designs That Would've Been Impossible without Computer Modeling" highlights the uses of CAD in the creation of an 8.5-foot-tall LEGO dinosaur, the Shanghai Tower, and the San Francisco-Oakland Bay Bridge. Popular movies such as *Avatar, Alice in Wonderland, Iron Man,* and *Harry Potter and the Deathly Hallows* use CAD software for visual effects. Explain that commercial industries use sophisticated CAD software such as AutoDesk AutoCAD and PTC Creo. Then present Tinkercad, the free online 3D design program, as an alternative to expensive commercial software.

Have the participants set up their own Tinkercad accounts. After they create their accounts, they will be prompted by Tinkercad to go through the "Basic Skills" tutorials. Have participants practice Learning the Moves, Camera Controls, Scale,

FIGURE 62.1 ....

Play-Doh models

FIGURE 62.2 ....

Participant using Tinkercad

Copy & Paste, and Creating Holes. After they feel comfortable with the design platform, give them a challenge. The easiest design challenge is creating a personalized keychain, which involves letters, copy and paste, and creating holes. An intermediate/difficult challenge would be to re-create their Play-Doh design in Tinkercad. Another difficult challenge would be to create a cookie cutter with a frame and baseplate/stamp. Other lessons and projects for teachers can be found under the "Teach" tab on the Tinkercad website. Playing with Tinkercad will take the majority of the program time, so plan for an hour for the participants to practice the "Basic Skills" and build their own designs.

Finally, show participants Thingiverse.com, a sharing platform where they can browse countless CADs submitted by other people. If you have a 3D printer, allow them to submit their creations to you in the appropriate file format for future printing.

LEARNING OUTCOMES

- Participants learn the fundamentals of computer-aided design: measurements, camera control, scaling.
- Participants understand how a 3D design becomes a model and the necessary qualities that make it print successfully.
- Participants practice problem-solving skills while building their own CADs.

RECOMMENDED NEXT PROJECTS

This project lays the foundation for several other programs. Libraries can offer a second advanced Tinkercad workshop with a focus on creating 3D models from 2D images. Alternatively, libraries can offer a workshop on 3D scanning, and preparing files for printing and operating a 3D printer. Other workshops can introduce different Autodesk free software such as Flame for 3D visual effects and Pixlr for photo editing.

Create a 3D Touch Display for the Library

JUAN DENZER / LIBRARY SYSTEMS SPECIALIST
Binghamton University Libraries

Type of Library Best Suited for: Public or Academic

Cost Estimate: $500–$1,000

Makerspace Necessary? Yes

PROJECT DESCRIPTION

Binghamton University Libraries wanted to create an exhibit that would engage patrons through touch, sight, and sound. Their goal was to bring various departments and talents together to make an exciting display. Those involved included faculty from the medieval studies department, the emerging technology studio, student sculpture artists, and library staff.

Illuminated manuscripts were the focused theme of the exhibit. A large 45 × 55-inch printed manuscript image from the J. Paul Getty Museum was the base theme. The display was created using 3D scanning and printing technology. Arduino technology is used to bring touch and sound to the exhibit. In addition to 3D-printed objects, sculptures were made to capture the artist's interpretation of the printed manuscripts. A custom frame made from a wood and vinyl lattice was built to house the touch print and Arduino technology.

FIGURE 63.1

Touch display

Courtesy of Binghamton University Libraries. Photo by Juan Denzer.

OVERVIEW

This project is designed to give your library step-by-step instructions on how to build an exciting 3D touch display that is 45 × 55 inches. The project can be scaled to fit just about any budget. The 3D touch display will help libraries promote their collections while providing a fun, informative, and interactive exhibit.

MATERIALS LIST

- Sculpey clay
- 18–20-gauge stranded electrical wire, 25 feet
- 18–20-gauge insulated ring terminals, 25+ count
- Tinfoil
- Bare Conductive electrically conductive paint, 50 ml (https://www.bare conductive.com/shop/electric-paint-50ml/)

- Bare Conductive Touch Board (https://www.bareconductive.com/shop/touch-board/)
- Black interior latex paint, 2 quarts
- White acrylic paint
- 45 × 55-inch foam poster board
- 3M spray adhesive
- Portable USB Bluetooth mini speaker bar, 4 × 17 × 4 inches or smaller
- 2-inch-wide Industrial 3M Velcro capable of holding 5 pounds or more
- #10 ¾-inch wood screws, 25+ count
- #10 1-inch wood screws, 25+ count
- 2 ½-inch exterior deck screws, 1 pound
- 1 inch × 6 inch × 6-foot wood, 2 pieces
- 1 inch × 6 inch × 4-foot wood, 2 pieces
- 48-inch × 8-foot vinyl lattice
- Large-format printed image, 45 × 55 inches

NECESSARY EQUIPMENT

- Electric miter saw or handsaw with miter box
- Cordless drill
- Impact cordless drill (optional)
- Multipurpose drill bit set
- Dremel or rotary saw with cutting disks
- Wire cutter/strippers
- Wire crimpers
- Pliers
- Set of quick grip clamps
- Laptop or PC with Windows 10
- iPad or iPad Air
- 3D printer
- PLA filament
- Slicing software
- Microsoft Kinect (Xbox 360 or Xbox One)
- Microsoft Kinect for Windows V2 adapter
- iSense 3D scanner
- Skanect software

STEP-BY-STEP INSTRUCTIONS

Step 1: Choose an Image

Begin by choosing a theme for your display. Choose something that will help promote a collection. For instance, suppose your library has a new collection of Superhero comic books. You could choose an image that has various superheroes from the Marvel Universe. Choose something that will capture the eye with lots of color. Be sure to choose an image that has multiple objects that stand out and are evenly spaced.

In our superheroes example, we would not choose an image of a single character posing because this would only have one object. Instead, we would select an image that would have several superheroes in an action scene. This might include explosions with cars, buildings, trees, and so on.

It is best to avoid images that are heavily filled with text. Since the goal of the display is to use sight, touch, and sound to interact with the patron, unnecessary text is not suited for it. Any accompanying text can be displayed outside the case, such as having a sign that reads, "For more information, please visit our collection in the children's department."

Other examples of images to choose are maps, the solar system, or still life art with fruit. Once you have chosen an image, it will need to be printed using a large-format printer. The display will be approximately 45 × 55 inches in size. You may choose to adjust the size by a few inches depending on the image selected. If a large-format printer is not available or if your budget is limited, a printed poster is an excellent alternative. Note that the standard poster size is 24 × 36 inches; this will make your display smaller than the one in this project. Mount your poster with spray adhesive to the foam board cut to the poster size.

Step 2: Choose and Create Relief Objects Using Clay

The objects that will be scanned should be carefully chosen. They should be key objects in the image that will help to either tell a story or draw the patron into the display. It is also important to avoid the clustering of objects. The display should have touch points that are spaced apart; this will not only help with the touch sensors' accuracy, but it will also help make the display stand out.

Which objects are best? In our superheroes example, let's imagine the image included Captain America, Thor, and Ironman. Choosing the entire character as a touch-point object is not a good choice. Instead, choose the iconic objects that the superheroes possess: Captain America's shield, Thor's hammer, and Ironman's helmet. This will help create a more focused narrative when creating the audio file for play-back. It also helps to focus on a specific object, so users don't get confused and think touching a specific area will play additional sounds. Remember that each 3D object will only have one audio file associated with it.

Once the objects are chosen, 3D relief models must be made so they can be scanned in 3D. Use modeling clay such as Sculpey, which can be purchased at any crafts store, to create the models. It is best to start with a flat base and work up to build the relief. If you are not skilled at sculpting, it is better to choose objects that are easily done, such as planets, fruit, hand tools, and so on. The more detailed your object is, the more complex your sculpture will be. The model does not have to be exact, since it is an interpretation of what you are choosing for the display. Do not be too concerned with fine detail, since the scanner and printer might not be able to capture this with precision.

It is important that the models should not exceed the 3D printer's print bed. Typically, the average size is 5 × 7 inches, so make sure to keep the selected objects to that size. Some objects might call for larger 3D prints. In this case you will have to create sections that will be pieced together.

Step 3: Scan and Print the Molded Objects

If your makerspace is equipped with a 3D scanner, use the scanner to make 3D scans of all the objects. If not, here are some low-cost 3D scan solutions. Each system is designed to achieve suitable scans for this project.

Solution 1: The original Microsoft Kinect for Windows, commonly known as the Xbox 360 version. Used Kinects can be purchased at any gaming store for under $50. This Kinect can be used with a free program called Skanect (http://skanect.occipital .com/). The website has tutorials on how to set up and use Skanect with the Kinect.

Solution 2: The newest Kinect for Windows V2 or the Xbox One version. This will require a PC adapter; both the Kinect and adapter can be purchased for under $150 from the Microsoft store online. Microsoft offers two free Windows 10 apps from the app store 3D Scan and 3D Builder. 3D Scan is designed to work with the Kinect V2. Scanning, editing, and saving 3D scans is easily done. The following link gives a detailed tutorial on how to use it: https://channel9.msdn.com/ Blogs/3D-Printing/3D-Builder-Tutorial-Part-5–3D-Scanning-with-Kinect-V2.

Solution 3: Use an Apple iPad. iSense is a 3D scanning adapter that connects to your iPad and can be seen in these videos: http//www.3dsystems.com/shop/support/ isense/videos. It allows you to scan objects in 3D and export the files for printing. The cost is around $100. Skanect also offers an iPad scanner for around $499, which includes the pro version of their software.

Once the scans are complete, edit and print them using your 3D printer. If your makerspace is not equipped with a 3D printer, the scans can be printed using online providers such as www.shapeways.com/.

Step 4: Build the Display Frame

Begin by laying out the 1 × 6-inch boards around the printed image. Leave a 1/8-inch gap between the edge of the print and the insides of the board. This will allow for easy removal of the print and make the frame reusable. After making the miter cuts, secure the frame with deck screws to make a portrait frame.

Next, cut the vinyl lattice to cover the back side of the frame. Secure the lattice using 1-inch wood screws. Once the lattice is attached, cut a 4 × 6-inch rectangle in the center of the lattice; this will be the access point for the Arduino board. Paint the entire frame black with interior latex paint. Make sure to include a 1-inch margin around the inside to cover the lattice. If the frame will be mounted on a wall, add three 1 × 4-inch boards to create a brace for the wall and frame.

Once the frame is dry, cut 3-inch strips of Velcro. Cover the corners and a few lattice pieces in the center with these strips. Drill tiny pilot holes in the Velcro and secure them to the lattice with wood screws. With the Velcro in place, carefully lay the print so the non-Velcro sections stick to the print. The end result will be a foam board print with fabric-side Velcro that will stick to the lattice Velcro.

Step 5: Record the Audio Files

The Arduino-based touch board by Bare Conductive (https://www.bareconductive .com/shop/touch-board/) is designed to be used right out of the box. No coding is needed. It includes a micro SD card that is preprogrammed for the project. Use any recording device to create MP3 audio files that will go with each 3D object. The board is capable of 12 touch points. Label the file for each point TRACK00.mp3, TRACK01. mp3, TRACK02.mp3 . . . TRACK11.mp3. Then overwrite the new files to the SD card and insert it into the board. Power the board using a micro USB cable, add a speaker, and test the audio by touching each contact on the board.

Step 6: Paint, Wire, and Secure the 3D Objects

Using the Bare Conductive electric paint, cover the flat side of each object with a thick coat. Take the white acrylic paint and fill in any micro holes on the front of the 3D print.

After the paint is dry, begin to wire and secure the objects onto the print. First place and hold the object on the printed side. Next, drill two to three tiny pilot holes from the back side of the print into the object. *Do not* drill all the way through the 3D print. Cut lengths of wire that are long enough to reach the holes and the center hole in the lattice. Strip the wire on each end, and attach a ring terminal to one end of each wire. The other ends will be twisted together with one ring terminal to be secured to the Arduino board.

FIGURE 63.2

3D print

Courtesy of Binghamton University Libraries. Photo by Juan Denzer.

Take #10 wood screws and begin to attach the wires and object to the board. Pass the screw through the ring terminal and add a piece of tinfoil to the screw point. Hold the object on the board and carefully hand screw the ring terminal. It should be on the back side of the foam board and tapped into the 3D object. Do this for all the 3D objects. Once they are all in place, Velcro stick the print to the lattice. Pass all the wire leads through the hole in the lattice and secure them to the corresponding touch point using a wood screw. Secure the Arduino board to the lattice using a few wood screws. Take a micro USB cable, power, and test the display by touching the 3D objects. You will see an amber light when a point is activated. Finally, add the USB powered sound bar to the top of the frame and plug a male-male audio cable from the speaker to the Arduino.

Carefully mount or secure your display to a wall or in a bigger case. Supply power to the speaker and Arduino board, adjust the volume, and enjoy your new interactive 3D touch display.

LEARNING OUTCOMES

Through this project, participants will learn . . .

- How to select, scan, and print 3D objects
- Basic electrical wiring for circuits
- Basic wood framing skills
- Programming Arduino-based boards

RECOMMENDED NEXT PROJECTS

The case in this project is designed to be highly versatile. Images and objects can be easily swapped out for other themes. The capacitive touch, which is the same technology used in smartphones that enables interaction, can be used with other non-3D-printed objects. This includes items such as fabrics, paper, plastic, wood, and so on. Additional frames can be built in various sizes. Libraries can also use ready-made picture frames to create low-cost interactive displays.

In addition to creating various low-cost exhibits, libraries can invite the community to help make exciting displays. Additional touch boards can be purchased to offer community classes on how to create your own touching-is-seeing display.

Index